D0593906

WE ARE
PROUD
BOYS

WE ARE
PROUD
BOYS

How a Right-Wing Street
Gang Ushered in a New Era
of American Extremism

ANDY
CAMPBELL

BOOKS

New York

Hachette Books
Hachette Book Group
1290 Avenue of the Americas
New York, NY 10104
HachetteBooks.com
Twitter.com/HachetteBooks
Instagram.com/HachetteBooks

First Edition: October 2022

Published by Hachette Books, an imprint of Perseus Books, LLC, a subsidiary of Hachette Book Group, Inc. The Hachette Books name and logo is a trademark of the Hachette Book Group.

The Hachette Speakers Bureau provides a wide range of authors for speaking events. To find out more, go to www.hachettespeakersbureau.com or call (866) 376-6591.

The publisher is not responsible for websites (or their content) that are not owned by the publisher.

Library of Congress Cataloging-in-Publication Data

Names: Campbell, Andy (Journalist), author.
Title: We are Proud Boys : how a right-wing street gang ushered in a new era of
    American extremism / Andy Campbell.
Description: First edition. | New York : Hachette Books, 2022. |
    Includes bibliographical references.
Identifiers: LCCN 2022019044 | ISBN 9780306827464 (hardcover) |
    ISBN 9780306827488 (ebook)
Subjects: LCSH: Right-wing extremists—United States. | Government,
    Resistance to—United States. | White supremacy movements—United States.
Classification: LCC HN90.R3 C35 2022 | DDC 322.4/20973—dc23/eng/20220519
LC record available at https://lccn.loc.gov/2022019044

ISBNs: 978-0-306-82746-4 (hardcover), 978-0-306-82748-8 (ebook)

Printed in the United States of America

LSC-C

Printing 1, 2022

All the work that went into this book,
and any good that might come out of it,
is dedicated to Tess, my beacon.

CONTENTS

WE ARE
PROUD
BOYS

INTRODUCTION

More Violence

Gavin McInnes wanted to see more violence from Donald Trump's people.

It was late in March 2016, in the heat of Trump's presidential push, and the national media had latched onto one bit of security footage from a Trump event. The video showed Trump's campaign manager, Corey Lewandowski, grabbing and pushing Breitbart writer Michelle Fields as she approached Trump and tapped his elbow. Fields claimed that Lewandowski left bruises on her arm. It was enough that police charged Lewandowski with simple battery, but prosecutors ultimately dropped the case. He shrugged off the allegation and the news cycle that followed, which left the pundits to bicker among themselves over the footage and decide whether an assault had occurred.

McInnes, staring slack-jawed at the footage during an episode of his reactionary talk show, couldn't believe it warranted media attention in the first place. A woman touched a presidential candidate and got what was coming to her, he argued. If anything, she deserved more.

"She wasn't randomly grabbed!" he groused, his voice pitching upward in aggravation as the video played. "I think there's not enough violence in today's day and age."

McInnes then launched into one of his signature rants, steering the conversation toward his keynote: America had gone soft in the waning years of Barack Obama's presidency, and there was no better evidence than the news media clutching its pearls over a woman being grabbed and pushed out of the way. Real Americans—real *men*—wouldn't give this story the time of day. Real men are hardened by a lifetime of violence.

"When we grew up, violence was everywhere . . . you got in fights!" he said. "I look at this video, and I don't see nothing."

He wanted more violence. And so he pivoted to show his audience an "awesome" Instagram account he'd found, which purportedly featured photos and videos of ISIS prisoners being executed in Iraq. He had his producer crank up some industrial metal while images from the account flashed across the screen.

"It's everything I've been hoping for," he said of the account. "Finally, some violence on our end! That's what I want. I'm done with capitulation."

Ultimately, as was often the case, his monologue didn't make the slightest bit of sense. At the beginning he was railing against Fields and the "stupid fucking push" that made her famous, and by the end, he was complaining about some Black people he saw on an episode of *The Real Housewives of Atlanta*.

"Same problems with African Americans in the rich community," he said. "Infidelity, violence, backstabbing. It just looked like the ghetto with a big fancy house behind it."

This was the standard fare on McInnes' show. He rambled his way through a long and bitter rant, ping-ponging between right-wing grievances and racist screeds until he ran out of breath and then moved on, sometimes in the middle of a sentence. He pointed out threats to his audience, but rarely brought any one of them fully into focus or spent much time considering the facts. He was *sick and tired of this crap*, and he left it to viewers to decide what *this crap* actually was. But where he was often vague about the enemy, he was very clear about his intent.

"I want violence. I want punching in the face," he said. "I'm disappointed in Trump supporters for not punching enough!"

His audience ate it up. They revered McInnes because he was more than just another bigoted shock jock who whines and complains and *tells it like it is*. That market was cornered long before his time. McInnes took his viewers a step further by turning to the camera and calling them to action. He whipped up a miasma of political anxiety and misogynist rage among the men watching his show and then captured it, nurtured it, and weaponized it. And less than two months after the airing of that episode, McInnes announced that he'd turned his audience into a gang.

He called them the Proud Boys.

——

THE PICTURE OF the American political demonstration changed forever the moment the Proud Boys began to show up at rallies.

Donald Trump had just won the presidency, and all over the country, despite the end of his campaign, his supporters were still throwing huge celebratory events in city parks and community spaces and parking lots, which came to be known colloquially as MAGA rallies. But something was off about them.

They featured plenty of patriotic familiarities: big American flags, bigger trucks, barbecues, prayer circles, the 9/11 remix of "God Bless the USA," you get the idea. But interspersed among the crowds of star-spangled patriots were these bizarre groups of men nobody had ever seen before, each with their own symbology and uniforms that designated them as members of different factions.

Among them were the Proud Boys, who appeared at first as a kind of Trump-humpy fight club. They were a group of mostly white men in their twenties and thirties, sporting beer bellies and MAGA hats and wraparound sunglasses, who would show up at rallies as one big group, clumped together in a throng of intoxication and noise. They distinguished themselves with a simple uniform, consisting entirely of a black Fred Perry polo with yellow striping. Some of them were suited up for battle, in army surplus gear or football pads and baseball helmets. They wielded American flagpoles as melee weapons and carried cans of beer in the pockets of their tactical vests, in place of hand grenades and bullet magazines. They marched throughout rallies together, hooting and hollering as they searched the crowd for someone to screw with, like a roving crew of bullies shaking down passersby for lunch money at recess. Their presence was off-putting, even for a Trump rally—they didn't have any discernible ideology or political motives, other than drinking and fighting.

They were flanked by other groups, each one weirder and harder to identify than the last. There were antigovernment extremists who described themselves as civilian military outfits, carrying AR-15s and other weaponry where permits would allow. There were minicelebs from far-right corners of the internet, barking racist rhetoric into megaphones. Then there were full-on hate groups that had been assembled online, draped in memes and innuendo to obfuscate and sanitize their intolerant ideology. Altogether, they looked like extras in a low-budget *Mad Max* sequel.

This stuff was utterly bewildering to see at the time. At one early event in 2017, I saw a young man standing amid a sea of red hats at a rally in downtown Portland, Oregon, wearing what appeared to be a riot helmet. He was wrapped in a big flag covered with unfamiliar symbols. Upon closer inspection, I realized the flag was meant to resemble a German Nazi war flag, except it was green rather than red and had the letters *KEK* in the center, where the swastika should be. He said the flag represented "the Republic of Kekistan," an ostensibly sarcastic internet faction born of racist Pepe the Frog memes and other sewage spewed into the world by 4chan, all in celebration of "Emperor Trump." A middle-aged woman standing near him said she'd never heard of Kekistan, but she was excited to see so many Trump supporters gathered in one place. These were the kinds of bizarre alliances that formed in Trump's early days, back when it felt unusual to see far-right gangs in makeshift body armor, internet Nazis, and your conservative aunt all hanging out in the park together at a political rally. By the end of Trump's term, that image was completely unremarkable.

But it was clear from the very beginning that the Proud Boys would emerge as leaders above the other street-level extremists. They weren't satisfied with standing around, holding a flag, and exercising free speech. They wanted violence. When they mobilized for a rally, they did so with the sole intention of fighting in the street, especially when they could fight leftists or anyone McInnes or Trump had a beef with at the time. That political violence, as we'd later learn, was baked into their rulebook, a guiding tenet by which they would commit all sorts of heinous crimes.

Even more concerning was the fact that they wore violent acts like badges of honor. Where other extremists concealed their identities behind masks or the anonymity of the internet, the Proud Boys wanted to be celebrities. They had public social media profiles and Proud Boys tattoos. They hosted semiregular street brawls against counterprotesters and happily spoke to the press afterward, using their real names. They lionized their most violent members with nicknames like "Rufio" and "Based Stickman" and promoted members who committed significant acts of brutality for the cause.

The Proud Boys are by definition (and by their own admission) a street gang, motivated almost entirely by political violence and bigotry. And yet this was not a net negative for their reputation. In just a few short years, they managed to captivate American audiences, secure ongoing support from the president and his closest allies, and position themselves as the Republican Party's extrajudicial enforcement arm. They did so with a heavy dose of patriotic propaganda, aimed directly at Trump's rabid voter base.

They like to describe themselves as an all-male fraternal organization of "Western chauvinists," a group of flag-waving drinking buddies who believe that the "West is the best." They call themselves a "drinking club with a patriotism problem," who are pulled reluctantly into violence by the right's dastardly nemeses: antifa, socialists, Black Lives Matter activists, Democratic politicians, Muslims, trans women, and random Twitter users, to name a few. It's a great public relations tactic for them, at least when it comes to the political right. As they make war with these enemies, they're cheered on today by Trump-era demonstrators and politicians alike. They've been extremely successful at marketing themselves to the right as an innocent organization of downtrodden Trump supporters.

But in reality, the Proud Boys have been on a yearslong fascist march through the country, attacking their political opponents in the street, destroying property, and committing mutinous crimes, all in the name of Trump and McInnes. If you can recall any act of far-right violence at a political event during Trump's presidency, you can bet the Proud Boys were in orbit, if not the architects.

A Proud Boy helped organize the deadly Unite the Right rallies in Charlottesville, Virginia, in 2017, which brought all sorts of hate groups under one banner and ended with a neo-Nazi murdering a protester. The gang turned Portland, Oregon, into an active war zone where the left and right have duked it out in near perpetuity, and they helped raise the national temperature to a degree that the specter of violence now looms over *any* American political demonstration. A group of Proud Boys led a felonious assault on demonstrators outside a GOP event in Manhattan in 2018, in what prosecutors at the time called "violence meant to intimidate and silence." Proud Boys were among the first to breach the US Capitol during the deadly insurrection on January 6, 2021, and prosecutors believe they had an outsized role in planning the assault. They continue their dirty work today.

What separates them from the other extremist groups around them is that they have secured mainstream appeal, through interpersonal relationships with the media, law enforcement, and the GOP, all the way up to Trump's inner circle. They have worked as a security detail for big-name conservative personalities and Trump sycophants like US Senate candidate Lauren Witzke and media pundit Ann Coulter. They were invited to give speeches at mainstream Republican events. They were the personal bodyguards, social media managers, and friends of Trump's closest confidant, Roger Stone. And now they're running for political office using the endorsements they've secured over the years.

Simply put, they're one of the most dangerous and influential extremist groups in America, thriving during a time when federal law enforcement agencies deem far-right extremism as one of the country's top threats. And yet they flew largely under the radar—past federal law enforcement, congressional oversight, and some sections of the mainstream media—until they stormed the Capitol, and by that time the threat they posed was existential.

The Proud Boys' meteoric rise in the Trump era highlights a slew of American crises and various failures to respond to them. They expose the violence and racism both embraced and incited by some of our top politicians. They show just how deeply extremist groups have penetrated law enforcement and military. They reveal how frighteningly easy it is to manipulate lawmakers and media personnel into regurgitating hateful ideology and sanitizing abhorrent beliefs. They demonstrate how easily the general public can be swayed. And they've proven that you can make it as a fascist gang of hooligans in this country, as long as you make the right friends.

In February 2022, ready to put the events of January 6 behind it, the Republican National Committee officially censured two of its own—Adam Kinzinger and Liz Cheney—for participating in the House panel investigating the Capitol insurrection. In a statement so galling it drew a rebuke from a federal judge days later, the RNC called the January 6 riot "legitimate political discourse." The deflection was dumbfounding and indicative of the moral decay that had creeped in during the Trump years, such that an invasion of the seat of government, resulting in the death of federal employees, could be justified by one of the two major parties. But viewed through the lens of the Proud Boys story, this rewriting of history was inevitable.

Over the past six years, extremism and violence have been normalized as part of American political discourse. While many might consider this a Trump story, that's only one side—in the sense that it leaves out a critical element, one that will long outlive Trump. And that element is the extremist playbook written by the Proud Boys, whose project has been to so carefully toe the line between an acceptable political group and a street gang that today there's not much difference between the two.

In the years since Trump took office, the story of extremism in America has been one of normalization. The Proud Boys brought forth a brand-new era of political violence and then helped build a support apparatus that included politicians, law enforcement officials, and media personalities to sanitize that violence into something more patriotic and palatable.

With this book, I hope to give you a better understanding of how a street gang, born of a reactionary talk show, went on to take the reins of the national far-right extremist movement and then normalize it for American audiences. I want you to walk away with a better understanding of extremist groups and their counterparts as they interact today and with an urgent sense that, left unopposed, the political violence and hateful ideology that this group fostered during the Trump era will continue to fester and grow in the future, until it crystalizes forever.

Chapter 1

THE GAVIN MCINNES SHOW

T he Proud Boys name first came to Gavin McInnes while he watched, with disgust, as a twelve-year-old boy with brown skin sang a musical number onstage at a school recital.

McInnes was pissed that he had to be in the audience at all. He'd already sat through performances of his son playing the drums and his daughter playing the guitar, and now here was this kid, singing a song from a Broadway musical. McInnes hated musicals. But because his wife, Emily, was sitting next to him at the time, he had to pretend like he was enjoying himself.

"Fuckin' musicals, man," he said during an early episode of his online talk show, *The Gavin McInnes Show*. "My wife's a fag hag so I had to sit there and just not laugh. I couldn't say to my boys, 'Don't ever fucking do that or I will be the opposite of proud.'"

He was ranting and waving his hands on the set of his show, a daily livestreamed video podcast on Compound Media that served as his bigoted sounding board for more than two years. He grimaced as he recalled the story for his guest, a comedian named

Aaron Berg, who sat giggling at the other end of an L-shaped news desk.

The recital was held in Williamsburg, the expensive and majority-white neighborhood in northern Brooklyn where McInnes used to live with his family. Despite the gentrification, it's still home to substantial populations of Hasidic Jews and Puerto Ricans, which were among some of McInnes' favorite punching bags.

"This little Puerto Rican kid comes out, and he goes, 'I'll make you proud boy!' It was the gayest fucking song," he said. "When I was watching I was like, this is obviously the Hispanic son of a single mom. He did high-five a grown man afterward, but it couldn't have been the real dad."

The song itself gave McInnes pause. He sang the words again and asked an off-camera producer about it—he wasn't sure where it came from, but he knew he despised it. The producer played the song over the studio speakers. It was a number from Disney's Broadway musical version of *Aladdin*, called "Proud of Your Boy." McInnes' face collapsed with revulsion.

"Oh my God, he was singing an *Aladdin* song? What a dork," he said. He sang the line again to mock the child: "'You'll be proud of your boy!' The worst part is, I don't think he was gay. I think he was just like, 'This is a good song, and I can really use my fuckin' diaphragm.'"

From that moment forward, the phrase "proud of your boy" became a running gag on the show. Callers would recite the line as soon as they joined, as if they were iterating on the classic radio call-in line "first-time caller, longtime listener." Within a few episodes, it took on a meaning of its own, an inside joke between McInnes and his audience. And soon, it would become a big part of their shared identity.

The origins of the Proud Boys, the nation's most notorious political fight club, can be traced to one reactionary bigot behind a microphone who hated a child he figured was a fatherless Puerto Rican. McInnes seems to embrace this characterization, though his wife is apparently appalled by it.

"She's pissed, she's like: 'So your whole thing, your whole organization, is mocking a twelve-year-old gay boy?'" he said. "And I go: 'That's such a crude way to put it but yes. Yes it is. Because that little boy personifies how far gone we are.'"

———

THERE ARE HUNDREDS of hours of Gavin McInnes' show available to stream online, but each hour is effectively the same, and it doesn't take a deep dive to get the gist. Let me spare you the misery:

McInnes is staring directly into the camera lens, raving. Each one of his features appears purposefully exaggerated, as if the sarcasm coming out of his mouth were built into his face. His left eyebrow is permanently cocked at a violent angle over his Wayfarer glasses, which amplify his bulging blue eyes and the dark, multilayered circles underneath. The bottom half of his face, covered by a meticulously twee handlebar mustache and manicured beard, opens and closes at a rapid clip but never fully reveals his teeth or tongue, giving the host a Muppet-like quality. His hair is slicked back, and he's wearing a tie and suspenders over a button-down shirt with the sleeves rolled up to his elbows. His hands are rolled into tight fists as he emotes.

He's howling about the decline of masculinity and patriotism in the face of encroaching liberal values, feminism, and globalism. He waxes poetic about the good old days (the early aughts) when men could openly embrace violence and misogyny and nationalism without fear of societal backlash. He might be sitting next to one of his guests—maybe a comedian or a porn star or a far-right figurehead—who serve as his muses between the serious moments.

This is a comedy talk show on its face, made to resemble the likes of *The Howard Stern Show* by pitting funny and shocking guests against McInnes' larger-than-life personality. But the real drive of the show becomes clear when McInnes turns to the camera and talks directly to his audience. This man sees himself as the leader of a movement, and he has an agenda for his followers. He repeats iterations of this directive often:

"Fighting solves everything. We need more violence from the Trump people," he said during an episode in early 2016. He'd pulled up a clip to show viewers in which somebody spat on a Trump supporter at a rally. He watched the clip, and then he turned to the camera and issued a command.

"Trump supporters: choke a motherfucker, choke a bitch, choke a tranny, get your fingers around the windpipe if they spit on you. That's assault. Don't fucking let anyone spit in your fucking face."

The casual savagery and hate on display aren't some cherry-picked snapshot or fluke—you'll see this version of Gavin McInnes on episode 1 just as you will on episode 400. This is the character he wants you to see. In real life, McInnes is a siloed media executive whose recent fighting experience includes sparring with neighborhood moms over email in his ritzy suburban neighborhood just north of New York City. But this man clearly wants you to believe he's clocking out of his day job and heading home to punch a block of wood. If you spend any amount of time watching one of his shows, you get the vibe immediately: Here's a guy who saw *Fight Club* and modeled his career around the Brad Pitt line: "We're a generation of men raised by women. I'm wondering if another woman is really the answer we need."

And it worked. McInnes built himself into a character, the last of a dying breed of free and proud Western patriots, and sold it to an audience of angry and anxious (and overwhelmingly white) men. He told them that their masculinity and patriotism were under attack, that their rights were being impeded by overreaching liberals and immigrants. He told them to fight back and to regard anyone who didn't join them as "pussies" and "traitors." His overtones were familiar—violent nationalism and bigotry aren't exactly new extremist concepts—but he dressed them up in the same hipster bro culture he helped popularize and commodify in the decades prior. He was building an army in his own image.

Gavin Miles McInnes was born to Scottish parents in the small town of Hitchin, England, in 1970 and immigrated to Ontario, Canada, when he was five years old. He casts himself in his early days as a drug-addled punk who thumbed his nose at authority and hung out around grimy music venues. But the stories written about him paint a picture of an obnoxious young student who was obsessed with attention. In high school he formed his very first street gang, the Monks, a crew of about a dozen stoners who punched each other for fun. He performed in punk bands as a teen, including one he started with his grade-school pal Shane Smith called Leatherassbuttfuk. He saw himself as a menace and an outsider, but he did his homework. He studied English at Carleton University in Ottawa and later at Concordia University in Montreal, and after he graduated, he traveled around Europe with Smith for a while before returning to Canada to find something to do.

In the '90s, McInnes began to look at his own brand of counterculture as a business venture. He started a zine in Montreal about his life experiences called *Pervert*, which was widely panned by local critics but became infamous after he sent a series of threatening letters splattered in his own blood to the writers who gave him negative reviews. He wasn't yet a fascist far-right gang leader, but he was never described as a good person either (an archivist in Montreal familiar with McInnes' work once described him to *Vanity Fair* as "the embodiment of smoldering rat shit"). Still, his hijinks got the attention of other burgeoning bros in media. He was introduced to Suroosh Alvi, who was putting together a new magazine called *Voice of Montreal* following a long and difficult battle with heroin. McInnes signed on shortly after the first publication, and his friend Smith wasn't far behind.

In 1994, the trio rebranded the magazine into *Vice*, a national lifestyle and counterculture rag that they gave out for free at record stores and streetwear shops. It was cynical and hip and crude, and it was immediately popular among young people in Montreal. They were ready to grow within four years: Smith, who ran the business side of things, managed to pull in ad revenue from fashion brands in the United States, investment capital from a media mogul in Montreal, and an offer to try their hand at success in New York City. They moved to an office in Manhattan in 1999, where they exploded in popularity. *Vice* was sought out by hip twentysomethings because it was different from other culture magazines: it was sleazy and apathetic and ignored mainstream media conventions. There were boobs and drugs and features written for young socialites, like their "Dos & Don'ts" column, containing snarky and off-color critiques of city fashion alongside some of the wildest, filthiest photos of partying you'd ever seen ("homeless golf pirate" is how they described the outfit on one guy, seen at a party with a woman's face crammed between his ass cheeks).

McInnes, known as the editorial voice of the early operation, used *Vice* to explore the boundaries of acceptable bigotry in pop culture. Mainstream media was already pretty vile in the early 2000s—this was the time of *Jackass* and *The Man Show*, when young men were celebrated for being aggressive and carefree, and young women were told to stop eating and having sex, through obsessive and misogynistic media coverage of the private lives of young famous women, like Paris Hilton and Britney Spears. But McInnes took the sordid machismo and voyeurism a whole lot further: the stories he wrote and oversaw were often disgusting, racist, violent screeds against women and Muslims and trans folks, each one practically begging you to be offended.

McInnes wrote, for example, "The Vice Guide to Picking Up Chicks," which may as well have been a guide for racist white guys to get away with date rape. It was a multisection primer on getting different women of color into bed, whether they wanted to be there or not. McInnes wrote:

> Besides the obvious coke and Viagra combo nothing turns you into a black man better than Adderall. It makes your dick into a fucking battle-ax. (It also makes you want to fanatically eat her ass, so you might want to avoid it if she's a square.) The rest of our advice is the usual. Once you have the go-ahead, do everything short of rape and almost scare the shit out of her.

It was published in *Vice*'s "Sex Issue" in 2005, alongside other repulsive works such as "Me So Horny," a gory vignette of a war photographer's "flicks of Iraqis with their faces exploded," a video and companion article about getting kicked in the balls, and a vox pop of interviews with (mostly) teenaged virgins, complete with a shopping list of what they were wearing at the time.

This is the kind of content that catapulted *Vice* from a local free magazine to a digital media empire that now boasts millions of visitors per month, so this is the content that filled its pages and its website for close to a decade. But by the end of the decade, *Vice* was also becoming a mainstream publication, beholden to more mainstream conventions. Suddenly, its founders were answering to investors and the general public, and McInnes' editorial vision was becoming more of a liability than a viable business plan. Advertisers grew uncomfortable with the content, as did McInnes' colleagues. As Alvi told *McGill News*: "It's hard to grow a business when it's like you're not going to play the game at all with bigger advertisers, especially in America." In 2008, Smith and Alvi parted ways with McInnes, who told me in a follow-up interview that they were "separated by creative differences."

Today, Vice Media Group is a legitimate worldwide news and culture operation, with valuation in the billions and investment worth hundreds of millions, which includes a deal with Disney and a surplus of properties and partnerships in its portfolio. McInnes' former ties to the company don't appear to impact day-to-day editorial choices; multiple Vice properties have covered the Proud Boys and McInnes critically in the years since his departure. But his previous work and legacy, and the question of what to do with it all, still haunt the newsroom. The entire catalogue of his godawful content was still featured on Vice's website more than thirteen years later, right up until I asked about it in 2021. Less than two weeks after I reached out to the company, "The Vice Guide to Picking Up Chicks" and other McInnes works were nuked from the site and replaced with this message: "We have concluded that this article does not meet Vice Media Group's editorial standards. It has been removed."

A Vice spokesperson confirmed by email that McInnes' works had been taken down. Furthermore, the rep said, McInnes hasn't had any stake or working role in the company "in any capacity" since he left, and today, the company "does not stand by his work." The statement reads in part:

> VICE and Gavin parted ways in 2008—many years before Gavin founded the Proud Boys. VICE unequivocally condemns white supremacy, racism and any form of hate, has

shone a fearless, bright light of award-winning journalism on extremism, the alt-right and hate groups around the world, and has created one of the most inclusive, diverse and equitable companies in media.

Nevertheless, the breakup wasn't at all disqualifying for McInnes' career. On the contrary, he was a media executive who helped build a brand that young people liked, and now he was back on the market. There was still an audience for his hypermasculine trash, and he set out to capture it, by pushing the envelope further and harder than he ever did at *Vice*.

But first, he needed to reclaim his audience. So he tried a little of everything: He launched an ultimately unsuccessful site for his content called Street Carnage, which Gawker at the time characterized as a *Vice* competitor. He did some acting and stand-up comedy. He wrote a memoir for Simon and Schuster titled *How to Piss in Public* (watered down as *The Death of Cool* for the paperback) in which he told "extreme-but-true stories" about himself, "featuring drunken fist fights, Satanic punk bands, afternoons on heroin, and multiple threesomes." He cofounded an advertising agency called Rooster, where he sat comfortably as its chief creative officer until the company got wind of an abhorrent diatribe he wrote for Thought Catalog in 2014, titled "Transphobia Is Perfectly Natural." As with anything McInnes writes, the article never once pretended to be a submission to some wider intellectual discourse. It was pure bigotry, through and through, and only worth repeating here to underscore the deep-seated intolerance he harbors:

"What's the matter with simply being a fag who wears makeup?" I think when I see them. You're not a woman. You're a tomboy at best. Get fucked in the ass.

The article provoked its own cycle of public outcry before it was scrubbed from the Thought Catalog site, and in short order Rooster released a statement that McInnes was taking an "indefinite leave of absence." McInnes didn't learn his lesson, though—the transphobia and misogyny would get much, much worse.

The next year, *The Gavin McInnes Show* launched on Compound Media, a subscription-based website that hosts a handful of right-wing reactionary talk shows, founded by disgraced shock jock Anthony Cumia. Cumia was ousted from his former gig, the popular *Opie & Anthony* show, after a racist meltdown on Twitter in which he fantasized about killing a Black woman he said he scuffled with on the street.

"Savage violent animal fucks prey on white people. Easy targets. This CUNT has no clue how lucky she was," he wrote as part of a now-deleted tweet thread, which led to his suspension from the platform.

This is the guy McInnes wanted to do business with. They joined forces in early 2015, when Compound Media was still operating out of Cumia's basement. The production was low budget, but it also had low standards—the perfect place for McInnes' next act.

You could see the Proud Boys' foundation start to take shape on the very first episode of *The Gavin McInnes Show*, which aired online on June 15, 2015. McInnes began with a monologue declaring that, despite the nature of his departure from Rooster, he wasn't racist or sexist. To prove it, he fired off a list of his personal beliefs in an extremely racist and sexist segment titled "How to Save America in 10 Easy Steps."

In his vision of America, everyone has a gun and stands prepared to shoot looters "during the riots in Ferguson, or any fuckin' riot this year." Welfare, which he likened to "giving Black people money to dump their boyfriends," is abolished. The borders are closed because, according to McInnes, if "you think most immigrants are sweethearts just coming here to clean your house, you're a fucking moron." And Americans would "venerate the housewife," as he blamed working women for declining fertility rates.

"All my friends from high school, their cunts are like rotten tea bags—baby free," he said. "And they will remain that way."

The list goes on in this fashion, each point as reprehensible as the next. One line in particular sticks out because it remains today as the Proud Boys' mission statement:

"I'm a Western chauvinist," McInnes said. "I've lived all over the world. I know a lot of other cultures and I know how much they suck shit. Multiculturalism reeks."

He continued by offering up a moral panic of his own creation: "If we could be more chauvinistic and more proud, and not be sent home on Cinco de Mayo from our own high schools for wearing an American flag shirt, you would see a ripple effect from that patriotism, of a lot more American things. We don't suck. We didn't start slavery; we ended it. Let's be a little more smug."

That string of words, along with all the steps laid out in McInnes' fantasy for America, would later become a set of guiding principles for the Proud Boys. His ultranationalist, misogynist, and anti-immigrant edicts were reminiscent of the white supremacist rhetoric put forth by so-called identitarian groups in Europe, which seek to sanitize age-old hatred for brown immigrants and their liberal supporters by positioning them as imminent threats to modern white culture and tradition.

In short, McInnes' Western chauvinism is really just old-school bigotry, dressed up as harmless intellectual discourse and issued alongside a bunch of vague existential threats: *They're coming for you, they're going to persecute you for your patriotism, and then they're going to erase everything you've built. It's time to fight back.* He honed and iterated the statement until it became a one-line motto, now recited by every new recruit into the Proud Boys organization:

"I am a Western chauvinist and I refuse to apologize for creating the modern world."

From the outset, McInnes used his show to indoctrinate his audience. He was building them a new collective identity, complete with their own language, and he was feeding them a bottomless helping of repellent ideology, through interviews with a revolving door of contemptuous far-right goons and violent videos he found on YouTube.

On one episode just two months into the show, he hosted both Milo Yiannopoulos, the former Breitbart writer most famous for being a petulant racist troll, and David Duke, the notorious former Ku Klux Klan grand wizard. McInnes, sitting next to a Black comedian named Chris Cotton, called Duke into the show to ask for his thoughts on a random assortment of prompts, like virility in young men, getting a good night's sleep, and various edible grains. The segment was meant to have an air of irony—*isn't it wild that we called David Duke and asked about bread!?*—but nobody challenged Duke's ideology or suggested that they were on opposite sides of the ball. In fact, McInnes lauded Duke for his viewership numbers on YouTube, handed him a humanizing softball interview, and ended the segment by plugging his website. He'd given his platform and his audience over to a hateful ideologue, and he'd continue to do so for the rest of his time on the show.

Over 407 episodes, McInnes hosted some of the most detestable extremists in the game: infamous neo-Nazi Richard Spencer; men's rights activist and rape apologist Daryush "Roosh" Valizadeh, who built his career off virulent misogyny (and now claims

to have renounced his past); neo-Nazi troll and genocide advocate Andrew "Weev" Auernheimer, who called Black people and
Jews "undesirables" on the show; Tommy Robinson, who made
a career as the United Kingdom's loudest Islamophobe; and dozens upon dozens of minicelebrities of the so-called alt-right—
right-wing reactionaries and white supremacists who rose to
prominence around the same time as McInnes. His show effectively served as a megaphone for racist grifters, who would otherwise have a difficult time reaching mainstream audiences. Duke
and Spencer didn't get many chances to air their ideology on the
major networks; McInnes' show was the closest they could get to
a regular mainstream audience.

And the show was successful. At a time when subscription-
based media wasn't the norm, McInnes was a cash cow for
Compound Media. The company was sitting on around twelve
thousand monthly subscribers at an $8.95 monthly rate, and as a
source close to the company at the time told me, McInnes was at
one point pulling in at least half of the company's daily viewers,
more than Cumia's flagship show.

Meanwhile, McInnes' online following was turning into a
real-life community, to the point where viewers started showing up to drink with him in the studio. Compound Media had
moved from Cumia's basement to its own space on W. 35th
Street in Manhattan right after McInnes signed on, and by early
2016 there were enough fan boys hanging around that the platform's hosts started partying with their audiences at a bar across
the street.

McInnes' parties weren't just after-work drinks with the fans,
though. They were weird, ritualistic affairs. He likened them to
"Knights of Columbus meetups," referencing the archaic Catholic fraternal organization, but told me that his version featured
"a bunch of dudes drinking beer and telling dirty jokes." They'd

get sloshed and rail cocaine, and then McInnes would pull out a copy of Pat Buchanan's *The Death of the West* and proselytize to them.

"The West did not invent slavery, but it alone abolished slavery," he read to them at an event in 2017. "The time for apologies is past."

The Death of the West is McInnes' favorite book to preach from at the bar and serves as the foundation for his concept of Western chauvinism and the Proud Boys. It's an almost biblical reference text for racists, dedicated to proving the conspiracy theory that brown people will replace the Western white population—which the book calls the "greatest civilization in history"—over the next few decades.

Buchanan has for decades been one of the most influential conservative thought leaders in America, an ally to multiple Republican presidents, who was described by his former comms director as the "pioneer of the vision that Trump ran on and won on." Throughout his illustrious writing career, Buchanan has couched blatant bigotry in pseudoscience, often involving male fertility rates and immigration, to argue that white men are being literally replaced by brown people. In his 2011 book *Suicide of a Superpower*, he bemoaned diversity in America and argued that the country is "disintegrating, ethnically, culturally, morally, politically." The Anti-Defamation League describes him as an "unrepentant bigot" who "demonizes Jews and minorities and openly affiliates with white supremacists." He saw a surge of popularity in the Trump era among extremists, who revere his works because they provide a seemingly intellectual route into white supremacist debates, without ever having to declare "I'm racist." Conservative columnist Jonah Goldberg described the tactic perfectly in a blog post back in 2002: "He offers red meat to the extremists while at the same [time] giving himself the wiggle room to deny he said anything controversial in the first place. This is no mean feat. To be able to say something that wins applause from racists and bigots without technically saying anything racist or bigoted is a great gift, for want of a better word."

There's arguably no better student of this tactic than McInnes. He taught his followers how to be coy about bigotry, by framing everything they say as either logical debate or unserious satire. There is some element of eye-rolling, teasing, or trolling in everything he says, which gives him the same air of plausible deniability that comedians like to claim when their jokes are unpopular (though most comedians don't run a gang). He argues to this day that the Proud Boys weren't built on a racist doctrine, and yet in each episode of his show—which are still available to view online as of this writing—he was openly teaching his followers that racism, white supremacy, and violent misogyny were hilarious playthings and that criticism was for liberal crybabies.

He often compared Black people to primates and threw racial epithets around like they were nothing: "My favorite monkey has to be Barack Obama . . . he's my favorite n—er," he said during one episode. He referred to trans people as "gender n—ers" and joked about rape constantly. He once got frustrated at the insinuation that the Nazi salute was offensive and threw a few up himself, saying, "It's not wrong, big fucking deal! *Sieg heil! Sieg heil! Sieg heil!*" During an interview with white nationalist Emily Youcis, he recited the fourteen words, a white supremacist mantra not totally unlike his own motto for the Proud Boys: "We must secure the existence of our people and a future for white children." Both maintained an air of sarcasm and a giggly demeanor throughout the interview, as if what they were saying could be (but might not be!) a joke. That's McInnes' entire schtick. But he also explicitly agreed with Youcis on her premise that "whites should be breeding, and breeding with other whites, and perpetuating the white race."

McInnes' show was a cesspool, and his audience was following him through the sludge. Within a year of his first episode, he'd built an army of pissed-off patriots who hung on his every word. They were more of a cult than a fandom, and McInnes nurtured and exploited that atmosphere. He started referring to his viewers as "disciples," and their meetups as a "movement." And on May 26, 2016, he announced on his show that he'd given this movement of men a name. He called them the Proud Boys, and he likened them to a gang.

"If there's a gang and they're called the fuckin' Murderers or something, those guys are pussies. You know the most dangerous gangs? They have names like the Crybabies and the Mama's Boys . . . those guys were fucking murderers," he said. "That's what we are. We're the Proud Boys."

The show took on a new tone after the announcement. It wasn't just a talk show anymore; it was a livestream of a fascist leader building out an army. Over the next four months, he shaped the Proud Boys' structure and credo on air, along with input from his viewers, who made up the earliest members of his new group.

Callers wanted to hear every detail of his vision for the Proud Boys. They wanted to know whom to associate with and what their ideology was. They wanted to know what tattoos to get. They wanted to know what to wear, when to masturbate, how to talk to their girlfriends. They wanted to know who they should be. McInnes spelled it all out, as if he were a lifestyle guru, and they clamored to join him.

He gave them a simple uniform—the black Fred Perry polo with yellow trim. It's a classic shirt, available in a variety of colors, that's been widely popular among preppy hipsters, ska punks, and the rude boys of London for generations, with its sleek trimmed collar and a small laurel wreath logo on the breast. The Fred Perry brand is clean and cool and affordable and maintains plenty of recent pop culture flair: Amy Winehouse worked on a collection back in 2010, for example, and the sexy gentleman agent known as "Eggsy" in the 2014 film *Kingsman: The Secret Service* wore the black-and-yellow polo as he fought his way out of South London. But the shirt has also been taken up by other extremist movements over the years. The neo-Nazi skinheads of England adopted the polo in the late '60s, and in the '70s, just as Margaret Thatcher and the Tories took power, the skinheads brought their new fashionable style of fascism into the street for political rallies. By the '80s, the Fred Perry polo had crossed the pond, where it was worn by white supremacist groups in the United States as Ronald Reagan was elected president. (McInnes was later questioned about the racist history of his gang's polo, and he threatened to sue the reporter who made the connection.)

McInnes and his viewers went over mockups of logo styles for the gang, including the letters *PB* surrounded by laurels and a rooster atop a weather vane pointing west, a reference to the Western chauvinist mantra. In one episode, he displayed an image of a Proud Boys logo concept one of the members sent him, a runic-style symbol.

"This is a little 'white power,' uh, I'm not against it, but I dunno if you'd wear that to a Jay-Z show," he said with a laugh. "But if you like that, that's great."

In the end, the black-and-yellow color scheme and Fred Perry's laurels stuck, a fact that the Fred Perry brand was not enthused about. In 2020 the company stopped selling its black-and-yellow polo in North America altogether, specifically to stop the Proud Boys from buying them.

"It is incredibly frustrating that this group has appropriated our Black/Yellow/Yellow twin tipped shirt and subverted our Laurel Wreath to their own ends," the company said in a prepared statement. "That association is something we must do our best to end. . . . To be absolutely clear, if you see any Proud Boys materials or products featuring our Laurel Wreath or any Black/Yellow/Yellow related items, they have absolutely nothing to do with us."

As the gang worked out their uniform and colors, McInnes was fine-tuning their ideology. In general he wanted the Proud Boys to follow the moral compass he established in his first episode: celebrate nationalism, reject multiculturalism and immigration, keep women at home, and punch anyone who disagrees. But callers wanted more specifics on their new belief system and, in particular, where McInnes placed them on the bigotry spectrum.

"Do you see the Proud Boys being a . . . subset of the alt-right?" one caller asked. The term, coined by Richard Spencer, described a portion of the extremist far right at the time that was recruiting young people to white identity politics using memes and social media. In other words, they were white nationalists with a fresh coat of paint.

"Sure," McInnes responded. The alt-right characterization was fine, he said, except that the alt-right was a little too outwardly racist. He told the caller that the Proud Boys were anti-immigrant and that all members should acknowledge and respect white men for creating American culture, but he didn't want exclusion to become their policy. The Proud Boys wouldn't be outwardly white nationalist, he said, but they would demand respect for white men.

"I'm a Western chauvinist," he went on. "If I lived in Japan, I would respect Japanese culture, and I would want to be included if there were Proud Ninjas. Same as it is here. If you're Black, Hispanic, whatever, I don't really care . . . I'm all about the culture. Now, part of that is recognizing that white males seem to be the ones who made it and respecting that, but it doesn't mean you're not invited to the party."

The caller dug deeper, and asked McInnes to expand on Proud Boys ideology, specifically as it related to "the Jewish Question"—a pre–World War II debate on what to do with Europe's Jewish minority, for which Adolf Hitler perpetrated the genocide-inducing "Final Solution." Essentially, the caller wanted to know if the gang would be antisemitic as a rule.

"I think there's a great argument that the origins of political correctness and cultural Marxism was Jewish," McInnes said. "The rationale was 'we don't want another Nazi party, so if white males start getting too proud, take 'em down a peg.' I think that's what [Jewish billionaire George] Soros' grandfather is going for, and I believe that's bad."

He added later that he only had one major "beef" with antisemitism: "To blame Jews for everything is to deny yourself culpability."

McInnes was sussing out the Proud Boys' worldview in real time. Callers would ask questions, McInnes would answer, and boom, the gang had new guidance. It was a haphazard and disorganized process, and it led to some pretty glaring contradictions in their worldview: McInnes wanted them to be racially inclusive but harbor a sense of white supremacy. They were violently anti-immigration, but they welcomed international adherents (and their leader, of course, was an immigrant himself). McInnes didn't want them to be associated with Nazi skinheads, but he understood if members subscribed to a few antisemitic conspiracy theories. The Proud Boys doctrine was—and still is—difficult to pin down in one sentence or soundbite, and that proved to be beneficial down the road: for years they were overlooked by the mainstream media and law enforcement agencies, which had no idea what to do with a group that wasn't voluntarily standing under a big sign that said "Nazis" or "Terrorists."

The truth is that McInnes didn't care who joined the Proud Boys. Any man could become a member of this national coalition of patriots, so long as they were willing to fight for the right-wing establishment's political ambitions. In fact, the only real politics held by the Proud Boys as a group involved supporting the Trump administration and opposing Democrats, McInnes told me.

"When Trump happened, the entire country was forced to pick a side. We happily picked Trump, and anyone who didn't like him voluntarily left the club," he said. "Proud Boy meetups became a safe haven where right-leaning men could talk freely in Dem-run cities."

All of it was in service of the real goal, which was violence. McInnes constantly celebrated violence on his show, particularly when it was carried out by Trump supporters in service of right-wing causes and grievances. Here are a few highlights:

- "Remember violence? Remember how fun it was? Remember fighting? There's no happier man than a guy who just won a fight. There's no beer more delicious than a man who just won a fight and drank that first beer."

- "We will kill you, that's the Proud Boys in a nutshell. We look nice, we seem soft, we have 'boys' in our name, but like Bill the Butcher and the Bowery Boys, we will assassinate you."

- "Get in trouble, get arrested, get fired, let's all get in this together. They can't kill us all."

- "I was on [Newsmax with host Steve Malzberg] yesterday and I go, 'It's fun to punch these kids because they've never been punched before.' . . . Malzberg was like, 'You're not advocating violence are you?' and I was like 'I absolutely am. In fact I'm mad at you for not advocating it in the past. It's a wonderful and effective thing.'"

- "I have all these conservatives bitching to me about Trump and saying, 'Can you believe the violence?' What's the matter with violence? Fighting solves everything."

- "If you're wearing a MAGA hat and some guy with a slightly punk demeanor comes up and says, 'Hey are you pro-Trump?' choke him. Trust your instincts. Don't listen to what he has to say. Choke. Him."

This rhetoric set McInnes apart from other far-right talk show hosts of his era. Conspiratorial, bigoted shock jocks were a dime a dozen when *The Gavin McInnes Show* hit the scene. Alex Jones, for example, had been a syndicated host for more than fifteen years by the time the Proud Boys were announced. And Jones certainly incited grievous acts among his audience: his repeated lies that the Sandy Hook Elementary School shooting in 2012 was a false flag using "crisis actors" led to years of harassment and threats for the parents of the young victims. But where Jones and the rest of the right-wing grievance apparatus pointed to threats and whined about their ideological opponents, McInnes told his viewers to get out there and fight them.

And the gang listened. Scores of Proud Boys have been arrested over the years on charges related to violent attacks, rioting, and destroying property at rallies and political events and anywhere else they congregate. More than forty of them (and counting) were collared over a single event, the insurrection at the US Capitol on January 6, 2021, where the gang played an outsized role compared to their fellow extremist groups. Members have been slapped with charges for brutalizing protesters, police officers, and members of the press using their fists and a variety of weapons. They've also been charged over gang assaults, racist attacks, harassment campaigns against their ideological opponents and death threats lodged against government officials, and conspiracy to commit violence prior to big national political events. They've been connected by federal agents to at least one assassination plot and many less-targeted plans to maim and kill their opponents at rallies. They are classified as a hate group by multiple extremist oversight agencies, have been investigated by Congress, and are formally labeled as a terrorist organization by the Canadian government, following the Capitol siege. And that's just the stuff on the books—the majority of their plots and threats and attacks have never led to significant consequences.

To support his demands for violence, McInnes created a structure for his gang that encouraged it. Organizationally, he built the group to look a bit like the Knights of Columbus. The Proud Boys launched chapters across the country (largely on Facebook and later Telegram), starting with McInnes' crew in New York City. Each chapter had its own leaders, who took guidance from McInnes and the inaugural chapter. The chapters were given a four-tier ranking system like the Knights called degrees. But unlike the Knights, who ascended the ranks through acts of Catholic ministry, a Proud Boy earned promotion through increasing displays of loyalty to the gang and acts of violence in service of right-wing causes.

McInnes denies today that bigotry and political violence make up the bulk of the Proud Boys' early education. Racism, he told me, is "not tolerated in any form," and the violence, he claims, is "always a reaction to left-wing violence." Whether he truly believes those things or not, they're just not borne out in reality. But his distortions of the truth nevertheless have worked to deflect attention from law enforcement, the media, and Congress for years. Almost every awful quote and violent decree McInnes issued over the course of hundreds of hours on his show has been readily available to view online from the start. But he knew that the people watching his show (who were now likely either members of his gang or sympathetic to its cause) were a completely different audience than the general public. In September of 2016, four months after he announced the Proud Boys on his show, McInnes introduced them to the outside world in a blog post on

Taki's Magazine, a webzine known for publishing the rantings of a neo-Nazi as viable political discourse. He described them not as a violent political street gang but as a patriotic fraternal drinking club, built in support of then candidate Donald Trump and in pursuit of "defending the West against the people who want to shut it down." The post was full of moral panic and McInnes' snarky brand of intolerance, but noticeably absent were his ongoing calls for violence:

"The fact that this group has exploded so quickly is a testament to how completely finished young American men are with apology culture," he wrote of the Proud Boys. "They tried being ashamed of themselves and accepting blame for slavery, the wage gap, ableism, and some fag-bashing that went on two generations ago, but it didn't work. So they're going with their gut and indulging in the natural pride that comes from being part of the greatest culture in the world."

This laundered image highlighted another foundational piece of the Proud Boys' early education that McInnes didn't often talk about outside his show: denial, deflection, and obfuscation. He incentivized violence and bigotry, but he also taught the Proud Boys to cover their tracks after the fact, using the same kind of language he used in the Taki's Magazine post. The hateful rhetoric was always slathered in a thick layer of irony so as not to be taken too seriously. And the violence was either deflected or denied outright, to avoid legal repercussions and societal backlash. Fighting and then lying about it are pillars of the Proud Boys' institutional instruction.

"Get the fuck out of there," McInnes said amid a racist rant about justified violence. "When the cops catch you, deny everything. Black kids have it right: deny, deny, deny."

The Proud Boys exploded in popularity just as Trump was rounding third base on his successful presidential run. McInnes said in his 2016 introduction that the gang already had chapters in the Pacific Northwest, Louisiana, Minnesota, Tennessee, New Jersey, and even some countries outside the United States. If that wasn't a true statement at the time, there's certainly some truth to it today: as of January 2022, the gang claims 157 active chapters and thousands of members in the United States alone, spanning all but three states, and claims to have international representation in Mexico, Japan, the United Kingdom, Brazil, Australia, and Canada, among other countries.

They got their early momentum on the coattails of Trump, who was known even in the early days of his campaign to attract violent bigots to his rallies and incite violence among them. In March 2016, Matthew Heimbach, then a leader in the now-defunct neo-Nazi Traditionalist Worker Party, was among a crowd of racists who accosted a Black woman protesting a MAGA rally in Louisville, Kentucky, immediately after Trump pointed out his detractors to his audience and shouted, "Get 'em out of here!" This was the tone that shaped Trump rallies throughout his presidency. Inciting violence became one of his recurring gags. He would fantasize onstage about beating up libs or media personalities or antifa, and the crowd would go wild. Some may not have taken the rhetoric seriously, but others carried out unspeakable acts of violence in Trump's name. A section of the president's followers embraced political violence, and for that reason they embraced what the Proud Boys were doing, too.

Once Trump was elected, Proud Boys began to appear at all kinds of political rallies in liberal enclaves on the West and East Coasts, like Berkeley and Portland and New York. They carried themselves the way McInnes taught them: they were aggressively patriotic, drunk as a skunk, and violent toward anyone and everyone who showed up to protest their presence or the Trump administration.

They quickly made headlines, at first because they were peculiar: America wasn't used to seeing people under the age of a mummified corpse at conservative events, and here was a sizable group of men in their twenties and thirties, with matching outfits, who had apparently assembled an entire club based on their adoration for the new Republican president. To the political right, this was a novel image, and to the media, it looked ridiculous. The *New Yorker*, in a story covering Trump's inaugural celebration at the National Press Club in DC, described McInnes as a "forty-six-year-old with a waxed mustache" who showed up with a dozen guys "a decade or two his junior, who he introduced as the Proud Boys." The story quoted one member, who used familiar McInnes talking points to describe the gang:

> "I find it strange," a Proud Boy from North Carolina said. "It's O.K. to be a nationalist, and it's O.K. to have pride in yourself. But you put either of those concepts together with being white, and suddenly you're an insane Nazi bigot."

But it didn't take long for the gang to reveal its true nature. Even in their earliest days, Proud Boys were known for showing up to events where they knew they might find leftists or counterdemonstrators and attacking on sight. They almost never left a rally without engaging in some kind of bloody brawl involving dozens of people. They made national headlines for the violence early and often, beginning in February 2017, after they fought with a group of antifascist demonstrators outside a New York University event where McInnes was scheduled to speak. McInnes celebrated what happened, saying later of his Proud Boys: "My guys are left to fight. And here's the crucial part: We do. And we beat the crap out of them."

Later that year, they led a hateful motorcade through Islamberg, a small community in upstate New York where numerous Muslim families had moved to get away from the racism and violence they faced in the city. The Proud Boys lodged bogus claims that those families were training jihadi terrorists, and as a result, the threats and bigotry followed them to their new home. Several members of militant right-wing groups were later arrested over plots to storm and attack the community.

Such violence and intolerance should have been immediately disqualifying for a group of self-described political activists seeking mainstream legitimacy. And for many of the extremists who reared their ugly heads during the Trump era, it was: some far-right groups disappeared from the scene altogether after events like Unite the Right in Charlottesville, when their violent tendencies and abhorrent beliefs were exposed to the public. But the Proud Boys continued to grow in power and political prestige, even after they organized and engaged in some of the most gruesome acts of political violence in modern American history. And now they enjoy a seemingly full embrace from the Republican Party, lackadaisical oversight from state and federal authorities, and a seat at the helm of a growing movement of violent extremism.

McInnes built an incredibly strong and resilient political monster and unleashed it on the world during a golden era for political monsters. The Proud Boys thrived in the vicious atmosphere they were born into and within months grew into a dangerous and national political force. They have McInnes to thank for that: he didn't just build a gang, he built a worldview for a generation of violent men.

Chapter 2

HOW TO BUILD A STREET GANG

Chace's first degree initiation ceremony happened quickly and seemingly at random, as he and a group of Proud Boys marched down a darkening street in Washington, DC. This was a demonstration mostly indistinguishable from several others he'd been to with the same group of guys. They would swarm a metropolitan city the evening before a big event, advertised on social media as a flag-waving hootenanny in support of then president Trump and good old American patriotism. They would cram into local bars and then march through the darkened streets, howling and carrying on until the early hours of the morning. They might be joined by a few buddies from other extremist groups—often the Oath Keepers and Three Percenters, perpetually armed antigovernment extremists who describe themselves as militias—but you could always tell a Proud Boys–led procession apart from other far-right events. This was a drunken, testosterone-fueled, black-and-yellow MAGA parade, a scene that would make any passerby duck into the closest alleyway to avoid making contact.

There were dozens of them on this night, in December of 2020, some decked out in their black-and-yellow Fred Perrys, while others wore flak jackets and MAGA hats or vests embroidered with the Punisher logo. They saw themselves as a battalion of freedom fighters, but they looked more like a wayward frat party. They followed their usual itinerary, Chace said, which meant their first stop was a local bar to get plastered. They couldn't show up at just any dive—activists would have already tipped off the local haunts that an extremist fight club was in town—but they knew a sympathetic bar owner or two in many metropolitan cities who would let them take over for the night. They took shots, ripped lines of coke, and traded war stories about their street brawls with antifa. Chace said "antifa" could have meant anything, though. It was a catch-all term.

"Anyone who disagrees with the Proud Boys on the street is antifa," he told me. "If it's a fifty-year-old man with a Biden flag or somebody in black bloc, they're all antifa."

When they were good and smashed, they marched out into the night.

They had two goals for this particular cavalcade. One was to show force. They roamed the sidewalks in a pack, screeching and chugging beer out of Solo cups. Sometimes they stopped and surrounded one another and gave speeches, fingers pointing and spit flying, about defending the US Constitution and bravery in the face of leftism. The whole raucous occasion was being recorded, via livestreams and videos that would later be posted to YouTube and other social media. They wanted locals to know the Proud Boys were in town for an event. If they marched all night unopposed, they considered it a win, convinced that their presence had intimidated the rest of the city into submission.

But what they really wanted was opposition. Their other goal, and their primary wish for any event, was to turn a corner and find a small group of protesters waiting for them so they could fight (preferably with an unfair advantage in terms of numbers). Most of them had traveled from out of town specifically for the next day's event—in this case, a massive and bloody MAGA rally on December 12, organized in protest of the 2020 election results—where they'd get a chance to pummel some leftists. They pontificated plenty about free speech and defending Western culture and right-wing values, but this group of potbellied bros in tactical gear didn't show up to listen to a few speeches and head home. They wanted to get drunk and fight. They'd have to wait a bit longer for that, though. It was early into their march, and so far they hadn't met any of the resistance they were hoping for.

At one point, out of nowhere, Chace was initiated into the gang. He said he's still not sure why he was asked to take the oath that night. He thinks his superior, a member of the Proud Boys in New York State, was perhaps overly sentimental from the booze—"hammered as shit," in Chace's words.

In a video recording of the big moment, Chace can be seen marching behind several dozen Proud Boys. The scene is jovial. They're parading down the street, there's a clash of classic rock music and shouting in the air, and a few of them are trading chants of "Fuck antifa." Chace's superior stops midmarch and whips around, stumbling a bit before regaining his posture and control of his beer. He finds Chace and slurs out the words, "You're gonna become a first degree Proud Boy. I want you to put your hand up."

"OK," Chace says.

The pair stands face-to-face, each with his right hand in the air. The superior barks out the first few words of the Proud Boys oath, beckoning Chace to repeat them, and he does. Eventually, through call-and-response, they get through all the words:

"I am a Western chauvinist and I refuse to apologize for creating the modern world."

And just like that, Chace is a member of the Proud Boys. They high-five one another and embrace.

"Congratulations," the higher-up crows. But what he doesn't realize is that Chace is not quite like other recruits. He attends monthly meetups and shows his face at rallies. But he's not working for the Proud Boys—he's an infiltrator and a mole. He didn't join up to punch antifa but rather to help antifascist activists in his community. He works against the Proud Boys from within by gathering information about their membership and events and leaks the info to other activists or the press when he thinks it might hinder a substantial act of violence. Several activists, posing as Proud Boys, spoke at length and provided information for this book, but Chace is one of just a few who does such work in person, at great risk to himself.

He said he didn't go looking to become an infiltrator. The opportunity arose when he found himself close to one of the New York State chapter leaders at a MAGA rally, which he attended, as he often did, to be a fly on the wall. He wanted to document the activities of any extremist group or far-right figure who might show up to the party, and perhaps try to identify a few or take some photos that could later be used by researchers to unmask a fascist. These are common tactics deployed by a broad range of antifascist activists. Chace's politics might differ from his immediate comrades: he told me he "used to be a regular Democrat, then a Bernie bro" and now said he's a more militant leftist, akin to socialist revolutionary groups like the Zapatistas in Mexico. But all these activists share a common motivation when it comes to extremist rallies: find a way to hinder the far right to protect their allies in the local community.

This time, Chace found himself in lengthy conversations with a high-ranking Proud Boy. He said the superior really took a liking to him, to the point where they were laughing and sharing inside jokes by the end of the day. Chace saw it as an opportunity to get closer to the gang and maybe feed some details about their movements back to his activist community. A big portion of antifascist work consists of gathering information about public events planned by extremists, and if Chace could get an inside track on those plans, he might be able to thwart an event or an attack before it was carried out. He decided right then and there that he would try to join the Proud Boys as a mole. But he didn't want to raise eyebrows by acting too desperate.

"That's the trick in getting in with these kinds of groups. You can't seem eager," he said. "You just have to be there and be perceptive or at least pretend to be perceptive to their ideas and their ideology."

It took several more events for him to gain the chapter's trust. Chace said he wasn't ever explicitly invited to anything in the beginning; he just kind of showed up. He didn't want to press the issue of joining, so he focused instead on getting to know members on a personal level. Most anyone can attend a public Proud Boys rally (so long as they're not wearing a black balaclava), but their drinking events, meetings, and prerally marches are more exclusive, for trusted members and pals of the gang only. Chace attended several of the public events and drank with some members, and eventually he was invited to a few meetings, which were not unlike the drunken ragers thrown by McInnes at the bar across from Compound Media. Once Chace was asked to take the oath, he knew he was set: now he had a member vouching for him, and he could relax a bit. He was still in danger of being outed as a mole (and whatever violent consequences that came with it), but some of the other guys seemed to like him, too. He was one of the Proud Boys now.

Eventually, they gave him all kinds of access to their inner circle, and he got a rare look at their organizational structure and personal lives. They invited him to private Telegram channels where members would gossip about other chapters, discuss ideology, brag about past fights, and fantasize about their next bouts. He received detailed briefing documents, directing Proud Boys on recommended attire, positioning, suggested routes, and attack plans at events. He said he witnessed regular assaults at those events, sometimes with mace and batons or other bludgeoning weapons. But he said he managed to stay on the outskirts of the melee without drawing attention to the fact that he wasn't doing much fighting, so he never had to lay a finger on an ally to prove himself. Because of his work on the inside, and the work taken up by an army of other researchers and infiltrators, we can now paint a pretty strong picture of the internal structure of the Proud Boys, as well as the ranking system that motivates members.

Taking the oath that night gave Chace the rank of first degree. But he was the lowest on the Proud Boys totem pole, an acolyte of sorts who couldn't speak for the rest of the gang nor expect anyone to come to his defense if he screwed up.

"They don't technically consider you a real Proud Boy until your second degree," he explained.

It's not all that difficult to pass the initial trials required for full membership. All a guy has to do is publicly declare his allegiance to the gang—as well as the Republican Party, which at the time meant Donald Trump—and accept any consequences that came with it.

"You make your Western chauvinism public and you don't care who knows it," wrote McInnes in his Taki's Magazine introduction to the Proud Boys. "If you support Trump (how can you not if you're a Proud Boy?) and it comes up in the cafeteria, you proudly state your stance. If that gets you fired, so be it."

There are four ranks within the Proud Boys, called degrees, which serve as a basic rule set each member must follow in his ongoing pursuit of promotion. Each degree requires an increasing amount of personal commitment and violence, and many Proud Boys boast their rank by displaying the degree symbol wherever they can, be it on their bodies or social media profiles (you might, for example, see a 2° or 3° symbol in a Proud Boy's profile picture on social media or as a patch on his gear).

The initiation experience can vary depending on which chapter a recruit belongs to. The Wisconsin chapter, for example, reportedly subjects newbies to a hazing ritual in which they're forced to watch and interact with a torrent of violent and racist imagery online, including graphic videos of Muslims being killed and memes making light of rape victims or Jews killed in the Holocaust. Over in New York, Chace had a different experience. He wasn't inducted until he had some face time with several members at multiple events. But where customs and ideology may vary between chapters, the degree system remains constant.

At the first degree, a new recruit has to declare allegiance to the Proud Boys, often and at every opportunity, whether it's online or in his personal life. In most circumstances, he's not allowed to hide his membership, including and especially when faced with social or legal repercussions. He must take and abide by the oath: "I am a Western chauvinist and I refuse to apologize for creating the modern world."

It's a deceptively binding contract. In theory, a Proud Boy can leave whenever he wants. This isn't exactly the Mafia, and he's not gonna meet his maker if he decides he wants out. But he's swearing fealty to a street gang with a demonstrated history of violent crime and close ties to all kinds of white supremacists and neo-Nazi types. That brand won't be easy to scrub away.

Plus, a first degree Proud Boy is at the bottom floor. He's inside, but he's not exactly trusted within the organization, and nobody of any import has his back. Other Proud Boys may fight alongside him, but they're not going to defend him when the law or the press come knocking. (He'll soon learn that almost nobody enjoys that benefit anyway; Proud Boys of all ranks have snitched on one another, inadvertently or in collaboration with authorities.) So for a first degree, the doorway out is effectively shut behind him as soon as he enters. His only way forward is climbing the ladder.

The second degree is a far more embarrassing and surreal process than the initiation, as Chace quickly learned.

With his initiation out of the way, preparations begin for his next promotion. He'll need to seek out and officially join a local chapter (which can be as easy as searching for one on Facebook or Telegram or whatever social media app far-right extremists have flocked to on a given day), as Chace did following his initiation.

Once leaders decide he's ready, the recruit is pulled outside and surrounded by a group of other Proud Boys. Then comes the big moment in which he obtains his second degree. A timer starts, and his fellow members punch him repeatedly, all at the same time, until he can name five breakfast cereals.

"The rationale here is we all need better adrenaline control," McInnes wrote in Taki's Magazine. "The bonding and camaraderie this violence produces is inspiring."

There are videos of the ritual all over Twitter and YouTube, and if they inspire anything, it's mostly cringe. In one video published to YouTube in 2017, a young man wearing a helmet, with safety goggles around his neck, can be seen surrounded by six other doughy young men, as well as a few onlookers holding American flags (the flag is a favored bludgeoning tool at Proud Boys rallies because it often falls outside local weapon restrictions). The man in the middle takes the Proud Boys oath, and the punches begin. The assailants don't seem to have their hearts in it; one man's pants begin to fall down, showing his crack, another loses his balance and careens face-first into the initiate's body, and a third is assailed himself by the cigarette in his mouth, which billows smoke into his eyeballs and forces him to squint. Through the punches, the initiate names five mediocre cereals, his voice burbling with each blow as if he were trying to sing while riding his bike down a gravel road: "Kiiiiiiix, Cheeeeeerioooos, Frosted Flaaaakes, Wheeeeaties, Raisin Braaaaaan." One of the top comments on the video reads: "I've seen harder hits in flag football."

Chace said he expected similar treatment during his second degree—some weak-willed punches from a few noodle-armed jabronis wouldn't be difficult to withstand. But somebody in the fray got him good, and he left with a cracked rib.

"They didn't really hit that hard, but one of them got a lucky shot on me," he said. But he didn't tell the other Proud Boys he was injured. Instead, he waited until he was on the other end of the initiation to get some revenge. "I made sure I got a really good shot on the next guy."

If the embarrassment of the punching ceremony isn't enough, a second degree Proud Boy is also expected to subscribe to one of the truly more bizarre facets of the group. This is the "no wanks" policy outlined by McInnes: he's only allowed to masturbate once a month, and he's otherwise only able to ejaculate when he's "within one yard of a woman with her consent."

Dating back to the early days of his show, McInnes was obsessed with the concept of no wanks. He was convinced that if men stopped jerking off to porn, they'd stay attracted to their

wives and girlfriends, enjoy better sex lives and heightened testosterone, and become better fighters.

"No wanks is a gift from the Lord where you don't beat
off," he said in an early episode of his show. "I have superhuman
strength. I'm smarter than ever before. I also crave my wife in a
way that's unprecedented."

In another episode, he said, with a greasy grin, that foregoing
masturbation "led me to raping my wife more, which has im-
proved our marriage tenfold."

These claims don't just sound ridiculous and disgusting,
they're also unproven. The notion of no wanks is pushed pri-
marily by right-wing pundits and so-called men's rights activists,
citing several highly disputed works, including an unreplicated
study conducted in 2001 with a sample size of ten, which claimed
that foregoing masturbation led to higher testosterone counts
(other studies have found that the opposite is true, that masturbation actually leads to higher testosterone counts). For years,
it's been a popular talking point among reactionary podcasters
and talk show hosts, who whip up anxiety around masculinity
and then generously offer to solve the problem by selling protein
powder and testosterone supplements to their audiences.

Some Proud Boys seem to take the no wanks rule as a joke,
and it was difficult to find anyone who would talk about it earnestly. But callers into McInnes' show said they were passion-
ate practitioners—one referred to no wanks as a "revelation."
McInnes described it as the "core of their existence" and declared
on his show that "no wanks is going on forever."

Once a recruit has joined a chapter and finalized his second
degree, he's known casually as a brother among Proud Boys.

At the third degree, things get permanent. The recruit must
get a Proud Boys tattoo or brand (plenty of them have done the
former, but there's not much evidence of the latter). The ink can

incorporate the gang's various symbols, which include the Fred Perry laurel wreath and the weather vane. But it must clearly say "Proud Boy." McInnes said he preferred to see a specific style, which is simply "Proud Boy" in a popular tattoo font resembling old-style freehand. Today, many third degrees bear that very tat across their forearm.

It looks like this:

PROUD BOY

Of course, a third degree is still expected to follow all the rules and regulations required of the first and second degrees. Now, this oath-reciting, rarely masturbating, tattooed brother is ready to gun for the gang's top honor.

To reach the group's highest order, the fourth degree, a Proud Boy must commit a significant act of political violence or get arrested on behalf of the organization. McInnes spelled it out during an appearance on *The Joe Rogan Experience* in February of 2017, on which he introduced the Proud Boys to Rogan's millions of viewers.

The two-and-a-half-hour episode was so toxic that it was removed from Spotify, alongside dozens of other controversial Rogan episodes, amid a deal he signed with the platform worth at least $100 million. But for the Proud Boys, it served as a huge platform. In fact, it sounded a lot like an episode of McInnes' show: the pair bantered over a variety of detestable topics, including a long, giggly debate about the line between rape fantasies and actual rape and when hitting a woman might be justified.

Later, Rogan handed the floor to McInnes to introduce his new gang and the degree system he came up with.

"I started this gang called the Proud Boys," McInnes said.

"The Proud Boys?" Rogan asked. "What's the Proud Boys about?"

"We have chapters all over the world, we meet once a month, we get drunk. It's like the Elks Lodge," McInnes said.

"Celebrating manhood?"

"Yeah, no women allowed. And we have degrees like the Knights of Columbus."

McInnes fired off the first three degrees, and when he brought up the violence requirement in the fourth, Rogan bristled.

"Fourth degree, you get arrested or get in a serious violent fight for the cause," McInnes said.

"Really?" Rogan asked.

"Yes."

"You get arrested? In a serious violent fight? So you're promoting violence?"

"Or some major altercation."

Rogan fumbled over his next words, suddenly uncomfortable with the direction of the conversation. "You shouldn't . . . ah . . . you should erase that part" from the rules, he suggested.

McInnes did not erase that part from the rules. The fourth degree remains today as a major motivating factor for any Proud Boy, and the title doesn't necessarily come easily. Proud Boys have to earn it, by proving to leaders that their attack was significant and public enough. One particularly violent member named Alan Swinney—who's been convicted for a number of assaults carried out as a Proud Boy, using various weapons including paintball guns and a revolver—bragged about his rank on Facebook in 2020 after he was seen dousing protesters with bear mace in Seattle.

"Oh hey guess what? I got my 4th degree again today," he wrote in a now-deleted post, which included a video of him holding a canister of pepper spray.

Proud Boys leadership clearly understands the problematic nature of the fourth degree. The group's survival depends largely on its leaders' ability to convince the news media, law enforcement agencies, and politicians that they are exactly what McInnes claims: a patriotic men's club standing in defense of right-wing values. But as many Proud Boys have learned amid the numerous assault cases they've racked up over the years, it's hard to claim self-defense when violence and martyrdom are written into your constitution. They've tried to scrub mentions of the fourth degree from their public-facing promotional material after a set of violent events in 2018 and continue to downplay it in the press.

McInnes maintains that members have never been allowed to "seek out" the violence required for the top rank. In an interview with me over email, he repeated his claim that the Proud Boys' violence is only ever reciprocal.

"The history of violence with the Proud Boys is always a RE-ACTION to left-wing violence," he wrote. "The Fourth Degree is a joke. The way it usually comes up is, 'Oh I guess that means you got your Fourth Degree' and the other laughs and says, 'Oh yeah, I guess you're right.' There are no special privileges or secret rooms you get to go into."

He doesn't like being asked about the fourth degree. On that topic, he left me with something that wasn't quite a threat: "This is not a club that's looking for violence. If it was, you'd be in the hospital."

He also doesn't like the Proud Boys being likened to a gang, despite clearly and repeatedly characterizing them as such. He wants the public to see them in a softer and more forgiving light, which is why he compares them to the Knights of Columbus and other fraternal organizations in interviews. Structurally speaking, they carry some similarities: the Knights have a Supreme Council on the East Coast that oversees local councils across the country and provides national support and oversight for local events, fundraising efforts, and individual needs.

The Proud Boys have the same in an Elders Chapter, formed in 2018 by the gang's lawyer at the time, Jason Lee Van Dyke, which includes eight chapter leaders and veterans from around the country. They write and keep basic tenets for each of the chapters beneath them to follow, organize and green-light rallies, raise and funnel cash, and oversee the gang's host of LLCs (we'll get to that later).

Chapters have always been organized online, first on Facebook, until the platform banned them in 2018, following a particularly brutal attack in New York City, and then dubbed them as a hate organization. Today, they organize and recruit largely on Telegram, an encrypted chat app that has generally been more lenient with extremist groups organizing on the platform. It hosts the majority of the Proud Boys' communications and organization efforts, both public and private, and many chapters are easily searchable there. Some chapters maintain websites: two in Oklahoma—one in Tulsa and the other in Oklahoma City—run a website called okfafo.com, a reference to the Proud Boys' favorite motto, "Fuck Around and Find Out." There you can buy Proud Boys merch or look at a gallery that includes photos from a river-rafting trip, in which members wore their gang colors and flew a black flag that read "Show Me Your Tits." The "about" section features a sizzle reel of sorts, a hyperpatriotic video slideshow depicting members marching through city streets, interspersed with images of a Proud Boy who was stabbed during one of their rallies in 2020. The sappy Americana of "Mr. Red, White, and Blue" by Coffey Anderson plays in the background. As a whole, the website looks like a GeoCities-era recruiting platform for the military. And it *is* a recruiting site: You can apply to join the Oklahoma Proud Boys at okfafo.com, though you'll have to provide a copy of your photo ID just to ask. Long gone are the wink-and-nudge days of the Klan.

Each chapter has a leader who reports back to the national organization, but McInnes built the chapter structure with a sense of autonomy in mind. In general, chapter leaders are free to throw their own events, recruit their own members, collect dues, and even sprinkle in their own rules and ideology, so long as they follow McInnes' basics. But their semisovereignty also means that they're largely on their own if they screw up or make the national organization look bad. The elders have publicly disavowed individuals after they committed indefensible crimes, got infiltrated by antifa, or leaked internal information to the press, for example. But if a group's crimes are deemed justified and worthy by the elders, they might instead enjoy support through fundraisers, promotional blitzes, and appearances on talk shows and podcasts of the Proud Boys' extremist affiliates. That's all up to the national leadership.

But a chapter's primary function is to serve as a local rallying point for recruiting and events. Chapter leaders can organize their own rallies and seek help from a network of other chapters to quickly gather bodies, funding, and equipment and then mobilize them when the time comes. Sometimes they latch onto Republican events they didn't plan, especially when they get wind of a counterprotest, signaling that they'll have a group to trade blows with. But they host the majority of the rallies they attend because they know that adding their name to a marquee will lure out antifascists and other demonstrators to fight. Some of their events are hyperlocal and small, organized in parks and downtown squares or in tandem with other politically charged events (today the Proud Boys add their threatening presence to antivaccine gatherings, school board meetings where race issues are being discussed, and antiabortion rallies, to name a few).

Other events are painstakingly planned, large-scale affairs that require input and mobilization from multiple chapters and their members.

They try to maintain secrecy around their planning materials, both to keep an upper hand against counterprotesters and to avoid leaving a paper trail behind criminal activity. But they have to do their event planning somewhere, and thanks to the work of researchers and activists, we have access to plenty of documentation showing the scope of the groundwork that can go into a Proud Boys event.

One such plan is detailed in a secret twenty-three-page document drafted by Randy Ireland, leader of the Hell's Gate Bridge chapter of the Proud Boys in New York City, and disseminated to at least nine other chapters in the Empire State and beyond. The "Strategic Security Plan"—stamped as confidential and provided for this book by an anonymous member of the Proud Boys—spells out in militaristic detail what roles and titles different members have in the field, what equipment to bring, which channels to communicate on, what routes to take through the city, and when to engage or disengage in combat. The Proud Boys wanted to send more than seventy members to act as a "security detail" to a "MAGA March" event planned for Manhattan on January 10, 2021, as one of the many increasingly violent extremist events held in Washington, DC, and elsewhere in the lead-up to and following the insurrection on January 6. This MAGA event (and several others like it) fizzled out after thousands of Trump supporters took the Capitol days prior, attracting the attention of every law enforcement agency and government official in the country. But the planning document provides a never-before-seen angle into the strategies (or, at least, attempted strategies) deployed by the Proud Boys in the field.

The gang was acutely aware of its reputation at this point in its illustrious career of violence. The Proud Boys were particularly nervous about events held in New York, where several of their fellow members were still behind bars over a vicious gang assault outside a political event back in 2018. And in the document, Ireland—fresh off his own arrest after he brought a knife and other weaponry to a gubernatorial campaign event—repeatedly reminds members that they're under intense legal scrutiny in New York City and should be careful about throwing the first punch:

> If any violence does spout off, all Proud Boys are expected to respond immediately—only so far as to eliminate and end that threat to them or others. VERY IMPORTANT: Once the threat has been neutralized, WE STOP!! If a Brother is going to the extreme, we pull them back and get them to the back of the line IMMEDIATELY! (**We have 2 Brothers serving a 4-Year Prison Sentence in NYS for the mere appearance of taking things too far.**)

Then he lays out a temporary chain of command, giving himself the title of "General of Security Detail," followed by a list of other roles identified by members' nicknames: Matt would work comms, JimmyZ would cover recruiting in the field, EmLIPB would be on overwatch or lookout, and so on. Ranking Proud Boys would talk over two-way radios, while the others would communicate in various channels set up for the event on Telegram and other chat apps. They would follow any orders given to them by police and provide a "back-up role and to force them to do their jobs, as may be necessary."

What's telling about the plan is that it never really spells out a necessity for the Proud Boys' attendance at all, beyond a vague desire to provide "security" and to "mitigate threats." The gang's "objectives" that day would be to "get everyone there and home safe, sound and without injury or arrest" and "stick to the plan at all times," Ireland wrote. The "purpose of this Event Security Plan," he argued, was to "implement a well-defined, strategic, and organized framework, with the chief of objectives being to keep all event attendees safe and secure." There is no indication that anyone outside the Proud Boys asked for any of this.

From there on, Ireland's plan veers into military fantasyland, where his team is an elite force of highly trained commandos capable of impossibly complex (and totally inadvisable) combat maneuvers under very specific situations:

> All Scouts will be dressed in dark clothing, complete with masks and hoods/hats/etc. All Scouts will NOT wear PB colors, for the sole purpose of blending in. Each Scout will immediately relay any threat sighted to the VP of Scouts, giving them the greatest amount of information regarding the threat as possible. If a scout sees many counter-protestors either forming, advancing, or about to penetrate our perimeter— they are immediately to sound a MAYDAY call to ensure the proper attention is given to the rising threat . . .
>
> If a threat is encountered, Security Team Officers will assess the threat and mobilize tactical teams by relaying the threat and location to the Team Leads. If only 1 or 2 or 3 Tactical Teams are required—all other Tactical Teams are Required to stay in place and NOT respond to the threat area. Doing so could jeopardize the Safety and Health of the other attendees—and open up our flanks to further threats.

In reality, the Proud Boys don't actually fight like they're SEAL Team Six or Spartan warriors, with scouts and tactical teams and structural perimeters. They march in big groups, single out smaller groups they can easily overwhelm, and then they attack with blind fury, throwing punches at their opponents until either the cops come or someone stops moving. But Ireland's plan reveals something interesting about the gang's perceived place in the world—namely, that the rank and file earnestly believe they're a necessary defense force against liberal protesters and a legitimate and accepted supplement to law enforcement. He finishes off the document with a series of maps showing where his tactical teams should mobilize, and a threat assessment reference sheet, which considers a group of "50+ Antifa/BLM or Counter Protesters" as a Category IV (basic level security threat) and a "1000+ Antifa/BLM Counter-Protest Group" as a Category I (maximum level security threat).

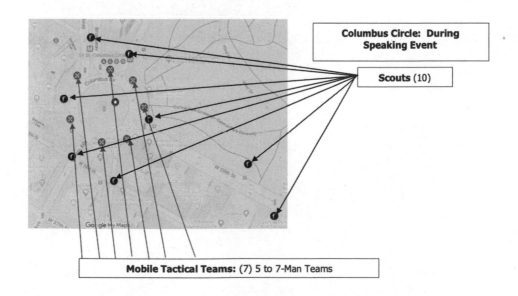

CONFIDENTIAL AND PROPRIETARY   **1/5/2021**

Still, the fact that the Proud Boys may not be tactical geniuses doesn't negate the threat they pose. Most of these guys don't give any thought to preparedness plans before rallies or falling in line when law enforcement is around; the majority just want to fight antifa.

The structure of the gang laid out by McInnes encourages each Proud Boy to push toward a common goal, the fourth degree, which invariably means each individual Proud Boy follows a similar path into violence and destruction for the cause.

Chapter 3

ANATOMY OF A PROUD BOY

On June 30, 2018, Ethan Michael Nordean became a folk hero among Proud Boys for an act of brazen political violence.

He'd been a member of the Seattle chapter for a little over a year, and he followed them to rallies up and down the West Coast, where they enjoyed a semiregular routine of getting completely hammered and fighting protesters at MAGA events. Though he hadn't yet acquired his fourth degree, he'd fought alongside them enough to earn their respect. By that point, everyone called him by his nickname: Rufio Panman, a reference to the punk leader of the Lost Boys in the 1991 children's movie *Hook*. And that day, during a particularly bloody rally organized in Portland, Oregon, Rufio became a legend on the far right, when he was captured on video knocking a man unconscious.

At just twenty seconds long, the video of the punch that went viral doesn't provide much context, but it sets the scene: Nordean is standing in the middle of a narrow street near downtown Portland, separated from the larger group of far-right hooligans he was marching through the city with that day. Behind him in the shot, just a few feet away, a crowd of more than twenty people is fully engaged in combat. Members of the Proud Boys and Patriot Prayer—their smaller affiliate group based in the Pacific Northwest—are trading blows with counterprotesters dressed in black, both sides mixed up in a viscous throng that careens back and forth across the street in broad daylight. Beyond them, a line of armored police officers approaches slowly but doesn't immediately intervene.

Nordean is in the foreground of the shot, wearing a backward cap and his Fred Perry polo. He looks back and forth, searching the fray for a target. He squares up as an opponent separates from the crowd and rushes toward him. The guy approaching is dressed in black clothing and wearing sunglasses, with a handkerchief covering his face (unlike the Proud Boys, counterprotesters tend to wisely prefer anonymity). He's smaller in stature than Nordean—a meathead who'd spent the previous few years bodybuilding and mainlining protein supplements—but he's armed with an expanded metal baton, and he takes a long, overhead swing at Nordean, who deflects the first blow with a forearm protected by padding. As the second blow comes down, Nordean grabs the baton with his left hand and, in a single, fluid motion, brings his right arm around for a haymaker, connecting with the side of the guy's face. The victim is out before his head slams into the pavement, glasses and mask flying off in different directions. The victim's comrades drag him away as the clip ends, his unconscious body stiff and straight as a board.

The Proud Boys called it the "punch heard around the world," and it instantly catapulted Nordean to celebrity status on the fringes of the far right. The video exploded across conservative media, presented as indisputable proof of leftist violence and as rationale for right-wing retribution. Alex Jones, the frothing right-wing conspiracy theorist at the helm of InfoWars, called the knockout punch "an incredible archetypal American moment" and invited Nordean onto his show two weeks later.

"This is the war against America," Jones said during the show. "You try to speak to them as humans. They disregard that and use it as weakness. But they do listen to your fist smashing into their face."

"Yeah, yes they do," Nordean replied. Jones kept playing the video on loop and cackled with glee watching Nordean's fist make contact.

"I just love that giant roundhouse right hook, and then shoving him down so his head hits the pavement. That probably hurt him more! God, I love it," Jones crowed. "How good did it feel once you saw his head hit the pavement?"

"Like Gavin McInnes says, violence isn't great, but justified violence is amazing," Nordean responded.

The video became a permanent fixture in Proud Boys promotional material, displayed prominently on their social media pages and in sizzle reels, featuring violent acts played to patriotic music that they use to impress would-be recruits. They held on to that moment because it painted them in their preferred light, as the antagonized, an opportunity they weren't often afforded. They were notorious by that point, having already been involved in so many major acts of political violence since Donald Trump took office, but the Nordean video, in all its brevity, showed them exactly as McInnes wanted them to be seen. Here was a Proud Boy overwhelming his opponent with his fists, in a purported act of self-defense, at a right-wing rally quite literally described as a "Freedom and Courage" event. As a bonus, his victim matched the right's description of antifa, the anonymous black-clad boogeyman who looms large in the imaginations of conservative pundits and politicians everywhere. McInnes wanted to convince the nation that everyday right-wing values were under siege from leftist aggressors, and the Nordean video gave him the perfect bit of propaganda, one that added weight to the "fuck around and find out" slogan they popularized.

Recruitment exploded in the month following Jones' fawning coverage. Six Facebook pages that the Proud Boys used to vet new members saw a 70 percent increase in prospective recruits over that time, totaling more than 820 new possible recruits, according to analysis by the Southern Poverty Law Center. As membership skyrocketed, so did their nationwide chapters: there were just three national chapters listed on Facebook in early 2017, and by 2018, there were forty-four.

To leadership, Nordean was the gold standard for a Proud Boy, and he's been cast that way since the video went viral. The gang would have you believe that members like Nordean aren't savage bloodthirsty goons but reluctant soldiers, forced out of their solemn observations of liberty and provoked into violence by the intolerant left.

"I went into this originally pretty passive," Nordean whined to Jones. "I wanted to try and debate with them. I wanted to see eye to eye."

Of course, Nordean never planned to debate anyone. Talking it out is in fact very much discouraged by McInnes. Remember: "Violence solves everything." And distorting the truth is part of a Proud Boy's curriculum.

It's no surprise, then, that local journalists, reporting painted a completely different picture of the rally than the video and Nordean let on. By their telling, the "Freedom and Courage" rally, organized by Patriot Prayer leader Joey Gibson, was violent from the start and only devolved from there into one of the most gruesome melees they'd ever seen. Members of Patriot Prayer and the Proud Boys marched through town, beating counter-protesters and activists with flagpoles made of wood and PVC piping and metal garbage can lids. Some shouted racial slurs at counterdemonstrators. One Proud Boy broadcast his violent anti-immigrant fantasies over a bullhorn.

"Illegals," he said, should be "smashed into the concrete."

Jason Wilson, a veteran local extremism reporter, said he was struck by just how bloodthirsty the far right was that day. An entire consortium of right-wing bruisers had come on Gibson's invite, hopeful that antifascist counterprotesters would show up, too. The crowd that responded ranged from Proud Boys to "stone-cold Nazi psychos," he said.

"That day," Wilson started, his voice trailing off as he gathered the words to describe it to me. "You've seen the videos, right? They've got, like, seven or eight people just kicking someone who's on the ground. Everyone knows that's a way to kill someone—you don't see a lot of that, kicking someone on the ground, because that person might fucking die. And that day, it was happening everywhere. There were scores of people who just did not care about the consequences. These people wanted to fucking annihilate antifascists, and it was clear that they had come specifically in order to get involved in that violence."

Another witness to the brutality was Alexander Reid Ross, a lecturer at Portland State University and doctoral fellow at the Centre for Analysis of the Radical Right, who showed up to observe. But the brutality he saw quickly turned him from observer to participant, as he tried to get Patriot Prayer members to stop attacking a protester.

"I saw several simultaneous melees occurring, but the most unnerving involved an immobile protestor lying on the ground while about seven Patriot Prayer protestors kicked and stomped him," Ross wrote in a first-person account of the day for *Haaretz* newspaper. He went on:

> Abandoning my attempt to observe, I intervened. Attempting to reason with the attackers, I yelled, "You're going to kill him!" Suddenly I was facing the other direction, heard a loud noise and felt pain in my cheek. Without having so much as raised my arms to defend myself, I had been sucker-punched by a Patriot Prayer supporter. . . .
>
> I kept trying to move the group away from the individual whose life they apparently intended to snuff out. The last remaining belligerent, a heavy-set white male in a bright blue T-shirt, put his knee on the counter-protester's neck and attempted to place him in a choke hold in a ridiculous imitation of a police officer. Since a choke-hold can be fatal, I pressed him to stop, while blood began to pool on the street beneath the counter-protestor's face.

Nordean's punch merely capped off an exhausting day of carnage at a rally intended to spark violence, which ended only after the Portland Police Bureau declared a riot and revoked Gibson's permits for the event. Nordean himself was briefly detained and marched away by police, as his crew chanted "Rufio" behind him. But he was never charged with a crime, adding what the Proud Boys interpreted as another layer of justification. His victim was reportedly hospitalized with a serious concussion.

None of the attendees I spoke to about that day downplayed the fact that some antifascists had clearly come ready for battle, just as the Proud Boys had. There are militant leftist factions who believe that fighting fire with fire is the best counter to far-right fight gangs, and it's those groups that the right loves to present as the ideological archetype for everyone left of Tucker Carlson. But witnesses who weren't a part of either side—Ross and Wilson included—generally agreed that the Proud Boys' characterization of themselves as some kind of reluctant defenders was totally misleading at best.

"This was entirely an event planned by the Proud Boys to fight the left. It was brutal and they targeted people," tweeted journalist Shane Burley. "I am fully convinced that the Proud Boys would have murdered someone today if they had not been stopped."

Nordean came out on the other side of the rally with an almost mythical status above other Proud Boys. He was awarded Proud Boy of the Week for his efforts, and a fellow member posted a blog in celebration of the big punch to their website, capped off with an iteration of their slogan: "They fucked around. They found out."

Shortly thereafter, he was rewarded with the title of Proud Boys elder, one of eight members of the secretive governing council on top of the organization. Going forward, McInnes presented Nordean as the Proud Boys' poster child and the punch as a game changer for the movement.

"Major wars, major events can pivot on the slightest thing," McInnes said on his show. "This entire war has just changed, and it's all because of this unbelievable punch. The greatest punch in the history of Trump's presidency."

Nordean's story is the perfect entry point into the chaotic world of the Proud Boys, a giant web of violent characters and extremist groups, fascist plots, antifascist countermeasures, and serious implications for the future of American politics. He's taken part in every facet of the Proud Boys experience, rising from the bottom to the gang's highest ranks, traveling with them to rallies across the country, organizing fundraisers and events, and, unlike some of his fellow leaders, actually standing at the front lines of the melee.

His story also shows the resiliency of the gang, which never seems to slow down despite numerous self-inflicted setbacks. He's been repeatedly arrested over the violence and destruction he's wrought, including his role in the Capitol riots, and yet he's always managed to bounce back quickly, due in large part to his gang's national support network. The Proud Boys don't have to rely on themselves to wriggle out of tight spots; they have help from the establishment, thanks to the inroads they secured with top-level GOP officials and popular pundits. When high-ranking Proud Boys like Nordean get in trouble, they have a deep fundraising apparatus to draw from, as well as free image laundering from politicians and media personalities with whom they've secured favor over the years.

Nordean is the ideal Proud Boy, a paragon whose story is presented by gang leadership as something to aspire to.

———

EVEN AS A young man, Ethan Nordean craved battle.

His father, Mike Nordean, hoped Ethan and his stepsister might grow up to take over Wally's Chowder House, one of the family's restaurants, which he opened in 1993 in Des Moines, Washington, a city of about thirty thousand crammed under the noisy flight path of Seattle-Tacoma International Airport.

But Ethan didn't aspire to the local restaurant business. He wanted to be a US Navy SEAL, an elite fighter that the military describes as "the one they're going to call for last-ditch reconnaissance missions and operations that 'never happened.'" He signed his recruitment papers immediately after graduating high school. But his dreams of special ops glory were over before they began—he was discharged after just five weeks, having never completed basic training.

The failure was hard on Ethan, and he was listless in the years that followed. He got into bodybuilding and eventually settled for a job as a dishwasher and then assistant manager at Wally's Chowder House.

On the side, he busied himself with right-wing politics. He grew up in a hyperconservative household in Auburn, a city near Seattle that's less liberal than its metropolitan neighbor but still blue enough that Ethan felt like his political and social beliefs were under siege. By his twenties, he was steeped in the right-wing moral panic and conspiracy theories being touted at the time by carnival barkers like McInnes, Jones, and Trump. He said later, during his interview with Alex Jones, that he'd become increasingly anxious about the fall of American masculinity and the rise of political correctness.

He didn't get those kinds of politics from his father, Mike, who was conservative but more soft-spoken about it at home. He reportedly took his political cues from his mother, Judy, who was an avid Trump supporter and, much like Trump himself, had a habit of posting conspiratorial word salads and Islamophobic statements online. By the time Ethan was a far-right celebrity of sorts, Judy had been prolific on Twitter for years, posting typo-laden screeds in which she railed against Islam and gay people and leftist values. She sometimes echoed Trump's lies and talking points, including his ongoing and false assertion that former president Obama was working in secret to bring about an Islamic state in America and that the Democrats and antifa were in cahoots with ISIS.

Ethan's upbringing effectively made him a model Proud Boy before he even knew the gang existed. His ideology ran parallel to Trump's: he felt threatened by encroaching liberalism, he was raised intolerant and conspiratorial, and he longed for an opportunity to fight.

He met a few members at a May Day demonstration in Seattle in 2017 and described the moment as his political awakening. He joined the Seattle chapter shortly thereafter, calling it "one of the best decisions I ever made." The Proud Boys, he said, "allowed me to network with like-minded men."

He was an eager new recruit, and within a few weeks, he was a regular face at Proud Boys and Patriot Prayer events held across the Pacific Northwest. He was on the front lines early and often and was accused by local activists of attacking demonstrators repeatedly at waterfront protests in Portland. His streetwear evolved, too, from the nondescript tactical gear he wore as a rookie to a custom black-and-yellow Fred Perry polo, adorned with an American flag patch and the word *Washington* across his chest, denoting his chapter's home state. His friend circle grew alongside his reputation, and within months of recruitment, he was seen hanging with some of the most notorious bullies on the Pacific Northwest protest circuit. After a rally in August 2017, Ethan posed for a selfie with his arms around Patriot Prayer leader Joey Gibson and Gibson's top brawler, Tusitala "Tiny" Toese, a massive and bloodthirsty bruiser from American Samoa. Toese—seen in this particular shot with a bandage loosely covering his bloody nose—was arrested at least four times in Portland over assaults and harassment he carried out at Patriot Prayer and Proud Boys rallies, and he once spent four months in jail for violating a plea agreement after he attacked a man on the sidewalk.

As Ethan gained notoriety on the local level, the Proud Boys were growing as an organization and making national headlines. In 2017, they cohosted a series of events in Berkeley, California, that attracted a full spectrum of white nationalists and extremist groups from the so-called alt-right. Like the extremist rallies happening in Portland, these events were billed as free speech affairs featuring a revolving door of bigots and grifters, designed to bait college students and antifascists into fights. The Proud Boys turned the city into an almost perpetual war zone from February through September, and taken together, the events were so grisly and injurious that they came to be known collectively as the "Battle for Berkeley."

Newsworthy as they were, the Berkeley events were mere precursors to Unite the Right later that year, a deadly series of extremist rallies organized in part by a former Proud Boy named Jason Kessler. The event attracted multiple gangs of neo-Nazis and other extremists, who goose-stepped their way through Charlottesville, Virginia, committing hate crimes. One prominent neo-Nazi, James Alex Fields Jr., rammed his car into a crowd of counterprotesters on August 12, killing local activist Heather Heyer and injuring many more. The Proud Boys, sensing bad optics, tried to distance themselves from both events despite their connection. But they had built a strong reputation for violence and bigotry by that point, enough to earn a hate group designation from the Southern Poverty Law Center.

Two months after Unite the Right, Ethan teamed up with a police officer in Washington State to launch a vitamin supplements company. For years, Ethan had reportedly sold homemade supplements for five dollars a bottle to his colleagues at Wally's Chowder House, but records show that in October 2017, he turned his hobby into a career. He launched Bangarang Elite Supplements LLC with Trevor Davidson, a US Marine Corps reservist and fledgling officer with the Everett Police Department. Davidson didn't disclose to his employer at the time that he was in business with a member of the Proud Boys, a decision that wasn't challenged until years later, after the insurrection at the US Capitol. Bangarang dissolved in 2019, and after January 6, Davidson's department launched a probe into his relationship to the Proud Boys. A disciplinary panel found that he broke a minor department disclosure rule by quietly launching a company with Ethan, but he was largely cleared of wrongdoing over the relationship.

Around the same time, local residents in Des Moines, Washington, began to make the connection between the Proud Boys and Nordean, the guy serving them soup at Wally's Chowder House. They started calling staff about Ethan and another Proud Boys employee there, asking whether Wally's was in the business of hiring racists. Unperturbed, Ethan reportedly hosted at least three Proud Boys meetings inside the restaurant. Locals called for boycotts. Ethan's wedding to a longtime Wally's waitress named Cory Dryden, to be held at Kiana Lodge in nearby Poulsbo, Washington, that fall, was canceled after the venue's managers learned of the couple's Proud Boys connection. All the drama swirling around Wally's became enough of a problem that Ethan's dad temporarily cut him from the payroll. He was given his job back in 2018, right around the time of his viral punch.

It wasn't until a few years later, in 2020, that the shit really hit the fan at Wally's Chowder House. Ethan and the Proud Boys were working overtime in support of Trump's reelection campaign, cranking up the frequency of their events as well as the violence. Their power and influence were peaking, and the gang had secured close relationships with a number of the president's associates, law enforcement officials, and top Republicans, who praised them in public and even took them on as private security for events. But with more power came more scrutiny: there were entire networks of activists and researchers online following their every move and exposing them wherever they did harm. Eventually, those networks turned their sights on Ethan's violent exploits, and suddenly, the local drama he'd caused for Wally's Chowder House became a matter of national interest. The restaurant was once again inundated with calls and bad reviews, and that summer, Ethan's ties to the Proud Boys finally cost him his job at his father's restaurant. In a now-deleted post on the restaurant's website, Mike Nordean announced that he'd fired Ethan and condemned the Proud Boys as a hate group. The note read in part:

> My son, Ethan, is involved with an extremist group called the "Proud Boys." Hindsight, as they say, is 20/20. Until very recently, my wife and I were blind to the ideology that our son supports. We were told by our son that this group was a "patriotic" group that were "protectors" who stood up for freedom of speech and traditional values. We regretfully believed him. . . .
>
> Because there have been rumors floating, let me be clear: Ethan no longer works for our restaurants. We do not share his misguided beliefs. We are disappointed and appalled that he has chosen this path.
>
> I want to say clearly that our restaurants respect diversity. Period. We reserve the right to refuse service, and members of hate groups are not welcome in our establishments.

Mike's decision had little effect on his son, who doubled down on his leadership role within the Proud Boys. It was the gang's most violent year yet, especially after Trump lost the election. Over the winter months, they punched and harassed journalists, defaced several historically Black churches, and were involved in multiple stabbings on top of their regularly scheduled fights. All the while, they acted under the assumption that the GOP had their backs; even after Trump lost, the Proud Boys enjoyed endorsements both tacit and explicit from right-wing politicians and police officers, some of whom had even joined their ranks with hopes of fighting antifa.

The police relationship, however, began to sour that winter after several Proud Boys were stabbed at two different pro-Trump events in DC. Enrique Tarrio was reportedly slashed across the stomach at one of them, held near the White House in November, and two Proud Boys were stabbed at a bloody Stop the Steal rally they hosted for Trump that December. Though the Proud Boys themselves stabbed multiple people in the melee, they were incensed that police hadn't done more to protect them that day, given their loyalty to law enforcement over the years.

"We are the ones that back you!" Proud Boys leader Joe Biggs screamed through a megaphone at a group of riot officers on December 12. "That thin blue line is getting thinner and thinner."

The Justice Department argues that Biggs and Nordean were instrumental in rallying their fellow Proud Boys to DC on January 6, the day that Trump sycophants saw as their final opportunity to thwart Biden's confirmation. In late December, Nordean began soliciting funds for communications equipment and "safety gear" in posts on the right-wing social media site Parler. On January 4, two days before the insurrection, he led a propaganda blitz on multiple platforms, characterizing the Proud Boys as soldiers in an upcoming "war," fighting against the Democrats on the side of the GOP.

And on January 5, less than twenty-four hours before he and dozens of other Proud Boys took part in the deadly insurrection, Nordean, now a true leader among Proud Boys, posted a public rallying cry for the other members on Parler:

It is apparent now more than ever, that if you are a patriot, you will be targeted and they will come after you. Funny thing that they don't realize, is we are coming for them. You've chosen your side, black and yellow teamed with red, white and blue, against everyone else.

Court documents allege that Nordean was granted "war powers" by the Proud Boys' acting chair, Enrique Tarrio, just before the attack on January 6. It remains unclear what those powers meant in practice (and Tarrio, for what it's worth, denied in an interview that it meant anything), but Nordean manned the front lines of the Proud Boys' effort that day. Prosecutors allege he was among the primary wave of right-wing rioters who overwhelmed police at the barricades surrounding the Capitol and again at their fallback position on the steps. Amid the chaos, he stuck close to a larger group of fellow Proud Boys, including Joe Biggs and Dominic "Spazzo" Pezzola, who first breached the Capitol by smashing a window on its West side, using a stolen police-issue riot shield. Prosecutors say Nordean was among the first inside along with Pezzola.

At least seven people died in connection to the attacks—among them Capitol Police officer Brian Sicknick—and hundreds more were injured, including 140 officers. That day was particularly brutal for journalists and police officers at the scene, who were targeted throughout the day by the unruly horde. Four officers who responded died by suicide later.

Despite international outcry over the insurrection, Nordean dug in his heels and continued to goad police in the days following. On January 8, he posted a photo of a Capitol Police officer pepper spraying a rioter on Parler and described police as "the honorable oath breakers."

"If you feel bad for the police, you are part of the problem," he wrote. "They care more about federal property (our property) than protecting and serving the people."

"BACK THE BLACK AND YELLOW," he added, revising the pro-police slogan "Back the Blue" to honor the Proud Boys instead.

Nordean was arrested February 3, 2021, on charges of aiding and abetting the destruction of government property, obstructing an official proceeding, and trespassing on restricted Capitol grounds, which totaled two misdemeanors and two felonies. More than a year later, federal prosecutors added a seditious conspiracy indictment on top of his case, arguing that Nordean and several other Proud Boys played outsized, architectural roles in the attack.

In light of the charges, Mike Nordean once again posted (and later deleted) a disavowal of his son to the Wally's Chowder House website:

> We have tried for a long while to get our son off the path which led to his arrest today—to no avail. Ethan will be held accountable for his actions. I want to thank our customers for their continued grace and support. We appreciate it more than you know.

But despite the severity of the allegations against him, some societal and familial backlash, and legal walls closing in on gang leadership, the Proud Boys' support network mobilized as soon as Nordean's arrest was announced. The redemption arc began, as it often does, with a fundraising and PR blitz. One of several campaigns, posted to the right-wing donation site Our Freedom Funding, described Nordean as a "patriot" and "a huge proponent of freedom" who was having "a very difficult time making ends meet." The site claims 328 people donated more than $17,000 to Nordean's cause before the campaign ended. The Proud Boys set up another donations page on GiveSendGo, the self-described "Christian crowdfunding platform" preferred by right-wing extremists who've been banned or otherwise deplatformed from more mainstream sites like GoFundMe, Kickstarter, and Patreon. The GiveSendGo campaign, titled "Ethan Nordean aka Rufio Support and Defense Funds," quickly raised nearly $6,500 before it was hacked, its title changed to "Ethan Nordean Piss and Shit on Myself Fund."

Meanwhile, conservative media and right-wing pundits from all over the spectrum were working to downplay the Proud Boys' involvement and to sanitize or obfuscate the insurrection altogether. Tucker Carlson, for example, continues to spew lies and conspiracy theories about the riots to Fox News viewers about the assault, including false assertions that nobody was armed that day, none of the attendees were white supremacists, and that antifa was to blame. The overwhelming majority of Republican lawmakers refuse, to this day, to admit that Trump's election loss was legitimate, and polling suggests that a substantial swath of Republican voters believe the lies. The right has a powerful and dangerous disinformation apparatus that has done great work for Nordean and the Proud Boys, not only after the insurrection but following each of their crime sprees.

With that wind at their back, the Proud Boys managed to capture the hearts and minds of a substantial slice of the American public during the Trump years. They enjoyed great public power and influence, despite sitting atop a colossal wave of violent extremism that was causing irreparable damage to the country.

To understand how they managed to build such an empire, you have to go back to the Proud Boys' first few months in action, when they were just starting to gain popularity on the right. Even then, they were playing a double-sided game, fighting out the right wing's grievances in the street while at the same time buttering up the right people in the upper echelon of the GOP.

Chapter 4

PORTLAND, THE POLITICAL WAR ZONE

onald Trump's rise to power came paired with an unprecedented surge in street-level mobilizations by radical right-wing movements and hate groups, emboldened by the new president's divisive rhetoric and convinced they now had an ally in the White House. A wide array of extremists, from neo-Nazis and white supremacist groups like the Klan to reactionaries and anti-immigrant groups like the Proud Boys, coalesced under the banner of MAGA and then flooded American streets, to celebrate and recruit and push their political agendas. Within Trump's first year as president, extremist groups were hosting public rallies almost every single week. And along with those rallies came an explosion of right-wing violence.

This all played out on a variety of different battlegrounds, but in the Trump era, Portland, Oregon, was the main stage. There were brutal (and ongoing) clashes between far-right groups like the Proud Boys, leftist demonstrators, and law enforcement, sometimes stretching into days or weeks without stopping. There were sweeping rallies for racial justice and equality, and the Trump administration responded with overwhelming displays of authoritarian violence, deploying federal agents to do battle against protesters in the streets. At its worst moments, Portland really looked and felt like an active war zone: explosions and sirens rang out in the night, the streets were choked with tear gas and smoke, cops clashed with civilians, and government agents disappeared protesters in unmarked vans as people fought and people died.

The Proud Boys were not only an ever-present force in this new era of political unrest for Portland, they were the catalyst that helped usher it in. Almost immediately after Trump took office, the gang began its work organizing a yearslong series of brawls disguised as patriotic demonstrations and chose Portland as their go-to locale for street-level violence. It was a strategic choice. The city didn't just magically transform into a coliseum for bloody civic engagement. It has a long history at the center of national protest movements and conflict along political and racial lines, which made it the perfect proving ground for the Proud Boys and their extremist allies.

Part of the reason they showed up in the first place is because they knew they could find leftist activists to fight there. Portland has a decades-long history with militant leftist action, particularly in response to far-right violence and bigotry, law enforcement, and right-wing policies.

For example: A series of demonstrations against George H. W. Bush and the Gulf War during the '90s led the former president's administration to nickname the city "Little Beirut." Wherever Republicans appeared, so would coalitions of demonstrators, which included students and single-issue activists standing alongside anarchists and antifascists dressed in black bloc. It's a tactic popularized by activists countering neo-Nazis in West

Germany in the '80s, in which they covered themselves in dark monochrome clothing and stuck together to obscure their movements and identities from police, and to avoid arrest and harassment from their right-wing counterparts. One of the largest of those events came together in 1990 when Bush's vice president, Dan Quayle, visited Portland to attend a Republican fundraiser downtown. Some three hundred protesters showed up, burned flags, and engaged in various acts of protest involving bodily fluids (a group of twenty-four Reed College students, calling themselves the Guerrilla Theater of the Absurd, swallowed different hues of food coloring in an attempt to vomit in red, white, and blue, and though the puking part was successful, their stomach acid turned the blue into green). Local cops were aggressive and violent at those events—one woman won a $25,000 settlement from the city after her treatment at the hands of the Portland Police Bureau.

In 1999, on the eve of the World Trade Organization protests in Seattle, a Portland-based activist collective called the Ruckus Society hung a gigantic banner off a crane overlooking the Space Needle, which read "WTO" on one side and "Democracy" on the other. Those protesters got bailed out of jail a day before the real demonstrations began and they joined thousands of protesters to completely shut down the city prior to the global trade negotiations. Some fifty thousand demonstrators mobilized to protest issues tied to globalization and the environment, groups ranging from anticapitalists and conservationists to labor unions and student groups. Though there were acts of civil disobedience and vandalism at the protests, they were described as nonviolent until the Seattle Police Department arrived and sprayed tear gas and rubber bullets into the crowd, triggering a free-for-all of fighting and destruction that cost the city millions in property damage.

If those tumultuous scenes feel familiar, it's because they're still playing out today. The typical demonstration in Portland features law enforcement and right-wing entities pitted against a broad consortium of leftist activists. Republicans, seeking to vilify their opponents as a group, often lump counterprotesters into a handful of blanket terms, such as *antifa* and *Black Lives Matter*, to project isolated and individual acts of violence or crimes at events onto the entire leftist spectrum. If someone's wearing a black balaclava and throws a rock at a rally, you can safely bet that "antifa violence" will be featured on Fox News the next day, regardless of whether anyone who identifies with antifa is named or any significant act of violence or property destruction even occurred.

There are a lot of lies and misinformation littering any right-wing conversation about antifa: Trump-era Republicans in particular love to ascribe dastardly deeds to the nebulous movement, which they define in equally nebulous terms. Trump famously (and without evidence) accused antifa protesters of throwing cans of soup at police at rallies and then claiming upon their arrest that the cans weren't weapons: "They say, 'No, this is soup for my family.'" He and right-wing talking heads throw the term *antifa* around a lot to describe a vague collection of things and people they dislike: Democrats, women, clergy, left-leaning news organizations, or anyone simply wearing black, to name a few. Antifa certainly exists to the degree that antifascist demonstration exists, and there are groups and collectives that describe themselves as antifa, but there are so many different factions and tactics under that umbrella that the term on its own cannot possibly describe any large gathering with accuracy.

But accuracy was never the end goal. Whenever Trump and company called out a leftist threat, the Proud Boys and their allies took to the streets to find it. And they saw Portland as a veritable hornet's nest of leftist demonstrators, the perfect place to rally their supporters and bait counterprotesters into the street.

"These guys think that Portland is just this horrible kind of leftist cesspool," explained local reporter Jason Wilson. "So they'd show up to demonstrate in favor of Trump or free speech, and when they'd get counterprotesters, they'd claim that Trump supporters didn't have free speech in Portland. That was the consistent message, and it kept people coming back."

Outside metropolitan cities like Portland and Seattle on the Interstate 5 corridor, the Pacific Northwest isn't exactly the liberal bastion it appears from a distance. Politically, Portland is a dark-blue stronghold in a state where Democrats are closing in on a two-thirds legislative supermajority. But that doesn't mean Oregon is particularly hostile to Republicans. Drive two counties away from Portland in any direction, and you'll find yourself in god-fearing, Confederate-flag-waving, truck-nuts country. And that's where you'll find a lot of far-right figures, including the Proud Boys, other militia types, and their allies. Joey Gibson, the founder of the local Proud Boys affiliate group Patriot Prayer, lives a ten-minute drive north of Portland, in Vancouver, Washington, which sits in a county that voted for Hillary Clinton over Donald Trump by just 316 votes in 2016. And it's here, at parking lots in Vancouver, where members of the Proud Boys and Patriot Prayer from other cities and states muster before descending on Portland en masse.

But it's misguided to think that Portland—or really any jurisdiction in the Pacific Northwest—is inherently repellent to the far right and the bigoted ideology they peddle. There's a kooky progressive version of Portland depicted in the sketch comedy series *Portlandia* that makes the city look like an amusement park for affluent hippies, and that reality exists, to a degree. It remains overwhelmingly liberal politically, it's one of the greenest and most eco-friendly cities in the nation, and it's chock-full of the twee shops and bohemian weirdos lampooned by the show. But even more than a haven for liberals, it's a haven for white people: it's the whitest major city in America. Portland is gentrified to an excruciating degree, and it remains a relatively cozy climate for intolerance. In fact, racism plays a huge role in the history of Oregon, a state founded quite literally as a white utopia.

Oregon was a whites-only territory even before it joined the Union in 1859, and its original constitution barred Black people from living there until the law was repealed in 1926. The Ku Klux Klan thrived in that environment, and by 1922 the Klan claimed fourteen thousand members in the state, with nine thousand living in Portland. The few Black families who came to reside and work in Oregon over the next few decades faced an uphill battle, to say the least, and many white-owned businesses across the state refused to serve people of color into the early 1960s.

The racism of Oregon's past still manifests today across the state, even in Portland. If you ever need an example of institutional racism, you'll find it in this city. A Black worker's income is, per capita, less than half that of a white worker's income in Multnomah County. Black youth are six times more likely to be charged with a crime than white youth and much more likely to be held in detention. There are gaping racial disparities in health care, unemployment, and child welfare—and the list goes on.

"Discriminatory policies in employment, education, housing, the criminal justice system, policing, and in economic development have had the effect of limiting the ways our community has been able to advance and thrive," write researchers for Portland State University in a data study on the local Black community. "The stress of racism has a profound impact on health and wellness, as do other social determinants of health, such as ongoing discrimination in housing, school discipline, and racial profiling by police."

Once Trump took office, the comfort that racists and extremists enjoy in the Pacific Northwest became more pronounced than ever, and you could see it in the streets. Some residents in smaller and outlying communities claim that there's been a new proliferation of Confederate flags and racist symbols in rural areas of Washington State and Oregon—areas not exactly remembered as Southern allies in the Civil War—and experts say the iconography showed up in direct response to social justice movements during Trump's presidency.

And then there are the modern extremist groups themselves: Washington State, Idaho, and Oregon are home to various neo-Nazi factions, aggressive antigovernment groups that call themselves militias, the KKK, and several far-right street gangs. Neo-Nazi Richard Butler—the founder of the Aryan Nations, who died in 2004—urged whites to move to the Pacific Northwest to build a modern white utopia, and in the 1980s, he constructed a twenty-acre compound in Idaho that became a national hub for white supremacists. (He was later implicated in a plot to overthrow the government and bring on a race war, though he was never convicted.)

Enter Patriot Prayer, who helped turn Portland into the ultimate rallying point for extremists all over the United States. To outsiders, Patriot Prayer looked a little different than the other far-right groups that were popping up during Trump's first year as president. They weren't outwardly racist, and their ranks were multicultural, at least among their leaders; Gibson says he's part Japanese, and his right-hand man, Tusitala "Tiny" Toese, is from American Samoa. Gibson worked hard to give his group an air of political legitimacy in the eyes of law enforcement and local conservatives. Some extremist groups had a hard time leaving the fringes of public opinion because they rallied explicitly around white anxiety and conspiracy theories, or antigovernment "accelerationism" that seeks a white supremacist takeover by hastening societal breakdown. But Patriot Prayer looked and worked like a chapter of the Proud Boys: it was dedicated almost exclusively to fighting leftists in the streets of Portland, and the groups were so tight that Gibson publicly swore Patriot Prayer's fealty to the Proud Boys. But as the name implies, Gibson added a prayer element that gave his events an air of religious and con- stitutional justification. He was known to kneel before attendees of his jingoistic events in support of Trump and lead them in a star-spangled Christian devotion ceremony.

That religious and patriotic cloak allowed him to host events alongside anyone he wanted—including explicit extremist gang members known to be violent, neo-Nazis and even Klansmen— and still secure permits, despite the fact that his events were per- sistently accompanied by acts of criminal violence.

Gibson held one of Patriot Prayer's first big rallies on April 29, 2017, in Portland's Montavilla Park. Though it was a "free speech" rally and march, it looked a lot like the far-right ral- lies that would characterize the Trump era: there were brawl- ers wearing capes and holding Gadsden flags (the Revolutionary War–era "Don't Tread on Me" flag that has been co-opted by the far right), racist goons showing up in support, and groups of counterprotesters who showed up with the hope of running them back out of town. Though Gibson often held prayer circles and gave politically charged speeches, these were "free speech" and "freedom" events in name only: at the end of the day, his rallies were big excuses to riot and fight and push propaganda for vari- ous extremist factions.

One of this rally's attendees was a local man named Jeremy Joseph Christian, then thirty-five, who was draped in an Amer- ican Revolutionary War flag. He marched through the park chanting the N-word and throwing up Nazi salutes. He told a local reporter he'd joined the Patriot Prayer rally specifically to espouse hate and express his loyalty to Trump. Before the rally he had been online, calling for the deaths of Muslims and Jews in an unhinged rant in support of Trump posted on his Facebook page:

> If Donald Trump is the Next Hitler then I am joining his SS to put an end to Monotheist Question. All Zionist Jews, All Christians who do not follow Christ's teaching of Love, Charity, and Forgiveness And All Jihadi Muslims are going to Madagascar or the Ovens/FEMA Camps!!! Does this make me a fascist!!!

He was quickly swarmed by antifascists and then police officers, who searched his bag for guns and ammo. Police had reportedly seen another post on his Facebook page in which he threatened officers working the rally that day: "Shoot to kill POLICE if they ATTEMPT DISARM." They didn't find any weapons on him at the time.

But a few weeks later, on May 26, Christian got on a MAX train—a popular above-ground transit option in Portland—and launched into another racist rant, directed at two teenage girls, one of them Black and the other wearing a hijab. This time, Christian was armed with a knife. He was confronted by several other passengers, among them Taliesin Namkai-Meche, twenty-three, Ricky Best, fifty-three, and Micah Fletcher, twenty-one. Christian stabbed all three of them and fled the train. Namkai-Meche and Best died, while Fletcher survived a stab wound to the neck.

Christian was arrested on murder and hate crime charges and later sentenced to two life terms without the possibility of parole. Gibson attempted to distance his group from Christian completely and claims to have had the man kicked out of his event in April. Two reporters who were at the event told me they never saw Christian physically removed, though some Patriot Prayer members said at the time that they weren't involved with the ranting racist.

Regardless, Christian's actions drew a strong connecting line between Patriot Prayer and hate-fueled violence, which Gibson and his allies in the Proud Boys would never shake. And for hate groups and other extremists, the event was a rallying cry. Less than a week after the stabbings, on June 4, Gibson held another rally, and this time he attracted a crowd of thousands, including Proud Boys in their Fred Perrys. On one side stood a broad coalition of leftists that included labor union reps, antifascists, local Democratic groups, and students. On the other side, Gibson was joined by a mash-up of hate leaders, bruisers, militia groups, and minicelebrities from the alt-right.

For anyone attuned to these kinds of events, there were recognizable individuals in the crowd. This was another characteristic of the extremist rallies of the Trump era: Some of the most violent regulars earned themselves nicknames and an almost mythical status among other extremists. Some of them wore silly outfits or had weaponry that set them apart in the crowd. But each of them was connected through various acts of bloodshed.

One far-right folk hero who attended Gibson's rally, a Proud Boy from the Bay Area named Kyle "Based Stickman" Chapman, got his moniker after he was seen beating counterprotesters with a wooden stick topped with an American flag at a Berkeley protest in 2017, which he later paid the price for in the form of a plea deal on a felony weapons charge. Like Ethan Nordean, Chapman was lionized for the violence, and the right glorified him with memes and photoshopped images depicting him, for example, as a valiant leader of Confederate armies. McInnes had Chapman on his show, and the Proud Boys built a partnership with his group, called the Fraternal Order of the Alt-Knights

(FOAK). It was a heavily armed battalion of hate-mongers who sought to destroy what Chapman called an "unholy alliance" of "globalism, radical Islam, and communism," and it became known as the Proud Boys' "tactical defense arm." But where the Proud Boys tiptoed around outward racism as a motivating factor in their attacks, Chapman steeped himself in it. According to a Southern Poverty Law Center dossier on FOAK, Chapman called for the lynching of politicians who let "dirty illegals" into America and encouraged his followers to fight "Islamic invaders." McInnes described Chapman and FOAK as a necessary part of the movement.

"The Alt Knights are warriors and so is he," McInnes wrote on the Proud Boys website around this time. "Based Stick Man has a slightly more aggressive stance on this but he too is against needless violence."

When Chapman arrived at the rally, he came ready for war. He stood alongside Patriot Prayer, the Proud Boys, and a smattering of white supremacist trolls and other alt-right miniclebs, including: Tim Gionet, aka "Baked Alaska," a white supremacist from Anchorage who would go on to march with neo-Nazis at Unite the Right and storm the Capitol on January 6, 2021; Tusitala "Tiny" Toese, Gibson's top scrapper; and John Turano, aka "Based Spartan," an exceedingly dense nationalist of few words who was known for dressing up as a Spartan warrior and bludgeoning people at protests. This motley crew of world-class buffoons was strange to see all together at the time, but today they're regular faces at political rallies.

They may have been an intimidating crew, but they were outnumbered—the crowd of far-right goons numbered only in the hundreds, while the counterprotesters who mobilized to face them were in the three thousand range—and though skirmishes did break out, there was never a full-bore clash between the two groups because they never got a chance. What surprised local reporters covering the event was that Portland police seemed to turn on the people of Portland—their own people—in defense of the far right that had descended on the town. This, too, would become a feature of far-right rallies in Portland and across the country, but at first, it was bewildering to see.

"Thousands of people showed up to let Joey know that he and his bullshit weren't welcome," Dave Neiwert, a longtime extremism reporter in the Pacific Northwest, told me. "And you could see from the start that the police actually found their own citizens, who they were supposed to be protecting, to be a bigger threat than the people who were there to cause violence. I remember seeing militiamen helping cops hog-tie antifa protesters in the street. It was a very, very unhealthy dynamic."

Gibson's rally was a proving ground of sorts for what was to come. After that, he and the Proud Boys knew they could host violent rallies in the city limits, invite any number of unsavory characters they wanted, and even expect support from responding law enforcement. It totally transformed the expectation for what you'd see at political rallies going forward, no matter who was hosting: bloodthirsty racists decked out in gang uniforms and homemade armor and weaponry became a mainstay at street-level protests after that point.

"I covered lots of contentious protests before, but this was a protest intended for nothing but violent confrontation, with hundreds and hundreds of people, Nazis and guys in [Pepe the Frog] costumes and the like," reporter Jason Wilson told me. "And that's how it is today. If you're hosting, say, a Black Lives Matter protest in Coeur d'Alene, Idaho, there's gonna be a counterprotest, and people are going to be armed. There's this constant looming threat of violence now, and people with weapons. This is the American protest now."

The Proud Boys and Patriot Prayer started using Portland as their personal playground and hosted events early and often. They went by different names—"patriot" events and "MAGA" rallies and even "protests" against "leftist violence"—but they all shared the same tone of violence. This was *the place* to go if you were a conservative looking to punch someone under the auspices of free speech. Terms like *clashes* and *skirmishes* became closely associated with Portland starting in 2017, and though there were arrests at almost every event, there was never a response from any level of governmental authority that led the far right to believe they had to stop. So they kept hosting events, and Portland became a breeding ground for extremist action.

The latter half of 2018 in Portland was particularly brutal, starting with the rally on June 30 that made Nordean—and his punch—famous. Wilson said it was the bloodiest rally he'd seen to that point and yet another indicator that the Proud Boys' violent activities weren't going away anytime soon. He was right. The gang and its allies continued their siege on the city with more events.

On August 4, 2018, Gibson hosted a rally ostensibly in support of his campaign for the US Senate in Washington State, though one could argue that his run was never very serious, and he got clobbered three days later, winning just 2 percent of the primary vote. Given his reputation for coalition-building on the far right and the free-for-all that took place on June 30, journalists and activists feared that the "Gibson for Senate Freedom March" would look more like a rerun of the Unite the Right neo-Nazi rallies in Charlottesville, Virginia, in 2017. It didn't quite get there, despite getting national media coverage, but it featured all the same sentiments.

I joined a number of reporters covering the rally from Gibson's side, which was a group of hundreds of Proud Boys and Patriot

Prayer members from out of town gathered in a cordoned-off area of Tom McCall Waterfront Park, a long stretch of strollable pathway alongside the Willamette River. Among them was Toese, who showed up wearing a "Pinochet Did Nothing Wrong" T-shirt, designed by a now-defunct clothing company called Right Wing Death Squads. The brand was a favorite among white nationalist groups and neo-Nazis who fantasized about, well, right-wing death squads. The back of Toese's shirt read "Make Communists Afraid of Rotary Aircraft Again" and featured an image of people falling from a chopper, referencing the Chilean dictator's habit of throwing his ideological opponents out of helicopters.

Across the street from Gibson's crew on the waterfront was an even larger crowd of protesters. There were hundreds of people in black bloc, many of them self-described antifascists, standing with locals in street clothes who had showed up to protest the presence of their far-right interlopers. They chanted the names of the victims of the MAX train murders and that of Heather Heyer, the activist who was killed by a neo-Nazi during Unite the Right.

The two sides traded projectiles and chants across the highway, but they didn't get many opportunities to close the gap. The Portland Police Bureau stood on the closed-down stretch of highway between them and largely kept them apart. But the line of officers stood with their backs to the right-wing crowd, and on that day the police were again described as the catalysts for violence against counterprotesters. Dozens of them stood in defense of a jeering crowd of Patriot Prayer and Proud Boys, lobbing so-called less-lethal crowd-control rounds into the mass of antifascists and other protesters across the street. One antifascist activist was struck directly in the head by a police-fired projectile. He was lucky to be wearing a helmet at the time because the round—described by protesters at the time as a flashbang—broke clean through and dug into his head. The wound required stitches, and without the helmet, his friends said he'd be dead. Several people went to the hospital with injuries, including a woman hit by a flash-bang grenade and a reporter with the *Oregonian*, who was struck in the head by an unknown object thrown by counterprotesters.

The threat of violence permeated these events, though sometimes that threat wasn't readily apparent. Portland mayor Ted Wheeler later revealed that police discovered several members of Patriot Prayer on a nearby rooftop in (legal) possession of long rifles, overlooking the protest below. They said they were awaiting orders as a "quick extraction team" for their comrades if things went south, an ominous threat that only hinted at what might have been should the order have come down.

Another rally, on October 13, highlighted a new facet of the extremist playbook that the Proud Boys employed. They held a flash march, a quick rally whose meetup details are kept secret until just before game time. Far-right groups love flash marches for several reasons. The first is for propaganda purposes, as neo-Nazi Richard Spencer demonstrated in Charlottesville: extremist groups march through town, taking tightly framed photos and videos of themselves to appear unopposed, to fabricate the notion that the community is either scared of them or OK with their presence. The second is that it obfuscates their movements in the eyes of law enforcement and counterdemonstrators. With less warning, there will be fewer protesters and police. Fewer protesters means they'll be easier to overwhelm, and fewer cops means fewer arrests. For that reason, flash marches are extremely dangerous, and this particular instance was no different.

It was night, and Proud Boys had joined Patriot Prayer members to march toward a vigil over the Portland police killing of a Black man the month prior. The Proud Boys, who showed up in uniform along with MAGA hats and Gadsden flags, reportedly attacked antifascist demonstrators at the vigil with batons and bare fists, and both sides blasted each other with pepper spray. Toese was back at it again, this time reportedly seen kicking a protester while he lay on the ground. One of his pals joined in and stomped on the victim's head. Eventually, police fired pepper rounds into the crowd and dispersed it. They reported seeing knives, firearms, hard knuckle gloves, and bear spray among attendees but made no arrests.

Gruesome scenes like these became the norm in Portland leading into the monthslong stretch of fiery protests there in the summer of 2020, ignited by the police murder of George Floyd. In May that year, Minneapolis officer Derek Chauvin killed Floyd by kneeling on his neck and back for nine minutes and twenty-nine seconds, cutting off the oxygen to his brain for nearly five minutes beyond the moment he uttered his final words. Chauvin was quickly fired and arrested on murder charges, but the justice was too little, too late for millions of Americans, who had for years been watching a spree of televised police killings of unarmed Black men. Floyd's murder was a final straw of sorts: it triggered nationwide and then worldwide demonstrations against police brutality and new, more mainstream discussions about the role law enforcement plays in the propagation of racism and authoritarianism.

Some protests tapered off in American cities by the end of the summer—but not in Portland. Downtown once again became a combat zone between demonstrators and law enforcement for close to a year. Droves of Black Lives Matter protesters, local residents, and antifascist activists teamed up and sparred with heavily armed police forces, who flooded the streets with military weaponry and tear gas. Scenes of police beating protesters and shooting crowd control munitions and pepper spray into groups of people became commonplace, as did videos of law enforcement buildings and equipment ablaze, as protesters set fire to police vehicles and building facades in isolated incidents that were played on repeat by the news media. For local demonstrators and reporters, going out into the street was like going to war every night.

"It's as close up to the line as you can get to actual war without live rounds," said Robert Evans, a conflict reporter who covered the demonstrations for some thirty nights, in an interview with the *New York Times*. There was so much tear gas in the air that it reportedly caused irregularities in the menstrual cycles of dozens of people, and Evans captured footage of the gas forming its own tornado downtown.

Trump used that violent imagery, along with reports from nationwide BLM protests, as a launchpad for an all-out assault against demonstrators. He called several state governors "weak" and demanded that they send in National Guard troops to "dominate" protesters. Eventually, he made that call himself and deployed federal agents to Portland to join the melee there. In turn, the violence and destruction got a whole lot worse.

Mainstream news outlets and reporters in the field were posting images of federal troops beating the snot out of protesters and disappearing them in unmarked vans in the middle of crowded streets. The *Washington Post* questioned whether Trump's deployment of federal troops was legal, and the *Times* compared it to similar federal deployments against Black demonstrators throughout modern American history, like Little Rock and the Rodney King riots. Right-wing media, meanwhile, ran footage of building facades and dumpsters on fire as anecdotal evidence that left-wing violence rivaled or exceeded that of the far right.

As the George Floyd protests began to wind down, the Proud Boys and Patriot Prayer continued their monthly brawls in Portland's streets through 2021 and beyond (as of this writing, there's no sign of that stopping, either). Their hold on this city remains a bit of an enigma. One would think that a local government could stop a gang of hooligans from turning the streets of a metropolitan city into their personal fight club. The Proud Boys and their allies have attempted to dig their heels into comparable cities across the country—including Berkeley, Denver, Philadelphia, New York, Boston, and Portland's neighbor to the north, Seattle—but they've had less success hosting rallies with the scope and regularity they have here. The through line between all those cities appears to be community resistance, as well as a strong governmental response, and officials' ability to navigate constitutionally protected demonstrations versus criminal violence.

Each jurisdiction handles these threats differently. Berkeley denied permits after the fight gangs that mobilized there made it clear they weren't showing up to demonstrate peacefully. New York, meanwhile, simply does not screw around with extremists: Proud Boys processions there are often vastly outnumbered by local protesters, and when there's violence, city officials throw the book at the guilty parties. In Philly, locals don't need help from the cops: when armed members of the white supremacist group Patriot Front held a flash march there on a hot summer night in 2021, it was community onlookers, not police, who banded together and chased them out of town.

In Portland, Mayor Wheeler's response to extremism in the Trump era was a complex jumble of missteps, embarrassments, and legitimate hardship. The most generous critique among locals was that he'd been dealt a rough hand: Portland has always been a flash point for political unrest, the president called him a "fool" and sent federal troops in over his head, state officials didn't seem eager to help until Trump got involved, and there's an issue with federal parkland in town, where Wheeler sometimes doesn't even get to make the final call. These problems are not easy to solve.

But locals largely criticized him as a nonfactor when it came to his response to extremism, unable or unwilling to work with the tools in front of him. Evans, for example, pointed specifically at Oregon's paramilitary laws, which he said could have been exercised to put a stop to the rallies after he and Wilson uncovered violent plots in chat logs from the Patriot Coalition, another group of pro-Trump, pro-police extremists connected to the Proud Boys.

"His First Amendment complaints just don't hold any water," Evans told me in an interview. "I don't think Ted Wheeler was in a hard position at all. I think he did what he thought would be the easy thing to do."

In the early days of Patriot Prayer and Proud Boys events, Wheeler struggled to maintain any semblance of authority over them. His appeal to the federal government to deny a permit to Patriot Prayer for an event following the MAX stabbings went unheard, and the Oregon ACLU called the request itself unconstitutional. In 2018, Wheeler proposed emergency rules giving himself and the police more power over local rallies, where he'd get to pick the times and places so they could respond more effectively. He didn't get the votes, but his plan would have proved ineffective anyway. Patriot Prayer demonstrations rarely stayed in cordoned-off areas provided by local authorities, and when they moved beyond the pens, Portland police had a habit of ignoring them and turning their weapons toward protesters.

Today, Wheeler just seems kind of fed up with it all. In the lead-up to a worrisome Patriot Prayer rally in August 2021, he joined a number of community leaders in a statement appealing to locals to "choose love" instead of hate and violence. Despite his calls, the rally looked a lot like previous rallies: Proud Boys and their local allies smashed cars, beat people bloody, and even lit fireworks near a gas station, all as police largely ignored them. At one point, a man pulled a gun downtown and fired several rounds at antifascist counterprotesters gathered there. Wheeler released a statement expressing his disappointment, though he claimed that "the Portland Police Bureau and I mitigated confrontation between the two events and minimized the impact of the weekend's events to Portlanders."

The Proud Boys, meanwhile, have made it a point to mock Wheeler with their presence. At one rally, Enrique Tarrio, then chair of the entire Proud Boys organization, finally admitted the gang's true intention for Portland: "We've wasted all their fucking resources to make this rally," he proclaimed in a speech to other members captured on video in 2019. "We want them to waste $2 million and we'll do it again in two months."

He also made reference to the fourth degree, which at that point the Proud Boys were trying to downplay in public. "This is a pure optics operation," he said. "If you're looking for fourth degrees this is not the event to do it."

This is the dichotomy of the Proud Boys on full display. They pitch themselves to the public as a men's club that moonlights as a heroic vigilante defense force, resistant to violence but willing to go there when leftists present a threat. But to one another, they characterize themselves as the aggressors, and they're very clear about their motivations: fighting their political opponents, destroying their property, and wasting their resources. Maximize impact, and minimize personal responsibility after the fact. The sleight of hand here is totally obvious, and yet they've had success with it in places where the establishment sees what they're doing and fails to react.

Portland was a sandbox where the Proud Boys could test the limits of violence disguised as constitutionally protected demonstration. Here, they grew personalities like Nordean and sent hundreds of members over the years to do battle with their enemies, largely unimpeded. And there's an argument to be made that the lackluster response by city and state leadership helped them strengthen their foothold in America.

But while such conditions enabled and empowered the Proud Boys, their greatest proponent by far—and really, the greatest ally to this entire generation of right-wing extremists—was the GOP establishment. Trump's administration and the right-wing media apparatus embraced the Proud Boys' brand of political violence and promoted it as something other Republicans should aspire to. They enjoyed a symbiotic relationship, one that revealed itself plainly in the first year of Trump's presidency, following one of the most infamous extremist rallies in modern American history.

Chapter 5

"VERY FINE PEOPLE"

S treet-level political violence works much like waves approaching from the sea. The smaller events, like the ongoing Proud Boys rallies held across the country, are ever-present threats, lapping up against the shore and eroding the bedrock over time. Further out, larger and more dangerous movements gain energy and swell, strengthened by the rageful storms at their back and compelled forward with every lashing of the coast by their forerunners. And every so often, a tidal wave reaches critical mass and moves inland, crashing down on the shore with the force of an explosion. It feels jarring and surprising in the moment, but its formation was observable and its arrival predictable, just like the waves before it, and just like the waves that will follow.

Unite the Right was not some unexpected surge of extremist violence. It was a planned and coordinated attack by a coalition of far-right groups, following more than a year of experimentation and field testing via smaller events, like those the Proud Boys held in Portland.

The two-day hate expo, held in Charlottesville, Virginia, in August of 2017, attracted all the elements of the extremism apparatus that had been coalescing since Trump took office. Fliers for the event hinted at the unholy alliance that would eventually show up: The scheduled speakers and attendees were Nazis, KKK members, neo-Confederates, militia groups, and a glut of new hate groups assembled online. There were Pepe the Frog memes mashed up with propaganda from the Confederacy and Nazi Germany. It was going to be "A Pivotal Moment For The Pro-White Movement In America," one flier read.

The result was a deadly parade of racist violence and hateful propaganda, followed by rolling endorsements both tacit and explicit from the president and his allies. Locals who showed up to counterprotest—including local activists, clergy, students and professors, antifascists and BLM demonstrators—weren't surprised to see the extremist coalition. The organizers were familiar to them. Several, including neo-Nazi Richard Spencer, were alumni of the University of Virginia (UVA) in Charlottesville, and locals already had plenty of experience countering fascist rallies marshaled in their hometown. But Unite the Right was the first time that the rest of the world would get to sit in on the violent conversation that had been taking place on America's streets for more than a year.

While Unite the Right is remembered today for its biggest set pieces—the Nazi torch march on August 11, the hate rally on August 12, the Nazi Germany flags, the murder of a young woman in the street—it was the failure to respond and react, both to the planning of the event and its aftermath, that truly exposed America's domestic extremism crisis. It also exposed the sheer size of the extremism web, which ties groups like the Proud Boys to neo-Nazis, and the lengths they go to cover their tracks when an event makes them look bad.

The Proud Boys are so good at covering their tracks, in fact, that they've all but removed their ties to Unite the Right from the historical record. But the fact remains: these rallies were organized by a second degree member of the Proud Boys named Jason Kessler.

Kessler was a relative unknown outside Charlottesville when he announced Unite the Right in early 2017. He was a white supremacist author and former UVA student who spent much of his time writing and whining about "white genocide," Islam, and what he called "disproportionate Jewish influence." He was also pals with Spencer, who that year had become internationally famous for getting punched in the face by an antifascist during a TV interview in the lead-up to Trump's inauguration. But Kessler hadn't yet achieved that level of national Nazi stardom. He was more famous in Charlottesville, where he was known as the racist blogger who'd dedicated himself to getting a local Black councilman named Wes Bellamy fired.

Kessler petitioned to have Bellamy taken off the council by angling him as a "black supremacist," in part because Bellamy voted to remove a statue of Confederate general Robert E. Lee in what was then called Lee Park. Kessler complained that removing the statue would erase "white history," despite the fact that the statue was not a historical document at all, but a monument to white supremacy. It wasn't commissioned immediately after the Civil War, but in 1917, at the height of the Jim Crow era, when laws were being passed to strip basic rights from Black Americans. Kessler ignored that part and maintained pressure on Bellamy.

Kessler told a reporter at the time, "[Bellamy] made clear that he did it to attack 'white supremacy,' a partisan left-wing term that most on the right construe as a pretense to attack white people and their history."

Kessler's petition was eventually thrown out, the process for the statue's removal inched forward, and Lee Park was renamed Emancipation Park. But Kessler's fight wasn't over: the Lee statue would become his rallying cry, which would eventually lead scores of bigots to descend on Charlottesville.

His reputation locally as a hateful loudmouth made it difficult for him to go anywhere in Charlottesville without some kind of confrontation. But he still had friends and allies in the Proud Boys, who were not only his drinking buddies locally but his biggest platform nationally. On June 17, 2017, Kessler was captured on video getting his second degree by way of the cereal initiation, held in Charlottesville (he went with "Cheerios, Rice Krispies, Raisin Bran, Weetabix, uh, Lucky Charms"). And just two days later, Gavin McInnes invited Kessler onto his show to tell a sob story about his oppression at the hands of local leftists, who, he said, showed up at a bar he was partying at with his fellow Proud Boys. He said the locals called them Nazis and got the bartender to stop serving them.

"They're in a liberal bubble here," Kessler told McInnes. "You have to learn how to conquer your fear if you're a right-wing activist. Whether you're in the Proud Boys or even just a Trump supporter. They will constantly call you racist, and they've made that a social stigma. . . . Do not back down to them."

It was there and then, on *The Gavin McInnes Show*, that Unite the Right got its first big platform. Kessler told McInnes' audience it was time to fight back against the big bad leftists, and he had the perfect venue to do so.

"I'm here in Charlottesville, Virginia, where we're gonna have Unite the Right on August 12," he said. "It's gonna be international news, so you won't forget Charlottesville, Virginia."

He admitted that Unite the Right would feature "some controversial speakers" like Spencer but argued "that's what free speech is all about." He said he hoped McInnes would show up in support and that the Proud Boys would come in droves.

"More people need to get involved in groups like the Proud Boys and in politics," he said. "And not be afraid to show them we have numbers."

"Yes, and to be an asshole and gloat," McInnes replied. "Thanks for coming on the show, I like you more than a friend."

As Kessler signed off, McInnes threw up an OK hand sign, the trolling hand gesture that has been co-opted by white supremacists and other extremists as a way to wink and nod to like-minded folks and upset any "woke" individuals (read: people who are not racist) who might be watching. The Proud Boys, ever willing to join in on a troll campaign, adopted the signal as one of their calling cards. You'll see them flashing the sign in group photos, and if you ask anyone about the white power thing, they'll call you a cuck and point to one of their members with darker skin to prove they aren't racist.

When Kessler hung up, McInnes took a minute to ponder the implications of the Proud Boys' involvement in Unite the Right. He knew that Spencer was involved—which meant neo-Nazis were involved—and he'd seen how the event was being advertised. The fliers were very explicit invites to white supremacists and bore the names of prominent white supremacist groups and figureheads.

"I go back and forth on that thing," he said. "It has Confederate flags on it and stuff. On the one hand, I'm not scared of being associated with Richard Spencer. On the other hand, I wanna get back to what we're really about, which is beer." In typical McInnes fashion, he had advertised the event and then given himself deniability.

Looking back at the interview, it's almost impressive that the leader of a neofascist street gang and the organizer of one of the largest American Nazi rallies in eighty years were able to keep straight faces as they complained about being called racists. But that kind of gaslighting works for the Trump-era generation of extremists. These guys position white supremacist ideology and political violence as a free speech issue under attack by the intolerant left, and that's how they were able to build coalitions of extremists and host events like Unite the Right in the first place.

McInnes invited multiple self-avowed white supremacists and would-be attendees of Unite the Right on his show in 2017, Spencer and Kessler among them. But he was always careful to put distance between his own ideology and some of those unsavory characters, and to this day he denies any organizational involvement in Unite the Right, despite Kessler's membership in his gang. But his part in platforming the event is undeniable: he brought Kessler on to promote it, and in doing so gave the Nazis a soapbox, a megaphone, and a crowd of thousands.

The Proud Boys' founder saw the forest for the trees when it came to Unite the Right. This was clearly going to be bad optics for his gang. Come August, the event was very plainly Nazi-centric, even as Kessler worked to sanitize it as a protest over the removal of the Lee statue. Locals were worried about what was coming; they had only recently countered demonstrations led by the KKK and other hate groups. But this one was getting national attention and gearing up to be the mother of all extremist rallies. Every Nazi and their mother was talking about it. City officials considered blocking Kessler's permit for the August 12 event but ultimately decided there weren't grounds to deny him based on the messaging alone.

To this day, some attendees and initial promoters of Unite the Right absolve themselves by pretending they didn't know what was coming, that they believed it was really about monuments and the preservation of American history. But one look at the promotional material or news reports in the days leading up to the event suggests that everyone knew what they were getting into. The *Daily Progress*, a local paper, made it very clear in a preview published on July 29 that year:

> The limits of constitutionally protected speech and freedom of assembly are being put to the test in Charlottesville. In less than two weeks, members of the National Socialist Movement, the pro-secessionist League of the South and hundreds of their allies in the Nationalist Front and "alt-right" movement will gather in Emancipation Park for the Unite the Right rally.
>
> Arranged by self-described "pro-white" activist Jason Kessler, the rally is expected to also draw hundreds of confrontational counter-protesters who will be able to gather at McGuffey and Justice parks, per event permits recently secured by University of Virginia professor Walt Heinecke. While the stage for Aug. 12 is nearly set, with massive demonstrations and protesters expected, questions regarding the enforcement of law and order remain.

McInnes knew what he would be signing on to if he gave his Proud Boys the green light to attend. So while members of the Proud Boys did go to Unite the Right, including Enrique Tarrio, then the president of the Miami chapter, McInnes forbade them from going in uniform. Tarrio told me in a later interview that McInnes advised him just before the event that he shouldn't go at all. He went anyway.

The decision to go in plain clothes worked fantastically in the Proud Boys' favor. It put just enough plausible distance between them and the Nazi groups that showed up, such that the Proud Boys left as one of the few far-right groups without their public image tied to the event. Other individuals and groups faced real consequences; activists and researchers worked to identify the attendees, leading to arrests, firings, and societal rejection. Several hate groups dissolved completely or were forced to rebrand. Identity Evropa, a white supremacist group that recruits on college campuses, changed its name completely after an antifascist media collective called Unicorn Riot published hundreds of thousands of its private chat logs, revealing the group's organizational ties to Unite the Right and the violent and racist ideology that its leader, Patrick Casey, was spouting to followers. Casey renamed the group the American Identity Movement, and thanks to a swath of activists keeping tabs on their every move, they were unable to fly under the radar from that moment on. Unite the Right was a bad look for any attendee, and it's easy to see why.

On the night of August 11, Spencer called to muster some 250 white nationalists for a flash march, starting at an area behind UVA's Memorial Gymnasium called Nameless Field. They stood in a tight two-by-two formation; organizers wore earpieces and radios as they moved up and down the ranks, barking orders into a megaphone. They lit Tiki torches and marched through campus, screaming chants of "Jews will not replace us" and "blood and soil" into the night.

The photos from that march are now emblematic of Unite the Right. The standout image featured Peter Cvjetanovic, then a twenty-year-old University of Nevada student with a fashy haircut and a white polo bearing an Identity Evropa logo. His mouth was wide open, and his face bulged as he bellowed the Nazi-era chants, his eyes black as the night sky despite the light from the Tiki torch in his hand. The photo drew immediate comparisons to historic images of the Hitler Youth marches and the crowd of frothing white Americans shouting down the Little Rock Nine on their way to their newly integrated high school in 1957.

The group marched through Nameless Field and up a grand set of steps to the rotunda, where a statue of UVA founder Thomas Jefferson awaited them, along with some thirty students and locals gathered in protest, arm in arm. The white supremacists attacked almost immediately, according to their victims, and sprayed chemical irritants and threw their torches at the crowd. The students relied on their friends for medical treatment; police and emergency services didn't arrive until after the damage was done. It was a terrifying evening, and it was merely a precursor to the main event.

There was a hopeful atmosphere among locals on the morning of August 12. The day began with an early procession of clergy and community leaders, who marched through the quiet streets of Charlottesville toward Emancipation Park. I stood with them at the edge of the park grounds. Some of them linked arms and knelt to pray in protest of the hateful throng Kessler had brought into town.

The park itself was mostly empty that morning, save for the statue of Lee and a handful of officers who stood in his defense. They'd cordoned off the area with metal barricades and tape to protect the monument and to create a space for Kessler's cadre. It was there, in front of one of the barricades, that we saw our first Nazi of the day. He was a scrawny, aging man in glasses, with a black T-shirt and jeans. He was talking to a few of the officers, and his back was to the counterprotest, so we could make out the words on the back of his shirt:

> Those who want to live, let them fight, and those who do not want to fight in this world of eternal struggle do not deserve to live. —Adolf Hitler

That was the last quiet moment of the day, and the last time we saw the local police come to the defense of anyone or anything. Huge crowds of extremists began goose-stepping their way into the park, chanting "Blood and soil," as antifascist protesters gathered on the south-facing street. There were neo-Nazis with full-sized German Nazi flags, banners with *sonnenrads*, Confederate flags, and extremist groups wearing MAGA hats and carrying shields and makeshift weaponry. The temperature rose quickly, and the clergy were pushed out of their prayer positions and away from the park altogether.

The rest of the day was an all-out war. Trash and projectiles flew through the air. Batons came down on makeshift shields. A layer of bear mace hung over everything. It was loud and chaotic; we didn't learn until later that a guy in the far-right crew had pulled out a pistol, shouted, "Hey, n—er" and fired into the crowd near where we stood. As the battle progressed it also spread, and soon fights were happening blocks away from the park, which served as the epicenter. White supremacists beat down a Black man named DeAndre Harris in a parking garage, and he suffered a broken arm and a concussion. Dozens of people were injured. Through all of this, a battalion of police—many in riot gear—stood by and watched, even as locals pleaded with them to intervene.

Three blocks away from the park, on Fourth Street, a twenty-year-old neo-Nazi from Ohio named James Alex Fields Jr. was idling in his Dodge Challenger, staring down the road at a peaceful procession of activists, before slamming his foot onto the accelerator. He hit the crowd at about 25 mph, sending a tangle of bodies and glass through the air as he made impact.

One of the victims, Heather Heyer, a thirty-two-year-old local activist, died from her injuries. Her mother, Susan Bro, sat down with me a day later in her home and said her daughter had joined the protest to stand up to injustice and the extremists who'd come to town.

"I don't want her death to be a focus for more hatred. I want her death to be a rallying cry for justice and equality and fairness and compassion," she told me. "No mother wants to lose a child, but I'm proud of her. I'm proud of what she did."

Heyer's death did become a rallying cry for justice—her face now appears symbolically at demonstrations against fascism and far-right extremism across the world.

Her death also turned the public's attention toward the people who had overlooked the threat of Unite the Right. Photos and videos on the news and on social media weren't showing backwoods neo-Nazis; instead, the country was looking at a murderous consortium of modern extremists, some of whom had shown up wearing MAGA hats and other regalia in support of the president. The people wanted answers, and their president gave them a doozy.

Trump's intent during his first press conference following Unite the Right is hotly contested to this day because of two quotes specifically: he said there were "very fine people on both sides" of the rallies, and separately, he said that neo-Nazis and white nationalists in the group should be "condemned, totally." The media latched onto the "very fine people on both sides" quote because one of the sides included murderous Nazis. Trump supporters latched onto his condemnation of Nazis and claimed that the media misrepresented what he was saying.

His words were not mischaracterized. The "very fine people" quote may not have represented the full conversation, but a deeper dive into the press conference doesn't change the context—in fact, it makes Trump look worse. He spent the entirety of his speech shifting blame away from the extremists and onto the counterprotesters and claimed inaccurately that there were regular upstanding conservatives on the neo-Nazi side, there to protest the removal of a statue.

A reporter at the press conference countered those assertions, saying, "But neo-Nazis started this thing. They showed up in Charlottesville—"

Trump cut him off.

"Excuse me, they didn't put themselves down as neo-Na— you had some very bad people in that group. But you also had people that were very fine people on both sides. I saw the same pictures you did. You had people who were there to protest, to them, a very important statue, and the renaming of a park from Robert E. Lee to another name."

There were no people discussing statues or protesting local policies on August 11 or 12. There were white supremacists and neo-Nazis and other extremists, who showed up on the promise that abhorrent racists like former KKK grand wizard David Duke would be speaking and rallying with them. Attendees came armed and immediately attacked those who showed up to protest their presence. Anyone who may have shown up on the morning of August 12 to join a regular conservative protest (and to be clear, I didn't see any evidence that any such people were there) would have either left the area once they saw whose side they were on or stayed and demonstrated alongside neo-Nazis. It's really that simple. There was no confusion about the ideology involved that day.

Whether he believed it or not, Trump was carrying water for Nazis. He decried them at one point, to be sure, but in the same breath argued that they'd been treated unfairly by the press. He even echoed Kessler in claiming that the removal of the Jim Crow–era Lee statue represented cultural and historical erasure.

"You're changing history, you're changing culture. And you had people—and I'm not talking about the neo-Nazis and the

white nationalists, because they should be condemned, totally—
but you had many people in that group other than neo-Nazis and
white nationalists. And the press has treated them unfairly." In
effect, Trump bought the kind of ambiguity the Proud Boys were
selling, and he helped them to market it.

He was attempting to obscure and redefine what we were
seeing right in front of us—a deadly show of force from the far
right—because that side of the demonstration included his followers. To the general public, his press conference signaled that
the spirit of Unite the Right wasn't going away and that we were
in for a lot more gaslighting in the future. To the extremists themselves, it signaled that the president was on their side and willing
to go to bat for them when it counted. Unfortunately, we were
all proven right. It set the tone for *anyone* faced with questions
about right-wing violence going forward: deny, deflect, and point
to antifa.

The Proud Boys went into self-preservation mode after the
events of August 2017. McInnes worked quickly to distance himself and his gang from Unite the Right, the alt-right, and especially
from Kessler. In his first live show after the fact, McInnes held up
a newspaper featuring Heather Heyer's face and expressed relief
that he and the Proud Boys weren't getting any of the blame.

"Hell of a weekend, boys, hell of a weekend," he said. "I've
been combing through all the media reports, going, 'don't say
Proud Boys, don't say Proud Boys.' Sorta like I assume Muslims
go through the same thing when a car drove through people.
'Don't be Mohammad, don't be Mohammad. Fuck!' I did pretty
good though."

He took aim at Kessler and called him back onto the show,
essentially to finger-wag at him for roping the Proud Boys into
the planning phase. Both were clearly flustered and started arguing immediately.

"I think you duped me," McInnes said. At one point he held up the newspaper and said, "The blood of this girl . . . is also on your hands."

"It's absolutely not, and you're trying to cuck and save your own ass," Kessler said. "You brought me up here to be a patsy for you."

McInnes was obviously worried about being connected to any of it. He published a (now-deleted) blog on the Proud Boys website later that month, titled "We Are Not Alt-Right," in which he ranted like a conspiracy theorist about outsiders working to sabotage the gang by wearing their uniform and purposely getting caught "doing terrible things." He made sure to point out that he was cool with Jews.

"We openly encourage Jewish and non-white members and want them to know they're at home with us," he said.

Meanwhile, the gang's lawyer at the time, a Proud Boy himself named Jason Lee Van Dyke, was getting touchy about any side-by-side comparison in the media between the Proud Boys and Unite the Right. He threatened to sue The Intercept over a short documentary film about the alt-right that included footage from McInnes' show.

The campaign to distance the Proud Boys' name from Unite the Right was ultimately successful. McInnes' decision to keep them out of uniform was likely the reason they were not named in a sweeping lawsuit against the organizers of the rallies, which slapped the likes of Kessler, Spencer, Identity Evropa, and two dozen other attendees and groups with millions in damages more than four years later.

And their distance from the event meant they also kept their reputation and momentum above the rest of the far-right groups of the era. Where other extremist groups had a Nazi brand stuck to them after the events of Unite the Right, the Proud Boys

emerged unfazed: they were still just a regular group of patriots out there fighting for Trump. And that ended up paying divi-
dends. Their next power grab involved distancing themselves
even further from their far-right counterparts, and cozying up
directly to the GOP.

Chapter 6

THE PROUD BOYS AND THE GOP

T he first real indication that the Proud Boys had political aspirations extending beyond their fists came after a GOP event
on October 12, 2018, when the gang attacked a group of
protesters outside a swanky Republican club in Manhattan.

McInnes was headlining a ticketed event that evening at the
Metropolitan Republican Club, which serves as the headquarters for the New York State Republican Party and as a ritzy,
members-only gathering place for the stuffy conservative elites
of New York City. Its previous members and guest appearances
include Richard Nixon, Teddy Roosevelt, Michael Bloomberg,
Rudy Giuliani, and Tucker Carlson. And now here was McInnes,
the leader of a far-right goon squad, chosen as their follow-up.

There was no question that the club organizers knew who
McInnes and the Proud Boys were when they plastered the event
across their social media pages. The gang had ramped up their
grisly efforts after Unite the Right, and they were organizing
and lending their violence to political rallies on a regular basis.
They'd also earned a hate group designation from the Southern Poverty Law Center, and they'd been banned from Twitter,

which characterized them as a "violent extremist group" ahead of a planned sequel to Unite the Right in DC that August, which fizzled out.

Club brass certainly knew what McInnes was going to do beforehand because he spelled it out in an Instagram post. He wrote that he'd be reenacting an "inspiring moment": the political assassination of Inejiro Asanuma, the former leader of the Japan Socialist Party, who was killed in 1960 during a debate on live TV when a far-right ultranationalist rushed the stage and put a sword between his ribs. McInnes advertised the event using photoshopped images of himself with the eyes and clothing of the Japanese assassin.

His announcement didn't faze his hosts, but it caught the attention of local activists, including the Metropolitan Anarchist Coordinating Council, who made a flier of their own and put the event on blast in a (now-deleted) social media post:

Alerta NYC! Gavin McInnes, the misogynistic founder of the Proud Boys, a violent fascist street gang who attended the fatal Unite the Right neo-Nazi rally, is speaking at The Metropolitan Republican Club in NYC this Friday. Call the venue and tell them to #CancelGavin!

The night before the event, the club was vandalized. Police said two unidentified suspects sprayed anarchy symbols across the front doors, smashed a window, and left a note, railing against various GOP policies, mass incarceration in general, and the club organizers for inviting McInnes and his gang.

"While these atrocities persist unabated, the Metropolitan Republican Club chose to invite a hipster-fascist clown to dance for them, content to revel in their treachery against humanity," the note read in part. The vandals were never found, but their work brought more attention to the McInnes event, including stories in local media.

The whole thing had become a circus for the Republican club, whose website declares in bold on the front page, "We Are Serious People." But rather than distance itself from McInnes and his clown show, the club doubled down and posted a very Trumpian announcement on Facebook that angled McInnes as a champion against the right wing's enemies.

"This Godfather of the Hipster Movement has taken on and exposed the Deep State Socialists and stood up for Western Values," the post read. "Join us for an unforgettable evening with one of Liberty's Loudest Voices!"

It was a small gesture, but it highlighted a wider shift in social mores among Republicans at the time. The blundersome reality show version of the GOP that former Alaska governor Sarah Palin introduced to America a few years earlier was no longer an embarrassment for the party but an entire platform under Trump. His conspiratorial word salads and lie-filled screeds were being adopted and regurgitated by politicians and pundits everywhere, to the point where you could start to hear his voice and mannerisms on the lips of other authoritarian leaders around the world. McInnes' odious brand of antiestablishment politics hit the stage in perfect stride with Trump's, and he was rewarded for it.

The night of his event, McInnes arrived carrying a Japanese-style sword as promised, flanked by a large group of Proud Boys. Members showed up knowing there'd be protesters to fight; McInnes events always attracted counterprotesters, and the last few had devolved into brawls. A year earlier, as the Battle for Berkeley raged on the West Coast, McInnes was giving a speech to a group of college Republicans inside a student center at New York University. A group of protesting students interrupted, chanting "No Trump, no KKK, no fascist USA!" McInnes laid down his mic and retreated outside, where his Proud Boys were exchanging blows with local antifascists. At some point in the melee, McInnes said he took some pepper spray to the face. Eleven arrests were made that night.

This time around, McInnes came with more guys. There were about thirty of them, a crew that consisted mostly of Proud Boys but also several members of two local skinhead gangs that McInnes had reportedly associated with in the past: the NYC-based 211 Bootboys, and Battalion 49, both of which are connected to neo-Nazi movements and several other attacks in New York City. This malevolent alliance would be McInnes' bodyguards for the night, and they flanked him wherever he went.

His assassination dance for the GOP club went off without a hitch. But the show didn't end inside. Footage from the scene shows McInnes exiting the venue and waving his samurai sword toward protesters in the street, before hopping into a waiting vehicle and disappearing down the road. Meanwhile, the Proud Boys and their skinhead pals stayed behind, left to their own devices on a darkening street with a handful of black-clad demonstrators who had amassed during the show. A new stage was set, and the Proud Boys performed the way McInnes taught them.

The attack came quickly and with little warning. Two photojournalists who captured footage of the ensuing brawl said that the Proud Boys charged after a protester knocked a MAGA hat off one of their heads. The reaction was brutal and one-sided, they said.

"They turned it into a pummeling," one of them, Shay Horse, told HuffPost at the time. "This was three people on the ground and people just kicking the shit out of them."

A group of about a dozen Proud Boys swarmed and overwhelmed four retreating protesters, pummeling them while they shouted homophobic slurs.

"Do you feel brave now, faggot?" one of the attackers yelled. Another screamed "faggot" as he kicked one of the victims already curled up on the pavement.

When the dust settled, the Proud Boys gathered together for photos and celebrated their apparent win. One yelled, "Fuck around, find out!" and bragged about his assault to the other guys: "Dude, I had one of their fucking heads, and I was just fucking smashing it in the pavement!"

The attack quickly grew into a national story, in part because the Proud Boys had also unleashed a substantial assault in Portland that same weekend. But the Manhattan incident got more attention because it happened on the turf of the New York Republican Party and by its own invitees. There was some plausible deniability up to that point between Trump-era Republicans and the dozens of violent acts carried out in their name. But now the attackers had explicit and direct support from the right-wing establishment. Suddenly, the GOP had something tangible to answer for.

New York's political and criminal justice apparatus came down hard on both the Proud Boys and the GOP club itself. You can understand why: the city is largely a Democratic stronghold, and the Republican Party had invited a bunch of right-wing thugs to unleash violence there. Plus, street gangs don't often go around attacking people in the tony Upper East Side, one of the wealthiest (and whitest) neighborhoods in the city, the kind of place where petty theft might be newsworthy enough to make the tabloids. The Manhattan District Attorney's Office said several Proud Boys helped "transform a quiet, residential street into the site of a battle royal, kicking and beating four individuals in a brutal act of political violence." Democratic governor Andrew Cuomo slammed state Republicans for inviting the gang to "their main club" in the first place, calling the event a "political tactic" designed to "fire up their base."

"It was either one of the dumbest acts or one of the most malicious and incendiary political acts I've ever seen," Cuomo said at a press conference. "You knew who the Proud Boys were. What did they think they were doing if not furthering the president's political tactic of polarization?"

The New York Police Department (NYPD) was criticized in the days following for not immediately arresting any Proud Boys. Not only was it clear within hours that the aggressors were Proud Boys, but activists had used footage and photos from reporters on the scene to identify all the suspects individually. Oddly enough, it was McInnes himself who reportedly arranged for the surrender of at least some of them. He told the *New York Times* that he would personally see to it that the Proud Boys suspects would turn themselves in.

"They are going to be in the Tombs," he said, referring to the notorious jail complex in lower Manhattan.

Ten people connected to the Proud Boys were collared over a slew of charges, including attempted gang assault and rioting, though several of the charges were reduced because the victims didn't cooperate with police or give any statements (that sometimes happens with antifascists, who don't usually work with cops). Turning, say, an *attempted* assault charge into an assault charge usually requires a victim statement, and there were none here. The pair that prosecutors characterized as the most violent that night—Maxwell Hare, twenty-seven, and John Kinsman, forty—were eventually sentenced to four years in prison each. At their sentencing, state supreme court justice Mark Dwyer likened the Proud Boys to the brownshirt movements of Nazi Germany before the gavel came down.

"I know enough about history to know what happened in Europe in the '30s when political street brawls were allowed to go ahead without any type of check from the criminal justice system," he said. "We don't want that to happen in New York."

But the GOP establishment didn't apologize. It didn't distance itself from the Proud Boys or throw McInnes under the bus. The Republicans doubled down again and defended the gang as one of their own.

The right-wing media's version of events, meanwhile, was a complete fabrication. The night of the Proud Boys' attack, Fox News focused on the spray paint graffiti from the night before and tweeted: "Antifa attacks again—swords and vandalism at New York GOP office." (Notice the absence of McInnes there in reference to the sword. It's just enough information to let the reader draw a connection between "antifa" and "attacks" and "swords" and "GOP office.") On the air, Fox quoted Ed Cox, then the state Republican chairman, as "calling on Democrats to cease inciting these attacks." Tucker Carlson suggested in a monologue that "the leaders on the left are causing this."

Local Republicans also worked hard to deflect for the Proud Boys, and their reactions were on a spectrum between "all violence is bad" and "antifa did this."

"Last night one of our state headquarter buildings was attacked by radical leftists," said Marc Molinaro, the Republican challenger for governor at the time. "This type of political violence and rank vandalism is unacceptable. We are one nation and one state. We must not revert to violence under any circumstances."

Later, it was revealed that Ian Reilly, the Metropolitan Republican Club member who reportedly invited McInnes to speak in the first place, worked in the campaign office for Republican state senator Marty Golden. It was proof enough that at least some section of the New York political establishment looked favorably upon McInnes. And as the pressure began to mount against the Proud Boys, the Republican club released a statement blaming protesters for the attack and ran interference for McInnes:

> We do invite speakers to the Club with differing political points of view—some we agree with and some which we do not. But we are staunch supporters of the 1st Amendment. We want to foster civil discussion, but never endorse violence. Gavin's talk on Friday night, while at times was politically incorrect and a bit edgy, was certainly not inciting violence.

A board member of the club, Alan Bialeck, said he believed McInnes was "joking" with his assassination reenactment and was exercising his "free speech." Bialeck made sure to note, in an interview with BuzzFeed News, that the Metropolitan Republican Club "is not a hate group."

It was concerning at the time to see the entirety of the right-wing political establishment rallying around and defending a brazen act of political violence on American soil, though of course we'd seen it before, following Unite the Right, and we'd see it again. But this wasn't just a blanket deflection, like the one Trump issued in the aftermath of a Nazi rally; behind the scenes, the GOP was building a deep and robust relationship with the Proud Boys.

The bond revealed itself slowly at first. Photos started making the rounds showing conservative politicians and pundits posing with the Proud Boys, like Rep. Devin Nunes (R-Calif.), Rep. Mario Diaz-Balart (R-Fla.), Sen. Ted Cruz (R-Tex.), Tucker Carlson, and even Roger Stone, one of Donald Trump's top advisers and confidants. The photos themselves weren't necessarily an indictment on their own (anyone can run up to a public figure and ask for a selfie), but they were adding up quickly. Carlson seemed to understand the negative connotation. A photo showed him and Stone with their arms around two Proud Boys inside a Fox News greenroom, reportedly just before Stone's appearance on *The Ingraham Angle*. When reporters asked about it, Carlson got snarky.

"I strongly support and endorse every personal belief of every person I take a picture with on the street, the subway or in the greenroom, and always have," he told The Wrap.

In February 2018, the Proud Boys posted a video to YouTube, appearing to show Stone getting his first degree initiation. He wore a suit and looked into a camera held by members as he took the oath:

"Hi, I'm Roger Stone. I'm a Western chauvinist. I refuse to apologize for creating the modern world," he said. A Proud Boy off camera shook his hand and thanked him for the address.

A month later, the gang made headlines again after Stone tapped them as security detail for his appearance at the Dorchester Conference, an annual Republican event in Oregon. Patrick Sheehan, the Dorchester board member who invited Stone, argued at the time that the Proud Boys were a necessary choice for someone like him.

"He was worried about getting killed," he told *Willamette Week* (Portland, OR). "He gets death threats constantly."

Few, if any, showed up to protest, let alone threaten anyone, but Stone was captured in photos drinking and smiling with members of the Proud Boys after the event.

For reporters covering the far right at the time, it wasn't hard to see what was happening. The Proud Boys were latching onto more mainstream elements of the MAGA movement by adopting right-wing grievances, like antifa and brown immigrants and feminism, and casting themselves as patriotic freedom fighters against those evils. And GOP leadership, desperate to appeal to a demographic younger than dirt, seemed happy to have them. The McInnes event at the Republican club was really a jumping-off point for the GOP into what would eventually become a full embrace of domestic extremist violence.

"It was a branding exercise. And subsequently, some in the GOP have really started appreciating the Proud Boys for the street goons that they are," said Kelly Weill, an extremism reporter who documented the courtship as it began. "They really embody this political violence that the GOP needs just a little bit of a proxy for. They can't personally be out there doing it, so they have the Proud Boys."

Some upper-crust Republicans tiptoed around the Proud Boys and, like Carlson, shied away from outwardly supporting the group. But others considered them the patriotic defenders they purported to be and endorsed them publicly.

"Thank God for the Proud Boys," reads a blog post penned by Ann Coulter, a longtime Republican pundit and racist troll whose other works include a book called *In Trump We Trust: E Pluribus Awesome!* She published several blog posts absolutely dripping with adulation for the gang—including one after the Capitol riots—whom she said she hired as her personal bodyguards for several appearances. Her posts were full of wildly inaccurate interpretations of reality, but they reveal how the right viewed the Proud Boys, as if they were the final safeguard between antifa and societal breakdown:

> A little more than a year ago, 2,000 antifa tried to shut down my speech at UC Berkeley. . . . Luckily, I'd invited about 20 Proud Boys from northern California chapters to attend my speech. If I hadn't, I might not have made it to the campus at all. . . .

College Republicans are absolutely fantastic, but generally are about as prepared for hand-to-hand combat as I am.

By contrast, the Proud Boys are brawny, tattooed brutes. Many are ex-military. Some worked security for a living, so my bodyguard planned to use a few of them as auxiliary troops, and the rest would get VIP seats so they could be spread throughout the audience in case of pandemonium.

But even as the Proud Boys began to enjoy a cozy relationship with the political elite, they also seemed to be buckling under the weight of the Metropolitan Republican Club attack and its consequences. The gang assault charges indicated that authorities were starting to consider them as a group, rather than individuals. And the feds were reportedly starting to pay attention.

In November 2018, right after the attack, documents were unearthed appearing to show that the FBI had classified the Proud Boys "as an extremist group with ties to White Nationalism," and warned local jurisdictions that the gang was recruiting and hosting violent events in college towns and metropolitan cities. The claim, made in an internal affairs report by the Clark County Sheriff's Office in Vancouver, Washington, led to speculation that the government might actually start cracking down on the Proud Boys where they'd seemingly failed to do so before.

In December, the FBI officially denied the report, stating that it hadn't listed the gang as an extremist group at all. But by then, the Proud Boys organization had undergone seismic shifts. Two days after the document dropped, McInnes said he was quitting the Proud Boys. In a bizarre, rambling, thirty-six-minute video posted to YouTube, he said he was stepping down as leader and claimed he was doing so to somehow alleviate the sentences of those arrested in the attack.

"As of today, November 21, 2018, I am officially disassociating myself from the Proud Boys, in all capacities, forever. I quit," he said. "I'm told by my legal team and law enforcement that this gesture could help alleviate their sentencing. Fine. At the very least, this will show jurors they are not dealing with a gang and there's no head of operations."

He may have also been worried about the implications of the FBI designation for himself. He had reportedly been nervous for years about being slapped with charges under the Racketeer Influenced and Corrupt Organizations (RICO) Act, which allows prosecutors to hand down strict penalties against leaders of gangs and other criminal enterprises.

It's hard to say what "quitting" the Proud Boys actually meant for McInnes, and it's not fully clear what role he plays today in their day-to-day operations. He's coy when asked about it, but he still has regular and very public contact with members and leadership on his current podcast, called *Get Off My Lawn*, airing on his own online network, Censored.TV.

At the time, though, his announcement created a destabilizing void at the helm of the organization, which led to a series of blunders that threatened to dissolve the whole operation. First, a new leader emerged. Replacing McInnes was their volatile and highly litigious lawyer, Jason Lee Van Dyke, who spent the majority of his time as a member threatening people with lawsuits and violence of his own. A law blog once described him as a "fraudulent buffoon, violence-threatening online tough guy, vexatious litigant, proud bigot, and all around human dumpster fire."

Van Dyke scrambled to release a new set of bylaws, much like McInnes' bylaws but chock-full of legalese, clearly intended to revitalize the gang's image. He declared among other things that the Proud Boys were now a peaceful fraternity and that there was no violence requirement for the fourth degree.

"Any requirement that a brother commit a violent or illegal act as a condition precedent to receiving a fourth degree is, by this bylaw, abolished," he wrote.

It was a total sham, of course—the Proud Boys' violence continues today, and members still pursue the violence requirement for their fourth degrees—but it would be a useful reference tool for Van Dyke, who was known to threaten anyone who spoke critically about the Proud Boys (sometimes with defamation suits, other times with violence of his own).

He also announced the Proud Boys Elders, a group of eight anonymous leaders on a shadowy council that would make top-level decisions for the rest of the group, such as fourth degree initiations and the formation of new chapters. They would hold power and responsibility over their fundraising efforts, dues, and legal action. A total of 121 Proud Boys voted on Van Dyke's new bylaws, and they were approved with an eighty-six-member majority.

But that iteration of the bylaws didn't last long, and neither did Van Dyke. When he released a PDF document to the press with the elders' names redacted, he made a substantial oopsie: the redaction didn't work. Simply highlighting the black bar covering the names revealed them in their entirety. On day one, the anonymous elders became not so anonymous. They were an unsurprising mix of chapter leaders and Proud Boys royalty: Enrique Tarrio, Patrick William Roberts, Joshua Hall, Harry Fox, Heath Hair, Timothy Kelly, Luke Rohlfing, and Ethan "Rufio Panman" Nordean.

Van Dyke lasted only two days as leader, and he was disavowed by the rest of the gang five days after that. On their website, the

Proud Boys commended him for his pro bono work and then threw him directly under the bus for the embarrassment. The post reads:

> JL Van Dyke worked tirelessly for the Proud Boys and sent a letter to every media source who called us white nationalist or racist or Alt-Right or anti-semitic etc. He did this literally hundreds of times—all for free . . . it's ironic that he worked so hard to help our reputation but also made some regrettable mistakes that could hurt our reputation. So, it pains us to say Jason Lee Van Dyke is no longer a member of the Proud Boys fraternity and will no longer be representing the fraternity in any legal capacity.

It looked at the time like the Proud Boys were falling apart. After all, who was going to steady the ship if Van Dyke represented the gang's second best after McInnes? I even published the headline "The Proud Boys Are Imploding," on HuffPost, and I was convinced that we were looking at the beginning of the end for the gang, at least in its current form. But they proved resilient, surviving that incident and several more rounds of self-inflicted catastrophe.

Enter Henry "Enrique" Tarrio, the president of the Miami chapter, who in late 2018 was voted in as the new chair by way of an emergency, overnight election following Van Dyke's ouster.

———

TARRIO WAS AN interesting choice for the new torchbearer because he was different from previous leaders. He mirrored McInnes' leadership style, to a degree: he was outspoken and outwardly bigoted (for example, he referred to Caitlyn Jenner, a trans woman who ran for California governor on a Republican ticket, as a man and a "tranny faggot" unworthy of right-wing support), and he portrayed himself as both a patriotic defender of freedom and an unserious everyman.

But he was more than just a loudmouth with a big platform and an axe to grind. He viewed the Proud Boys as marketable to the mainstream right and saw potential in gaining favor with the GOP for the coming culture wars. He characterized McInnes' Proud Boys as a fan club and his version as a political force.

Tarrio came to the table with skills most Proud Boys had never seen before: a bit of political savvy and business experience. Plus, his backstory and his brown skin gave the Proud Boys some diversity at the helm, a fact that remains as one of their go-to counters whenever anyone points to all the racists in their ranks and the bigotry at their core.

Tarrio grew up in Miami's Little Havana neighborhood, the son of Cuban immigrants, running side hustles and latching onto political campaigns. He dropped out of high school to be his own boss and along the way got into legal trouble. At twenty, he got three years' probation for stealing a $55,000 motorcycle, and in 2012 he was indicted on federal charges for his role in a criminal operation that resold stolen diabetic test strip kits. He got a sixteen-month prison sentence for that one.

In an interview over the phone, he told me he was introduced to the Proud Boys in May of 2017, at a lavish mansion party thrown by Milo Yiannopoulos to announce his lawsuit against Simon and Schuster. The publisher reportedly canceled Milo's $250,000 book deal after a video surfaced showing him defending sexual relationships between adult men and young boys. He then sued for $10 million in damages (a suit he later dropped) and threw himself a party. The *Miami New Times* described it as "a bacchanal that included a live python, semi-automatic weapons, and a whole lot of outwardly directed hate and inwardly directed loathing" and featured Roger Stone as a surprise guest.

Tarrio, who says he was campaigning for a Florida senate hopeful at the time, ran a small company of bouncers called Spie Security LLC, which was hired on as door security for the Milo event. He said he used his time there to rub elbows with like-minded conservatives. At some point during the party, he met "these guys with these black and yellow polos." One of them, a fellow Cuban American named Alex Gonzalez, wooed Tarrio with conversations about local politics and business and eventually steered the conversation toward the Proud Boys. Tarrio said he was intrigued but not convinced—he wanted to meet more of the guys.

So they decided to make the introduction by throwing a barbecue for the South Florida chapter of the Proud Boys. Tarrio offered to host the event in his backyard and told Gonzalez to "bring a few dead animals and some beer." He spent a whole day cleaning up and prepping for a big party, but only two guys showed up.

"I'm like, ah fuck, this is retarded, but I'm like, whatever, this is cool," he said. The rest is history.

He hit the political pavement early and hard on behalf of the Proud Boys. He already had some political cachet, he said, from his days campaigning for Republicans like Ron Paul, in his failed presidential primary bid in 2012. More recently he knocked on doors for Trump ("at least forty thousand doors" in South Florida, he claimed). But now, instead of working for candidates, he was showing up at civic events and demonstrations with the goal of promoting the Proud Boys and enlisting more members.

"We started going to these events, and we started recruiting," he said. "I was always involved in local politics with my chapter,

and I would say [to the others], hey, we're at this fucking campaign event, you guys need to fucking step it up. And then the
organization started doing it too."

One of the political events he got excited about was Unite
the Right, which he saw as an opportunity for the Proud Boys
to show what they were made of. He said he and others went,
despite McInnes' warnings about the optics, because he was
"really fucking against tearing down history" (referring to the
Confederate monuments in Charlottesville). He tiptoed around
his involvement in the rallies themselves and claims that he only
showed up "to record" alongside a film crew from InfoWars and
members of the Proud Boys' paramilitary arm, FOAK. He said
the ensuing neo-Nazi rally on August 12 was "the craziest shit I
have ever seen in my life" and claimed that he and his crew left
shortly after it started.

But he was inspired by Unite the Right to push the Proud
Boys into politics and spread their influence beyond street-level
events. If they were going to outlast some of the far-right groups
that dissolved after Unite the Right, they needed endorsements
from mainstream politicians and pundits.

His new plan was to cash in on all the investments he'd put
into Republicans over the years and, ultimately, put Proud Boys
in office. He even tested the water himself and filed paperwork
to run for Florida's 27th Congressional District in 2020, a seat
held by Democrat Donna Shalala. His run wasn't exactly serious,
though—in a statement to the Federal Elections Commission, the
campaign said he didn't even raise money to the $5,000 thresh-
old that would have required him to report contributions. But
his main priority was securing the trust of other, more powerful
politicians.

"You could get more followers, you could change people's
minds, you can put together rallies with thousands of people," he

said, and "that's nothing compared to the drying of the signature of a congressman or a senator or a member of city council."

He planned to push members to run for seats of their own, no matter how small.

"The best way to make change is to become that change," he said. "Taking local GOP seats, for example. Those are super easy to get."

With time, if they lapped up enough seats in a small jurisdiction, perhaps they could secure a voting block in an agreeable county somewhere. They could build a Proud Boys hegemony, where all decisions move in their favor. And once they got some momentum, maybe they could even run for higher office.

It's a sobering prospect, even if it's a pipe dream. The vast majority of Proud Boys aren't exactly US Senate material. But what keeps extremism experts up at night is Tarrio's baseline ambition—picking up small offices around the country—because it's not a tall order.

"At the local level, it's often really easy to take over," said Melissa Ryan, a former Democratic campaign strategist who tracks extremism via her newsletter *Ctrl Alt-Right Delete*. "If you can pack a meeting with forty people, you can elect your slate of candidates," she said. And eventually, "they're making laws, they're turning their ideology into legislation. They have raw political power. And it also creates a pipeline of other extremist candidates. The next Marjorie Taylor Greene might be a state legislator or a school board member."

Tarrio estimates that more than thirty Proud Boys are running for office in 2022, from local committee seats to state senate bids. That number is hard to verify, and Tarrio said some of them aren't publicizing their membership as part of their campaigns. But local news stories about Proud Boys hopefuls paint a concerning picture nonetheless.

Richard "Dick Sweats" Schwetz, a forty-seven-year-old Proud Boy from Reading, Pennsylvania, who reportedly runs the Lehigh Valley chapter, revealed on Telegram that he was running for a state house seat in 2022 as a representative of the so-called Patriot Party, a sputtering pro-Trump movement cobbled together on Facebook and Telegram. He made the announcement in February 2021, in tandem with an invite to a Patriot Party rally, to be held in a parking lot in Harrisburg.

"Please join me," he wrote. "This is how we take our country back. Spread the word. Vote for the candidate who will fight for you both figuratively and literally."

He signed off with, "I am Dick Sweats and I approve this mother fucking message."

His policy platform, detailed on his now-defunct website, Dick2022.com, covers a gamut of obscure right-wing gripes, including "equal rights" for "those with traditional values and conservative beliefs" and the criminalization of doxing, the act of publishing personal information about someone online, often with malicious intent (and a term thrown around loosely whenever antifascists reveal the identity of a Proud Boy photographed at a public political rally).

About thirty people showed up to Schwetz's parking lot patriot rally, among them about eight people wearing Lehigh Valley Proud Boys hoodies. Interestingly, Schwetz tried to distance himself from the Proud Boys in attendance when reporters questioned him.

"This isn't about the Proud Boys. It's about the Patriot Party," he told CNN. Asked about the Patriot Party merch in the back of his car bearing the Proud Boys' black and yellow colors, he stumbled over his next words: "No, I don't, I—I just had yellow vinyl. I'm sorry. That's all I had left over."

He didn't say why he was so nervous about the Proud Boys connection in that moment, but an event he attended with the gang provides a clue: he led a group of Proud Boys on a spree of assaults in Washington, DC, a few months prior, during a Stop the Steal rally in the run-up to the insurrection at the Capitol. He reportedly screamed "fucking pussies" before allegedly attacking two women who showed up to protest the Proud Boys' presence and then laughed in the face of responding officers (though none of the Proud Boys were immediately arrested).

"We got numbers, let's do this!" he said. "Fuck these gender-confused terrorists! They'll put the girls out first—they think that's gonna stop us?"

Dick Sweats is probably not going to win a house seat. As of this writing, it's not even clear what he's running for. He said on Telegram that he would be running against incumbent Dan Meuser, a Republican in Pennsylvania's Ninth Congressional District, whom he described "as fake and fraudulent as Beijing Pedo Joe and Dominion software," but on his website he claimed to be gunning for a seat in another district entirely. The most immediate concern about Schwetz's run—and those of his fellow Proud Boys—is the work being done to mainstream violence, conspiracy theory, and bigotry in political circles. His would-be colleagues in Congress, like Reps. Marjorie Taylor Greene in Georgia and Paul Gosar in Arizona, were stripped of their House committee assignments for merely supporting acts of violence against their political opponents, and they're considered fringe politicians. Any successful Proud Boy run represents a normalization of that mentality. And plenty more of them are running for office.

Edgar J. Delatorre, the former leader of the Schaumburg, Illinois, chapter and an attendee of the Capitol riots, said he was collecting signatures to run for the Illinois senate. His political hopes were rendered unclear when he was arrested a few months after January 6 for attacking someone at an anti-Biden rally he organized.

Joel Campbell, who's running for city council in Topeka, Kansas, claims that he left the gang to focus on politics after January 6, though he still reps the Proud Boys with a tattoo on his forearm denoting his third degree and said he has no desire to get it removed. In fact, he claims his membership and the stories written about him have only helped him.

"The truth is, I haven't spent one campaign dollar. I haven't asked for one donation yet. And I'm probably the most well-known person in Topeka," he told NPR.

Josh Wells, another Kansas resident who ran a failed bid in 2021 for a school board seat in the tiny town of Haven, said he's held leadership positions with the Proud Boys and other extremist groups. He's also a white nationalist who has a soft spot for Nazi imagery and celebrates the deaths of Black people, all facts he revealed in private messages that were compiled and released by a group of antifascists online.

Tarrio acknowledged that some of these guys don't stand a chance in their elections. But he told me he encourages them anyway because each run gives the group a little more political prestige. There's an unearned kind of confidence in his voice when he talks about his aspirations for the gang. He attributes it to a single moment when then president Trump called the Proud Boys out directly on national TV. It happened during one of the 2020 presidential debates, when Trump was asked by Fox News moderator Chris Wallace whether he was willing to condemn "white supremacists and militia groups."

There was a back-and-forth, and Biden offered the Proud Boys as an example of one of the groups Trump should disavow. Trump's next words were a game changer for Tarrio and the boys: "Proud Boys, stand back and stand by."

Now, one could argue—the same way they might argue against anything Trump says—that the president didn't speak correctly, that he wasn't trying to give the Proud Boys marching orders, that he's not responsible for his sentences because he's never demonstrated an ability to put one together. But even his closest allies argue that he knew exactly who the Proud Boys were when he said those words. His longtime personal attorney Michael Cohen—who pleaded guilty in 2018 to charges related to tax evasion and lying to Congress—went further during an interview with CNN.

"I think he's actually doing it on purpose. If you look at who the Proud Boys really are, they're an army," he said. "This is Trump's army. . . . And when he loses, he's going to use them to try and keep control of power."

And anyway, to the Proud Boys, the president's intent didn't matter. "Stand back and stand by" was big for them.

"We got mentioned, and my life has not been the same since then," Tarrio told me. "As soon as the words came out of his mouth, my phone started blowing up off the hook. I had ten fucking news trucks at my house the next morning. I didn't sleep for, like, two days."

Proud Boys across the country celebrated what they saw as a direct nod from the president, whom they'd supported since day one. Tarrio was preparing "Proud Boys Standing By" T-shirts to be sold on the gang's merch site within minutes of the quote, and at the same time, he was recruiting. He claimed that they had to shut down their website due to the waves and waves of membership requests rolling in.

Trump and company shrugged off the moment, but Tarrio saw it as a needed boost for members, many of whom he hoped would be running for office in the next election. And when the time came, if any of them even got marginally competitive in their races, Tarrio had another political ace up his sleeve, a further boost from the guy who pushed him into politics in the first place.

He had Roger Stone.

▬▬

ROGER STONE HAS been the troll sitting on the shoulder of powerful Republicans since Richard Nixon's presidency. His "dirty trickster" moniker derives from a career of cutthroat weaseling for the right people: during Nixon's 1972 reelection campaign, Stone posed as a socialist and donated money to Nixon's primary opponent and sent the receipt to the press. Then he hired an operative to infiltrate the George McGovern campaign. He played a small role in the Watergate scandals at the age of nineteen and a large role in the rise of Donald Trump half a century later.

Throughout the Trump years, Stone remained one of the president's closest friends and loyal allies. He'd been a presence in Trump's life for three decades before he was hired for the presidential push in March 2015. He got fired a few months later for being what Trump called a "publicity seeker," but Stone continued his work behind the scenes well into Trump's presidency, especially when it came to obscuring the president's movements and sliming his political opponents. He worked to get dirt on Hillary Clinton during her presidential bid and launched a smear campaign against her, including the formation of an anti-Hillary group called Citizens United Not Timid, an acronym that got its own news cycle and merchandise campaign.

Eventually his dirty work caught up to him: he was convicted on five counts of lying to Congress over his efforts to secure emails obtained by Russian agents that would damage Clinton's 2016 campaign. He might have spent three years in prison, but

Trump pardoned him during his final weeks in office (along with many other loyalists), and he walked free.

Stone is sometimes secretive about his political dealings (which makes sense, given the crimes), but his persona is louder than life. If you didn't know him by name, you'd know him by photos: he goes almost everywhere wearing a pinstripe suit and tie, round teashade glasses, and a fedora, with a wide and crooked grin and a wider forehead, like a poorly written Batman villain scrapped for being too on the nose. He has a tattoo of Nixon's face on his upper back and even cribbed the former president's signature gesture of throwing up a double peace sign in front of news cameras.

He's also just really weird. He's incredibly self-important and, unlike most lawmakers, always seems to answer calls for comment, from anyone, despite his proximity to the upper crust of the Republican Party and all the security implications that entails. He's had the same cell number for years and answers almost every text he receives, which sometimes gets him in trouble when his messages show up in news stories.

He also has close ties to multiple Proud Boys and chapters, especially those most involved in Florida politics near his home in Ft. Lauderdale, and he remains without a doubt the gang's closest connection to Trump's inner circle.

One of his Proud Boys acolytes is Jacob Engels, a trolling blogger who counts Stone as his mentor. Engels has written multiple stories in Stone's defense on the Gateway Pundit, a far-right blog that pushes conspiracy theories, and his own site, the Central Florida Post. (He has repeatedly claimed, for his part, that he's not a member of the Proud Boys, though he openly attends their meetings and events and has been pictured in their uniform.) The Daily Beast once described him as Stone's "Mini-Me." He's known to show up to political events with a megaphone, leading Republican crowds in chants against Democrats or George Soros and joining in on protests, despite characterizing himself as a journalist.

In 2018, he appeared alongside the Proud Boys and Rep. Matt Gaetz (R-Fla.) at a Republican protest at the Broward County elections board, spewing conspiracy theories about missing ballots in the recent election. The Daily Beast's Will Sommer likened the scene to a similar and infamous ballot-blocking effort in 2000, known as the Brooks Brothers Riot, which Stone also had a hand in fomenting:

> The attempt to stop the Broward ballot count echoed a similar effort from the 2000 election, in which a group of rowdy Republicans intent on winning the state of Florida for George W. Bush staged a protest in Miami-Dade County to stop a Florida ballot count. That moment, forever known as the "Brooks Brothers Riot," was organized by Roger Stone, a longtime dirty trickster who went on to advise one Donald J. Trump.
>
> That Engels would adopt Stone's tactics some 18 years later is no surprise to those who know him. Stone, after all, is his mentor.

But Stone's closest Proud Boys relationship is with Tarrio. The pair has appeared together on numerous occasions dating back to 2018, and they make no secret of their mutual respect. Tarrio makes press appearances in defense of Stone whenever he ends up in court, and Stone boosts the Proud Boys and attends their events. In December 2018, the pair stood together in a video address to the gang, and Stone called on the Proud Boys to fight back against "globalists" and Special Counsel Robert Mueller, who was at the time leading the investigation into election meddling and ties between Trump's camp and Russian officials.

"Keep the faith. Don't let them wear you down—the global-ists, the two-party duopoly, Robert Mueller, the deep state, the *Wall Street Journal*, the *New York Times*, the *Washington Post*," Stone said. "They want to wear us down. Never give up the fight. We will prevail."

Both of them get a little coy when you ask about their rela-tionship. Tarrio told me he met Stone at a book signing in 2014, and that they've been friends ever since. Stone said he doesn't recall when or how they met. Of course, that's what they say to a journalist, to whom neither have a vested interest in telling the truth. But when they're put in the hot seat—in front of a judge, for example—the picture of their working relationship gets clearer.

In 2019, amid hearings in his federal obstruction case, Stone got in trouble for posting a photo on Instagram that depicted US district judge Amy Berman Jackson, who was overseeing his case, next to crosshairs. The judge had already gagged him from talking to the press about the case, so she wasn't exactly pleased to find a threat against her posted to his social media.

Stone claimed under oath that it was one of his "volunteers" who posted the photo. Asked to elaborate, Stone admitted that several Proud Boys were acting as his social media managers and did "a lot of clerical work" for him. He named a few familiar names: Enrique Tarrio, Jacob Engels, Tyler Whyte, and Rey Perez, all Proud Boys in Florida. He said they had access to his Face-book and Instagram accounts and even his phone and that his house was "like a headquarters" to them. He said he couldn't pin down which Proud Boy was around at any given time, though.

"People come and go. They're all part of the same group," he said. "It's a revolving situation."

Around the same week, Tarrio was spotted in a live audi-ence standing behind Trump at one of his speeches in Miami. He waved his arms and cheered, wearing a black shirt that read in bold white type "Roger Stone Did Nothing Wrong." The shirt would become a mainstay for Tarrio at Trump-related affairs; he wore it again while posing for a photo with Donald Trump Jr. and former Fox personality Kimberly Guilfoyle, Trump Jr.'s girlfriend and an adviser to his father.

What's always been interesting about Stone and Tarrio is their power imbalance. Obviously, Tarrio and the Proud Boys stand to benefit from a partnership with the president's fixer, but it wasn't clear until recently how Stone might benefit from a relationship with members of a fight gang, who by 2018 were only making headlines over their violence.

Stone agreed to an interview with me in May 2021, during a time when he was under immense public scrutiny over his proximity to the January 6 insurrection at the Capitol. He maintains that he was in his DC hotel during the riots. But he made various appearances with the Proud Boys in the days surrounding the event and, on the morning of, was captured on video flanked by a group of Oath Keepers, some of the gang's closest allies. He was later subpoenaed by the House panel investigating the Capitol attacks, though he refused to cooperate with the probe.

Interviewing people like Stone is a complex and confounding kind of dance. He's a celebrity, a convicted liar, and a Trump sycophant, and like a child born of all three, he's prone to self-serving word salads sandwiched between half-truths and deflections.

He couldn't decide from question to question whether he was close to the Proud Boys or not; in one breath he said he didn't associate with the gang but "befriended specific individuals who happened to be members of that organization." In another, he lamented that the Proud Boys, and Tarrio in particular, had been "stigmatized" by the media. He suggested that the Proud Boys were never violent or racist, despite a mountain of evidence proving otherwise.

"When a lie is repeated enough times over and over again by these powerful assets, you get unfairly labeled. And I think that's what has happened to the Proud Boys," Stone told me. "'They're racist, they're white supremacists, they're violent, they're criminal.' No, none of these things are true. Not in my experience."

From the start, and throughout the twenty-five-minute conversation, Stone repeated the claim that if the Proud Boys were a criminal enterprise capable of carrying out violence or an insurrection, he had no idea about any of it, and he had no part in it. And in any case, he argued, anything criminal attributed to the Proud Boys was the act of an individual, not the group.

"You can't condemn everybody who's an Italian American because some Italian Americans broke the law. It just doesn't work that way."

He worked hard to deflect for the Proud Boys, even when there wasn't any apparent need to do so. Some of that seemed to be for the sake of self-preservation; whenever he's asked about his relation to the gang or his whereabouts during a Proud Boys event, he launches into a spiel about the media's mismanagement of his and the Proud Boys' image. But it was also clear that he had invested a considerable amount of emotional and professional capital in Tarrio.

In fact, Stone admitted that he's been advising Tarrio and the Proud Boys directly for years, perhaps much in the same way he might have advised Trump. He said he provided his professional and personal input on their political goals and on several occasions gave them advice when they got into legal trouble or did something that was bad for their optics.

"I encouraged [Tarrio] when he wanted to run for Congress, even though I thought it was probably a hopeless exercise," Stone said. "Enrique is somebody who's had a tough life. But he is charismatic. And I do think he's got a great future if he wants one.

Although I fear [he] will constantly be stigmatized by the creeps at CNN, the real haters, the folks who really are intolerant, the folks at MSNBC. . . . It's a false imagery. And it's really tremendously unfair."

Asked whether he thought the Proud Boys could make a solid collective run for office going forward, Stone suggested they might be too "radical" to earn his support.

"I don't see them as an elective political force. That's just not how I see them. I see them as individual patriots who support Western values," he said. "If you're on the left, you can transcend your radical past. It's not clear whether you can transcend a radical past on the right for a political future. Just not clear. Too early to say."

As for the attack at the Metropolitan Republican Club, Stone said he believes the convicted Proud Boys might have been exonerated completely if they'd listened to him and hired a better lawyer, one who could cast the blame on antifa and stand up to the New York establishment. He said he told McInnes the same.

"They should have hired a former state attorney general who could have taken [New York governor] Andrew Cuomo on frontally," he said. "If the Proud Boys are violent, then antifa and BLM are violent. You can't have it one way. Gavin [McInnes] knows I feel this way: I think they should have been better represented."

After Tarrio took the reins, Stone told him that the gang's image was growing too toxic for public consumption and suggested that he should just change their name and start over.

"Candidly I told him a good two years ago that I think he should change the name of the organization and completely rebrand them. I think they've been so thoroughly stigmatized."

When I asked whether he had any ideas for their new name, he shot back immediately.

"Yes, I would have called them the Ancient Order of the Orange Men."

It was obviously a reference to Trump and his iconic orange hue that comes from a thick layer of TV makeup. Was Tarrio receptive to the new name?

"Not in the slightest," he said. "I would say completely disinterested."

While Stone didn't seem super optimistic about their chances at real political success, he didn't count the Proud Boys out completely, though he said he wasn't aware of any other members running for public office. Asked whether he'd endorse another Tarrio run, Stone said he would wait to gauge how the charges stemming from January 6 affected him and the rest of the Proud Boys.

"I'd like to see the results of the current situation. I mean, you know, every American is entitled to the presumption of innocence until proven otherwise."

Even his openness to endorsement means a lot. The Proud Boys climbed to higher heights in their first few years of existence than any other extremist group around them, specifically because of their high-level political connections. Endorsements from the likes of Matt Gaetz, Ann Coulter, and Roger Stone would have been a game changer for *anyone* looking to make it in political circles, let alone a right-wing goon squad. And those relationships have helped launder the Proud Boys' image for the general public.

They're now celebrated on the right as freedom fighters and sought out for their security. They were welcomed as heroes by an evangelical pastor hosting an antiabortion rally outside a Planned Parenthood in Salem, Oregon, in 2021.

"We have the Proud Boys across the street," said the pastor, Ken Peters, on a livestream during the event. "Oh my goodness, thank God for the Proud Boys. We heard that antifa might be making a showing tonight but we're gonna be OK."

In the same city, just days after the Proud Boys stormed the Capitol on January 6, they were touted by a QAnon conspiracy theorist running for US Senate named Jo Rae Perkins, who stood on her rally stage and thanked them for their service.

"For those of you who don't know the Proud Boys, they're a great group of men," she said. "They love this country and they love this state. They are there to make sure we don't lose our rights."

The gang's relationships make their baseline goal of fighting in the street much easier to pull off. They have the Republican Party at their side, often literally so, which gives them a veil of political legitimacy. Now they're able to disguise their ambitions as protected demonstration and continue securing rally permits and freelance gigs as bodyguards.

But while their relationship with the GOP is a valuable asset, they know they can't continue their vicious fieldwork without the good graces of the press and the police. These two entities are the only watchdogs present at their street brawls, and winning them over can mean the difference between prison time and what essentially amounts to constitutionally protected violence.

Chapter 7

THE FIST AMENDMENT

The first time you see a line of armored police officers standing in defense of a group of extremists and firing "less-lethal" munitions at their own citizens, your blood runs cold.

It's a common sight at Proud Boys events. I saw the scene play on repeat while reporting on extremist rallies in cities across America during Trump's presidency, and it never got easier to stomach. One scene in particular sticks out in my memory:

It was August 2018, in Portland, Oregon, during the bloody rally held ostensibly to kick off Joey Gibson's Senate run. I was on one side of a highway separating the downtown area from Tom McCall Waterfront Park, and I was standing next to a raucous group of Proud Boys and Patriot Prayer members. They were jeering and chanting "Fuck antifa" at the much larger crowd amassing across the street, a gigantic coalition of leftist protesters that included local hippies in tie-dye and militant antifascists dressed in black bloc, protesting together as one group. Standing among them was my colleague, a fellow extremism reporter named Christopher Mathias, who was covering the growing demonstration from the perspective of the counterprotesters.

One major difference between the two sides (besides their ideology and reason for being there) was their connection to the locale: many of the Patriot Prayer and Proud Boys attendees were out-of-towners, who had descended on Portland from their homes in Washington State and beyond to draw out the community for a fight. The crowd that had gathered against them was full of locals, who were acutely aware of what happens when fascist groups feel empowered to organize. Unite the Right was still fresh in their minds, and they said as much, chanting "We remember Charlottesville!" They came to drown out the Proud Boys, and in that sense, they were victorious, outnumbering the opposition by about four to one.

Standing between the two groups was a battalion of heavily armored Portland Police Bureau officers who, from the very beginning, stood in formation along Naito Parkway with their backs to the interloping group of neofascists (at least one of whom, you'll recall, was wearing a "Pinochet Did Nothing Wrong" T-shirt), keeping their "less-lethal" munitions pointed at the counterdemonstration. The event was largely peaceful, until police announced over a loudspeaker that the locals would have to disperse or face arrest and "impact weapons." The pretense for that order remains a bit of a mystery: police claimed they'd spotted antifascist protesters with weapons. But the Proud Boys side was clearly armed from the beginning, and though weapons were seized from several members, the group was never given a dispersal order.

Some time passed, and after a few more warnings, police launched an attack against the counterprotesters. They started firing projectiles and chemical irritants, and with every pop and explosion that rang out, the Proud Boys at their back cheered. A cloud of smoke rose over the crowd, and they retreated from the street and into downtown. A small group of armored police broke from their ranks and gave chase, firing tear gas and flash-bangs at the protesters as they pursued. Mathias, who was among those being fired upon, described the scene as a war zone.

"I've covered a lot of extreme police tactics in my career, but what Portland police did that day was the most aggressive I've ever seen," he told me in a follow-up interview. "They started shooting some kind of nonlethal munitions at us. I got hit with something in the leg, and I remember seeing someone get hit next to me. I started screaming that they were going to kill someone if they didn't stop."

Mathias ran toward the officers, begging them to stop, and when he got close enough, the looks on their faces gave him pause.

"I remember, vividly," he said, "that one of them was smiling."

To the Proud Boys and their pals, the scene was something to celebrate. Patriot Prayer's Tiny Toese called it "beautiful" and thought the police "did their job." To his cheering compatriots he crowed: "Today was a victory for America!"

———

THE PROUD BOYS wouldn't survive as a group without the convincing public image they've built for themselves. As they and other extremist groups have learned, you can't just go around attacking people on the basis of hate and ideological differences without facing legal and societal backlash.

This gang is able to continue its campaign of violence by maintaining a veneer of patriotism. They use star-spangled imagery, military garb, MAGA hats, and pro-police messaging to appeal to mainstream media and law enforcement. When the cameras are on, the Proud Boys want the press and police to see a group of patriots holding up American flags because that imagery looks a lot like constitutionally protected demonstration. They also want to use those American flags as bludgeoning weapons against leftists, but the bar for making war look like protected speech can be pretty low.

While there's sometimes an element of deceit involved in winning over the media and police, often that support is just baked in. It's not like police are inherently repelled by groups like the Proud Boys; sometimes they're one and the same. US police and military forces in particular have a long and fraught history with white supremacy and extremist infiltration. And though some progress has been made since the civil rights era, when the Klan penetrated all walks of law enforcement and government in the United States, researchers and intelligence agencies alike warn that the threat has ballooned again over the past fifteen years or so, alongside the rising threat of far-right violence. To this day, extremist groups are working to form and nurture symbiotic relationships with law enforcement in order to push their causes forward unimpeded.

A 2006 FBI intelligence assessment warned that police departments across the country faced a new threat of white supremacist infiltration. Neo-Nazis and other racist factions were working to infiltrate departments and, the agency warned, might use the intelligence gathered there to hamper investigations, recruit officials into their ranks, or target elected officials for violence. The groups were purposefully sanitizing their appearances and messaging to appeal to broader society and in particular law enforcement officials, whose favor came with some obvious legal benefits:

> The term "ghost skins" has gained currency among white supremacists to describe those who avoid overt displays of their beliefs to blend into society and overtly advance white supremacist causes. . . . At least one white supremacist group

has reportedly encouraged ghost skins to seek positions in law enforcement for the capability of alerting skinhead crews of pending investigative action against them.

Almost a decade later, another FBI document—a classified counterterrorism policy guide from April 2015—revealed that its "domestic terrorism investigations focused on militia extremists, white supremacist extremists, and sovereign citizen extremists often have identified active links to law enforcement officers."

These and other warnings from the intelligence community, alongside those of academics and activists, have gone largely unheeded for decades. A Brennan Center report, published by former FBI agent Michael German in 2020, stated that the US government was "strikingly insufficient" in its response to known racism, white supremacy, and far-right militancy within law enforcement.

"The failure of federal, state, and local law enforcement agencies to aggressively respond to evidence of explicit racism among police officers undermines public confidence in fair and impartial law enforcement," the report states. "Worse, it signals to white supremacists and far-right militants that their illegal acts enjoy government approval and authorization, making them all the more brazen and dangerous."

A police lieutenant in DC was placed on leave in February 2022 after an internal investigation revealed that he had close and unethical contacts with prominent Proud Boys, including Enrique Tarrio. The details of the investigation weren't clear at the time of this writing, but Tarrio told reporters that he had a close working relationship with the officer, a twenty-two-year veteran of the force named Shane Lamond. He claimed that he gave Lamond a heads-up when the Proud Boys were coming into town, and in return, that Lamond revealed the positions of coun-terdemonstrators during their marches.

"He was just a liaison officer for when we held rallies," Tarrio told the *Washington Post*.

There's danger beyond this kind of direct influence, though. Undermining the public's trust doesn't require a police officer to align fully or even directly with an extremist group. The small-est gesture can project a lot of information, whether the officer means it or not.

In 2019, on the Fourth of July, a Proud Boy was captured on video pounding fists with a cigar-smoking DC police officer on duty. Another officer was overheard by reporters joining in on the Proud Boys' chants of "I like beer," a nod to Supreme Court justice Brett Kavanaugh, who uttered the phrase during his con-firmation hearings, in which he stood accused of multiple sexual assaults. Both of these decisions by police officers were relatively small but had cascading effects on the public perception of their entire department. It makes sense: Would you trust an officer who was chummy with a Proud Boy to protect you against them during a violent altercation?

Proud Boy Luke Rohlfing said after that that he wasn't sur-prised the police were "being friendly with people who aren't calling 'oink oink bang bang,'" given that he and the other Proud Boys had been chanting "Blue lives matter" that day, he told DCist.

He may be right, but as anyone demonstrating against the Proud Boys would argue, policing isn't about protecting the peo-ple that officers might feel more comfortable around; it's about protecting the community from harm. And the Proud Boys have always been very clear about their intention to cause harm to protesters, and they make good on that promise every time they show up.

To continue that dirty work unimpeded, the gang works really hard to nurture its cozy relationships with local authorities.

The Proud Boys often incorporate pro-police messaging into their patriotic tableau at rallies. The thin blue line flag, for example—a popular white-and-black American flag featuring one blue stripe, the so-called thin blue line, a symbol for police solidarity—is a mainstay at extremist events, in part because the far right sees it as a symbol of intimidation, counter to antifa and BLM. The flag's creator, Andrew Jacob, reportedly invented the flag in response and opposition to the Black Lives Matter movement and protests against police. Jacob also began to mesh those pro-police symbols with the skull logo of the Punisher, a crime-fighting Marvel comics character from the '70s who used extrajudicial murder and torture as a means to an end for law enforcement. Extremist groups love this imagery because it serves a dual purpose: as easily recognizable countermessaging against their sworn enemies and as a symbol of truce with police when they are in the field. The thin blue line flag and Punisher logo were both featured prominently at Unite the Right, alongside the German Nazi war flag and the Confederate flag. There are legitimate connections among those symbols now.

The thin blue line flag has become the centerpiece of the so-called Blue Lives Matter movement, an aggressively procop countermovement to Black Lives Matter. BLM was born amid street protests after the acquittal of George Zimmerman, who killed an unarmed Black teen named Trayvon Martin in 2012, and Blue Lives Matter reared its head in 2014 alongside the thin blue line flag, after the murders of NYPD officers Rafael Ramos and Wenjian Liu in Brooklyn, New York.

But the Blue Lives Matter movement and its symbology were problematic from the start: wearing a thin blue line flag wasn't just a patriotic salute to police, it was clearly an anti–Black Lives

Matter banner, and for that reason it was criticized as projecting a message of violence and racism. It solidified perceptions that police and Black citizens were part of two factions on opposing sides of a violent campaign and signaled that the person flying it had chosen the side of the police.

As it happens, much of the Trumpian right sees pro-police messaging as synonymous with patriotism and that standing in direct opposition to Black Lives Matter is an inherently good thing, so it makes sense that more mainstream right-wing characters have adopted the thin blue line imagery. US senator Pat Toomey (R-Pa.), for example, has repeatedly tried to push his idea for the "Thin Blue Line Act," which would pose harsher punishments for those who kill officers or first responders in the line of duty, increasing the chance that perpetrators would face the death penalty. Toomey positions the act as patriotic, while critics call it an empty gesture that would raise already high tensions between police and the communities they serve (it hasn't yet gone anywhere in Congress). Trump, meanwhile, had a gigantic thin blue line flag displayed behind him onstage at an election campaign rally in Wisconsin in 2020.

But seeing Republicans display thin blue line imagery is one thing. Seeing it worn by officers in uniform, despite the implications, projects another. Police officers across the nation have worn their own iterations of the flag while sparring with Black Lives Matter protesters, making demonstrations look more like war campaigns. Departments in San Diego, California, and Columbia, Missouri, banned black-whie-and-blue masks after multiple incidents of active duty officers wearing thin blue line face coverings while they scuffled with protesters.

Some police chiefs banned the symbology outright. University of Wisconsin–Madison police chief Kristen Roman announced that her officers were prohibited from wearing any thin blue line symbols on duty, likening them to "hateful ideologies" despite what she described as some well-meaning applications.

"I am moved to enact specific measures to distance UWPD from the thin blue line imagery and the fear and mistrust that it currently evokes for too many in our community," she said in early 2021. "The balance has tipped, and we must consider the cost of clinging to a symbol that is undeniably and inextricably linked to actions and beliefs antithetical to UWPD's values."

Other law enforcement entities have leaned into the symbology. The Fraternal Order of Police, the country's largest police advocacy organization (and an aggressive opponent to police reform), uses thin blue line imagery in just about all of its PR material. The police department serving Mount Prospect, Illinois, revealed its new officer patch, featuring the thin blue line in the background, just four months after Unite the Right. A press release from the Mount Prospect Police Department states that it "honors the law enforcement officers who have made the ultimate sacrifice for their communities." It sparked a massive outcry, and the patch was later removed from uniforms, despite pushback from a local officers' union. In the wake of the George Floyd protests in 2021, the *Wall Street Journal* ran an op-ed by the author of a book titled *The War on Cops,* which suggested that banning the thin blue line imagery was anticop because "police officers aren't making minority neighborhoods unsafe; criminals are." The piece failed to mention why anyone might be offended by the imagery in the first place.

It might seem overly vigilant to give much thought to cops who fly a procop flag. But there's a reason officers wear uniforms in the first place: they're supposed to be easily recognizable in an emergency situation as legal arbitrators and public aid workers. Departments often have strict regulations meant to keep up those appearances. The Urbana Police Department in Illinois, for example, bars on-duty employees from using their uniforms to support, oppose, or otherwise engage in politics or religion. The department regulates everything about an officer's appearance, from patches on the officer's uniform to his or her grooming standards. Police department regulations often resemble those of the US Armed Forces, which generally forbid any sort of customization to the on-duty uniform at all, let alone regalia showing membership in or support for a political movement or group.

So when the accoutrements worn by officers begin to match those worn by extremist groups, the messaging changes dramatically. Something that might seem insignificant—like a thin blue line gaiter—looks to the public like the cops have chosen a side.

On the other hand, sometimes it's a department's actions that suggest improper allegiances. The Portland Police Bureau, for example, was repeatedly accused of standing aside while Patriot Prayer and Proud Boys members beat protesters. In August 2020, at the height of the BLM protests there, the department issued an announcement that officers would no longer intervene in fights "between willing participants," following a particularly bloody day at the hands of the far right, in which a Proud Boy named Alan Swinney pointed a gun at someone's head, and other members attacked protesters with a variety of weapons, including pepper spray, paintball guns, fireworks, and aluminum bats.

"Each skirmish appeared to involve willing participants and the events were not enduring in time, so officers were not deployed to intervene," the bureau said in a statement to the *Washington Post*. "PPB members have been the focus of over 80 days of violent actions directed at the police, which is a major consideration for determining if police resources are necessary to interject between two groups with individuals who appear to be willingly engaging in physical confrontations for short durations."

When the bureau did get involved, it was usually with the Proud Boys at their backs and its arsenal pointed at counter-protesters, or defending the Proud Boys while they marched. In one instance in August 2019, officers escorted the Proud Boys, led by Tarrio, through the city and across a closed-down Hawthorne Bridge, where the gang took triumphant photos of themselves that they still use in their promos today, even though they had been brutalizing the city for almost two years by that point.

Sometimes Portland police coordinated directly with Proud Boys and their affiliates, too. Text messages between Portland police and Patriot Prayer leader Joey Gibson obtained by *Willamette Week* revealed a chummy relationship that critics say went beyond what could be considered intelligence gathering for the bureau. Lieutenant Jeff Niiya, the commanding officer on the Portland Police Bureau's rapid response team, at one point advised Gibson on what behavior at rallies would force him to arrest Tiny Toese on his active warrant and what he could reasonably tolerate and look the other way.

"Just make sure he doesn't do anything which may draw our attention," Niiya texted to Gibson in 2017. "I don't see a need to arrest on the warrant unless there is a reason."

In another exchange, the pair discussed what Gibson's Senate run might mean for Niiya's workload:

Gibson: The hate against me will multiply because I am running for office, so when I come into Portland and Seattle the energy will be high. I know it's a pain in the ass for you guys, but I will do the best I can to work with you.

Niiya: You're running for office?!! Good for you. County level?

Gibson: Running for US Senate. Will take a miracle for me to win but people are backing me so we will see what happens. I will be using Portland and Seattle protesters as a part of the campaign so it will impact you guys unfortunately, so I apologize now ahead of time.

Niiya's boss at the time, former chief Danielle Outlaw, also carried some water for Gibson when she joined conservative talk-radio host Lars Larson a year later to talk about police violence at several violent protests. She likened officers' clashes with antifascists to a schoolyard fight, blamed protesters for their own injuries, and then ran deflection for Patriot Prayer. *Willamette Week* also published a transcript of that chat, which read in part:

Outlaw: I'll use this analogy: I tell you, 'Meet me after school at 3:00. Right? We're gonna fight. Right?'

Larson: Yeah. [Laughs] Yeah.

Outlaw: And I come with the intention to fight. And then you get mad because I kicked your butt. And then you go back and you wail off and whine and complain because you thought when you left that you were going to come and be the victor. And that didn't happen. Nobody's calling that. Why?

Larson went further and tried to get the chief to agree with his assertion that antifa was a "terrorist group." She didn't bite, but she did complain that she'd been called a "protector of those who are believed to be white supremacists" in Patriot Prayer, for whom she deflected.

Outlaw: You know, I'm not a subject matter expert on [antifa], but I will tell you this: The fact that I, as a very obvious African American female police chief, have been accused by those within that group or those who support that group, as being a supporter and protector of [Patriot Prayer] who are believed to be white supremacists—if that's even the case—is ridiculous. Right?

Larson: Yeah, I would agree with you.

Local officials were outraged. Outlaw was criticized for appearing to side with the fight gang running amok in her town, and furthermore misrepresenting her own officers' role in that violence. The conversation suggested that the bureau didn't have a clear understanding of *any* faction battling it out in their streets, let alone Patriot Prayer, and by that point the gang's members and their allies had already been connected to a swath of criminal attacks on the local populace.

It's a conflict of interest at best, and some officer–Proud Boy relationships extend way beyond conflict of interest. On-duty cops have been revealed as active members on multiple occasions. But even then, their departments don't always know what to do with that information. Some have been fired outright for their affiliation, including a sheriff in Washington State who wore a Proud Boys sweater, and a Fresno, California, cop named Rick Fitzgerald who rallied with the gang at violent pro-Trump rallies. "Such ideology, behavior and affiliations have no place in law enforcement and will not be tolerated within the ranks of the Fresno Police Department," Fresno police chief Paco Balderrama said in a statement about Fitzgerald. "Public trust and accountability are paramount in our ability to fairly police this community."

But other officers weren't found to have broken any rules at all, despite multiple civil rights groups, government agencies, and some law enforcement watchdogs labeling the Proud Boys as an extremist group with very strong ties to white supremacy.

In 2019, a civil rights group investigating police ties with extremists revealed that an officer in East Hampton, Connecticut, named Kevin P. Wilcox was not only a member of the Proud Boys but also made dues payments to the gang.

The Lawyers' Committee for Civil Rights Under Law found Wilcox while conducting a national inquiry into "law enforcement with known ties to white supremacist and extremist organizations." Wilcox's dues payments, the group suggested, were helping to fund the Proud Boys' "violent or otherwise illegal" activities. In July the group called on East Hampton police chief Dennis Woessner to investigate Wilcox and conduct a review of his stops and arrests to check for bias allegations.

"Police officers who affiliate with white supremacist groups contribute to a climate of fear and mistrust, infect the ranks with bias and racism, and exacerbate the divides between communities of color and the police," said Kristen Clarke, president of the group. "We call for the removal of Officer Wilcox from the East Hampton Police Department given his confirmed ties to the 'Proud Boys' and call for a Justice Department investigation to determine whether the officer and the department have violated federal civil rights laws."

Woessner obliged and launched an inquiry. It lasted two months. In September, Woessner announced that Wilcox hadn't actually broken any policies. Wilcox, he said, "adamantly denies being associated with white supremacist groups," and that denial was apparently enough to exonerate him.

Reached later by the Associated Press, Woessner said that "there is no question that [Wilcox] is not a white supremacist."

Asked what he knew, if anything, about the Proud Boys, the police chief admitted, "Only what I searched on the internet." Wilcox retired shortly thereafter, and on his way out claimed that Clarke's ulterior motive for the inquiry was to "silence conservative voices" using "far-left propaganda" in her letter, parroting language used by both extremist groups and the mainstream right.

Another officer based in Chicago, Robert Bakker, was exposed by local antifascists to have extremely close ties to the Proud Boys. Chicago Antifascist Action released a dossier on Bakker that included his private chats with other Proud Boys in a chat room called "Fuck Antifa," dating back to 2019. The screenshots appear to show Bakker coordinating Proud Boys meetups in the area and bragging about his contacts with "high police," which he said he was using to track antifascists' movements. He also claimed he had "government connects" through which he was pushing to get antifa labeled as a terrorist group. The Chicago Police Department launched an investigation in 2020, but Bakker was reportedly still active on the force two years later, despite outcry from civil rights groups.

"CPD should not, and need not, give cover to white nationalism within its ranks," wrote the Lawyers' Committee for Civil Rights Under Law in a letter of inquiry to the department in January 2022. "The First Amendment protects the right to speak and associate freely and assemble peacefully, including as a Proud Boy, but not to serve the community as a police officer or other government employee."

Police forces carry a tremendous amount of responsibility and political power at Proud Boys rallies. Every decision they make projects to the crowd whose side they're on and how violent things are going to get. When they show favor to far-right factions, they not only signal that those groups can keep coming back, but they also further aggravate tensions with the people who show up to protest them. It's a dangerous feedback loop that can quickly spin out of control, as we've seen in Portland. And at the end of the day, police are in control of much of the Proud Boys' power, whether they like it or not: they can be a barrier to the violence, or join in and be a propellent.

—

THE PRESS, IN a perfect vacuum, is supposed to be an unbiased overseer, one who has the ability to extract the truest truth from any story and whose own opinions have zero bearing on the narrative. If only it were that easy.

The press bears similar responsibility when interacting with the Proud Boys and other extremist groups but with different implications. Instead of being the arbiters of physical violence, the media has significant control over their ability to disseminate and sanitize their ideology for the masses and promote themselves. And just like police, members of the media play a variety of important roles in the ongoing survival of the Proud Boys: some cast light on the threat they pose and the damage they cause, some embrace them and promote them as allies, and others become hapless pawns in the gang's promotional efforts, whether due to ignorance or negligence or any number of other factors.

Reporting on modern extremism is a difficult and ever-evolving dance, one that we're still building best practices for. The press' job generally boils down to seeking out and reporting the most fair and accurate depiction of events possible, in service of the public interest. But in extremism land, the route toward that goal isn't always clear. This is a different kind of journalism, in which the subject is actively trying to wrest control of the narrative and distort it for personal gain.

Take the Proud Boys, a violent political street gang that very much does not want to be presented that way to the public. So they make themselves available to the media for interviews, and relentlessly push their own version of the narrative—that they're not a violent gang but a patriotic men's drinking club—with the hope that someone, anyone, will parrot their talking points uncritically. Some outlets see through it and make note of all the violence or recognize that their leader very clearly describes them as a violent gang on his podcast, and refuse to allow the Proud Boys to define themselves. But eventually, the "men's club" half-truth makes it into a news article or TV interview and further assists the Proud Boys in pushing misleading characterization, whether an outlet means to or not (*Forbes*, for example, once described them as "a provocative club for men who love America but hate political correctness while vehemently denying any connection to the alt-right").

Another pitfall of extremism reporting comes with the "both sides" mentality. Traditional journalism asks reporters to keep an unbiased posture, seek out as many perspectives as possible, and give each of them equitable space so that the audience walks away with a deep understanding of the topic. There's merit in using that strategy as a guideline. But when it's employed as an immovable tenet (as it often is in mainstream media), it can impede good journalism, especially when people with harmful and dehumanizing worldviews are involved. Not every issue requires debate, and not all perspectives deserve a platform. There's a big difference between, say, a story that takes a political issue and asks both Democrats and Republicans for their opposing opinions, and a story that gives equal space to the perspective of a person of color and someone who questions that person's humanity. The latter sounds like an easy one to avoid, but you'd be surprised how often iterations of that story come together, even at the hands of well-meaning journalists.

In August 2018, reporters descended on Charlottesville, Virginia, to cover the dark anniversary of Unite the Right and its ripple effects on the local community. I was there interviewing Jalane Schmidt, a Black Lives Matter activist and associate professor of religious studies at the University of Virginia, as she gave a tour of the city and the monuments to slavery and Confederacy that still dot the landscape. As a scholar of Charlottesville's racist history, she's intimately familiar with the role law enforcement and the media play in the propagation of violent extremism and bigotry; as a street-level activist and community organizer, she's witnessed the worst of it from the front lines.

She remembers several hate-fueled rallies that preceded Unite the Right, smaller extremist affairs in the months prior that were all but forgotten once their larger and more deadly successor took the stage. In particular, she's haunted by a rally held there in July of 2017, at which fifty members of the Ku Klux Klan traveled hundreds of miles from North Carolina, ostensibly to protest the impending removal of a Robert E. Lee statue, and wormed their way into a local park, chanting "White power." Schmidt joined a crowd of about a thousand counterprotesters with the aim of making the Klan feel unwelcome in her community, and it worked—their rally lasted only about a half hour. But she was struck by what she saw next: a battalion of armored police escorted the Klansmen back to their cars, their munitions pointed at local protesters. They fired pepper spray and three tear gas canisters into the crowd, arrested some two dozen people, and sent at least three people to the hospital.

"That was a real wake-up call for us, in terms of who the police see as the enemy," Schmidt told me.

Schmidt stood holding a cigarette in the parking lot of First United Methodist Church, which overlooks Market Street Park, where extremist factions of all walks had marched a year before. I happened to be standing next to her when she took a phone call from an Associated Press reporter, who posed an idea for a story: Schmidt, a Black woman, would be interviewed alongside Jason Kessler, the white nationalist organizer of Unite the Right, for some kind of reckoning on the anniversary of the Nazi rally. For Schmidt, the request was a total slap in the face. Why would she want to appear in a story that tries to find middle ground between her and someone whose cadre questions her humanity? She declined the interview, hung up the phone, and rolled her eyes. "Hell no," she said.

That kind of request was—and still is—all too common in Charlottesville, whose activists field a swath of interview requests every time Nazis make the news. It's why the local activist community now takes requests through a group called the Charlottesville Anti-Racist Media Liaisons, who give a green light to interviews under one simple but strict condition:

"No platform for white supremacy," said the group's cofounder, Mimi Arbeit, in 2018. "No platform to spread their violent views and actions."

That rule, for extremism reporters, is generally pretty easy to follow. Most journalists in this space understand the perils of trying to force a "balanced" narrative where no balance exists and work to accurately portray groups and ideologies as they are, not as they claim. (This is why I refer to the Proud Boys as a violent gang in my reporting and throughout this book: those are the words Gavin McInnes uses to describe them internally, for one, but also, that's how they function.) This approach can help reporters avoid being manipulated. But there's no industry standard for ethical extremism reporting, and for that reason, some news reports come out looking more like extremist propaganda.

A ten-minute-long ABC News feature on the Proud Boys, which aired in the aftermath of the Metropolitan Republican Club brawl in Manhattan in 2018, is a shining example of what can go wrong when you hand an extremist leader the microphone. In it, former network correspondent Paula Faris sits across from McInnes in a softly lit studio and lists off quotes and anecdotes for him to deflect. He claims that the Proud Boys aren't racist, misogynist, a hate group, or an extremist group and that any violence they engage in is "justified violence," like "protecting some woman who was getting beaten up."

"So what do you guys do? You just get together and you drink?" Faris asks.

"Ninety-nine percent is meeting at a bar once a month and drinking beer, just like everyone else," McInnes responds.

"What's the other one percent?"

"The other one percent is escorting conservative speakers to and from their cars, or wherever they're going."

The lies and obfuscations continue throughout the segment, as McInnes and a handful of members interviewed by Faris paint a picture of a misunderstood group of drinking buddies—an argument that, again, belies the reason they're on camera in the first place, which is constant and rampant bloodshed across the nation. Faris does ask McInnes about specific acts of violence carried out by his gang and his intolerant pronouncements. But the two key missteps in the segment were allowing him to lie at length in response to those questions and overextending to humanize his dehumanizing behavior. Near the end of the segment, viewers are brought inside the McInnes household for an intimate moment between Gavin and his wife,

Emily, who's given the narrative role of making her husband look like a tolerant family man. Emily is shown packing cookies for a child's lunch and then sits down with Gavin for a heart-warming conversation about the diversity of political views in their household.

"I'm a diehard Democrat," she says to her husband. "So, your politics evolving this way in the last few years has been a challenge, but I respect anyone's right to have their opinion."

Ultimately, the segment handed the gang a gigantic mainstream platform (and a significant amount of time) to push an inauthentic narrative about themselves, one that still reaches the top of some Proud Boys search results online.

Crucially, Faris didn't disclose in the segment her close personal proximity to the McInnes family. She lives in the same ritzy upstate New York neighborhood as McInnes, and their children go to school together, two facts that raise questions about how the segment came together in the first place. In a follow-up interview, Faris told me she disclosed to her bosses at ABC News that she lived near McInnes and that then president of ABC News James Goldston nevertheless wanted her to interview him and cover the Proud Boys, who were in the news.

There's no evidence pointing to foul play in the creation of the segment. But it reveals a universal truth about interviewing far-right gang leaders: *any* reporter trying to maintain a neutral stance in the face of extremist ideology will invariably end up as a megaphone for it.

An oft-cited example of earnest neutrality gone wrong is "A Voice of Hate in America's Heartland," a humanizing two-thousand-word feature in the *New York Times* about the quiet daily life of Tony Hovater, one of the founding members of the neo-Nazi Traditionalist Worker Party, which helped organize

Unite the Right. The reporter's heart was clearly in the right place with the piece: his editor argued at the time that he was just doing what reporters do and tried to help readers understand what kind of person might support such an abhorrent movement. And that's kind of the point: in doing so, he handed his platform to one of the architects of a deadly neo-Nazi rally, who's now described in the paper of record as "the Nazi sympathizer next door" and quoted as saying Hitler was more "chill" than other Nazis and that the Holocaust was "overblown." The backdrop for each story beat is an adorable slice of Hovater's life outside his hate group: he goes shopping, he discusses his thoughts on Nazi Germany at a Panera Bread, and he's described as "polite and low-key" and a fan of *Seinfeld*. The takeaway, regardless of the reporter's intent, is that Hovater and his views may be unsavory, but they're not outside the realm of normalcy. The article was widely criticized for the platform and polish it gave to hateful rhetoric and serves today as a prime example of what *not* to do when covering extremists.

None of this is to say that poorly framed stories and softball interviews with fascists bear sole responsibility for extremist action and hateful rhetoric. It'd be really nice if this entire conversation revolved around ethics and best practices among well-meaning journalists. But they're just one piece of a gigantic puzzle. There exists a tremendous right-wing media apparatus that actively props up extremists, pushes disinformation and hateful rhetoric into the mainstream, and casts the right's political opponents as the true threat.

Now, let's get one thing straight, if you're looking to do real reporting: the data available, published by government agencies, mainstream news outlets, and all sorts of accredited researchers, indicates that right-wing extremists disproportionately commit violent crime as opposed to leftist forces, which Fox News likes to blame for all societal ills. ("January 6 is not the greatest threat to America—it's the Democrat Party," contends Fox News host Mark Levin. The Trump administration said in a Facebook post: "Left-wing violent extremism is a serious threat to American lives and American freedom.") Data on the subject, even that compiled by Trump's own appointees, concludes that far-right violence vastly outweighs that on the left and remains one of our greatest domestic terrorist threats, beyond that posed by international terrorists.

But conservative media don't care for data when they're trying to push the violence needle away from the right and toward the left. Data doesn't support that characterization, so they'll use solitary anecdotes and imagery from isolated incidents as evidence of broader trends. They especially love to drum up fears about BLM and antifa. "Antifa marches through NYC as fears of political violence heighten," reads a Fox News headline, published in January 2021, five days after throngs of Trump supporters led an assault on the Capitol in DC. The story that follows is not an account of political violence, nor is it evidence of "fears" of any kind, but rather a peaceful demonstration at which nothing happened: "'Burn it down,' marchers chanted as they passed a New York police substation in Times Square. There were no reports of violence and no arrests were made."

The story highlights a key tactic utilized by right-wing disinfo peddlers to incite their audiences and ascribe hate and violence to the left, without actually saying anything substantive. They pin all kinds of criminal acts and existential threats to street-level movements like antifa and BLM, which, unlike real people, can't easily sue for defamation or accuse them of lying. In the fantastical universe invented by the likes of Fox News and the Trumpian right, antifa and BLM were directly responsible for: the insurrection at the Capitol, the Proud Boys' attack at the Metropolitan

Republican Club, terrorism, fascism, divisiveness in America, wildfires, kidnappings, Nazis, police killings, plots to overthrow the government, and so on, ad infinitum.

These connections almost never hold up to the slightest bit of scrutiny, in part because the accused parties here aren't usually part of structured groups but decentralized social and political movements. There are many organizations that coalesce under the banners of antifascism and Black Lives Matter, and even local groups bearing those names, but there's no inherent rule set shared by the entirety of the movement, and nobody speaking for all of it. I could assume, for example, that a third degree Proud Boy in Austin has a similar tattoo as a third degree Proud Boy in Seattle, because they both follow the tenets written by their founder, Gavin McInnes, and those upheld by their chapter leaders. But I could not assume that your grandma employs the same street tactics as a BLM rally organizer in Chicago just because she put a Black Lives Matter sign in her window.

The nebulous nature of these movements, however, is what makes them such perfect punching bags for reactionary media. The right has created faceless monsters who are responsible for everything and fundamentally incapable of denying it. The cumulative effect of the constant scapegoating of protest movements is that, now, people really want to kill protesters. A substantial cutout of the Trump-supporting right is absolutely bloodthirsty for anything even remotely resembling "antifa" or "BLM," which generally amounts to any and all people in the street demonstrating against the right or the establishment. Protesters have been shot repeatedly at political events, often by people who weren't even involved in those events. The *Washington Post* tallied nineteen incidents of vehicles plowing into crowds of protesters in just the first four weeks following George Floyd's death. A man named Daniel Peña revved up his chain saw and moved toward a group of antiracist protesters while spewing racist slurs, an act that was caught on video and shared approvingly on Twitter by Mercedes Schlapp, then a senior campaign adviser for Trump. Even Roger Stone seemed to support the practice: in the days leading up to the 2020 election, amid the chaos and tension at nationwide Black Lives Matter rallies, one of Stone's aides put forward the idea of driving trucks into crowds of protesters, and Stone replied, "Once there's no more election, there's no reason why we can't mix it up. These people are going to get what they've been asking for."

Extremists and their allies in the media understand the miasma of rage they've whipped up over protest movements among the Trump-supporting right and that it can be utilized as a weapon. Not only does the right's constant hypothetical droning about big scary leftists invite random acts of extremist violence, but they can peg individuals as sympathetic to antifa or BLM and expect a torrent of harassment, threats, and violence to follow, all with an air of plausible deniability. This tactic is called stochastic terrorism, which Trump deployed regularly by calling for nonspecific aggressive action to be taken against the left and allowing his audience to interpret his words as they may. He so regularly targeted the media—which he referred to as the "enemy of the American people," in league with his ideological opponents—that in August 2018 experts with the United Nations officially condemned his rhetoric, calling on him to "end these attacks." Two months after that press release dropped, pipe bombs started showing up at the addresses of prominent Democrats across the nation and at the offices of CNN, mailed by a fervent Trump supporter who wanted to kill and intimidate the president's enemies.

Among the Proud Boys' allies, nobody has more experience with the tactic of provocation by proxy than Andy Ngo, a far-right internet reactionary who was martyred by conservative media after he was hit with a milkshake, punched, and kicked at a joint Proud Boys and Patriot Prayer rally in 2019. Since then, he has built a lucrative career out of vilifying antifa on Twitter in support of the far right. He spends a considerable amount of his time lodging outrageous claims of leftism against random people and drawing connections between individuals and antifa, resulting in their harassment.

For example, he wrote an op-ed for the *New York Post* that cast doubt on a bunch of gay residents of Portland, Oregon, who said they'd been the victims of hate crimes, often citing his own inability to get a hold of them as evidence that their stories were "suspicious" and that the total picture of gay hate crimes in Portland constituted a "moral panic" and a "hate crime hoax." The piece ran in defense of the Proud Boys, whom he framed as wrongfully accused parties in a series of hate crimes, based apparently on a single Instagram post that accused the gang of "terrorizing the queer/trans community lately." He also quoted several members, including a self-described gay Proud Boy who used Ngo's platform to cast positive light on the gang. "The Proud Boys is the most welcoming organization that I have ever been a part of," he said.

As is often the case with Ngo's reactionary brand of writing, this piece led to threats against the community. When a local chapter of the Council on American-Islamic Relations pushed back against the op-ed, Ngo accused the civil rights organization of "terrorism," leading to dozens of threats sent their way. In another case, a reactionary online magazine called Quillette, where Ngo worked as an editor, published a piece falsely calling fifteen reporters who covered extremism "Antifa journalists." The spurious story, written by a known far-right troll named Eoin Lenihan, resulted in the names of all fifteen journalists (including my colleague Chris Mathias) being included on a neo-Nazi's hit list called "Sunset the Media" and disseminated online. Though the Quillette piece, which threatened journalists' safety, was debunked, Ngo continued to promote it as fact on social media.

The issue with Ngo and his work, beyond the immediate threats, is that he's positioned by the right-wing media (and sometimes even left-leaning outlets) as a mainstream journalist, legitimizing his every deceptive claim. He makes regular appearances on Fox News and across conservative websites, where he is labeled as a journalist and an "expert" on antifa, worthy of audiences' trust despite ongoing breaches of basic journalistic ethics and rampant misleading and inaccurate claims in his writing. He also reportedly maintains questionable relationships with the far-right actors he's defending: video released to the press by activists in Portland appeared to show Ngo standing alongside members of Patriot Prayer as they plotted what would later become a felonious assault on an unsuspecting group of antifascists. He never reported on the Patriot Prayer plot and instead blamed antifa for the violence that day. The source who leaked the video to local media claimed Ngo had an "understanding" with Patriot Prayer, that they'd protect him from antifa in exchange for favorable coverage.

Jacobin magazine in an article ("Portland's Andy Ngo Is the Most Dangerous Grifter in America") identified Ngo as a dangerous provocateur for a reason. Not only is he a vector for far-right extremist rhetoric, but his disinformation blasting on social media about nebulous antifascist threats has been a key galvanizer for the Proud Boys.

"[His antifa narrative] got a lot of media attention and it reinforced something the Proud Boys have pushed for years, which is the real threat is the violent left," said Keegan Hankes, a researcher at Southern Poverty Law Center.

"Most dangerous" or not, Ngo is just one cog in the machine. Mainstreaming a street gang requires work from the entire spectrum of media. The Proud Boys got here with help from Joe Rogan's platform and the millions of viewers who tuned in to McInnes' fourth degree introduction. They were boosted, perhaps inadvertently so, by swaths of hapless news organizations, who handed their mics over to a group of veteran manipulators. And finally, they were gifted far-right reactionaries sitting on the fringes of mainstream journalism like Ngo—and there are many like him—who intentionally deflected for them and offered them up to mainstream conservative media, saying, "These guys aren't so bad." The Proud Boys might not have a direct line to the *New York Post* for their sob stories, but Ngo certainly does, and he's already shown that he can use the tabloid to clean up the Proud Boys' dirty laundry. This is a full support network, through which the Proud Boys have funneled disinformation and PR.

They would be nothing without these kinds of relationships, and they're using them to great effect, for both social credit and monetary profit.

Chapter 8

FUNDING POLITICAL VIOLENCE

In the weeks leading up to the riots at the US Capitol on January 6, 2021, the Proud Boys were on a fundraising blitz. They sent hundreds of members to Washington, DC, as part of a coordinated, monthslong effort with the wider Trump-supporting community to upend their president's failed reelection bid. And that kind of mobilization costs a lot of money.

Running a national crime gang is expensive. These guys have an exorbitant overhead to think about, and their costs can vary wildly depending on what kind of trouble they're in on any given day. At the very least, individuals and their chapters have to raise money for travel expenses and tactical equipment for their events, which happen practically every weekend in some capacity. Then there are court fees, bail funds, damage costs, and medical bills to consider, because Proud Boys rallies often involve blood and crime.

The Proud Boys mobilized large groups to three events in DC between November 2020 and January 2021, where they joined a series of increasingly violent and desperate demonstrations in rejection of the election results. There they packed out area hotels—they preferred the Harrington Hotel, which can cost upward of $150 per room each night—and bought up tactical equipment and supplies for members in what would effectively become a weekslong siege of the city in the run-up to January 6.

Those expenses add up quickly, and they're layered on top of the bills already stacked up from previous rallies—their ongoing criminal cases, for example, soak up a significant amount of cash. On paper, the Proud Boys should have an exceedingly rough time meeting their budget needs. They can't even fundraise on many of the platforms that would give them free access to large audiences. They've earned themselves bans from Facebook, Twitter, and YouTube and a number of payment processors, banking options, and donation sites.

Yet despite themselves, they're able to generate huge sums of money in short order. In desperate times of need—prior to a big event or when they need to post a member's bail, for instance— they've managed to pull together hundreds of thousands of dollars in short order.

Those efforts were kept in relative secrecy for years. Questions remain about how the Proud Boys have been able to fund their weekly ritual of sending their goons from state to state, cramping area hotels and partying, and then brawling their way into jail, only to do it all again the next weekend. And unfortunately, they haven't been gracious enough to open their books voluntarily. But after some hard work by data researchers, journalists, and activists and a series of screwups by the Proud Boys themselves, their once-private business practices are becoming more transparent every day. We now have a deeper understanding of where all the money's coming from and a clearer view of the people and enterprises funding and supporting domestic extremism.

The Proud Boys are not particularly prolific in any one money-making venture, but they make up for it by casting a wide net in terms of funding streams. They've got a network of LLCs and side hustles going, they collect dues from and sell merch to other members, and they are constantly tapping the MAGA contingent for donations via online fundraisers. When they need a big infusion, say for a costly court battle or an insurrection at the Capitol, they tap all those resources at once. And like a bunch of teenagers pooling all the quarters they found in their parents' couches, eventually they can afford that pack of smokes.

Some Proud Boys have tried opening small businesses, though few appear to have had much success. Ethan Nordean's supplements brand, Bangarang Elite Supplements LLC, was a short-lived affair that mostly served to put his police officer business partner in hot water. Robert Piccirillo (known to the Proud Boys as Bobby Pickles) runs a merch company called Fat Enzo, Inc., dedicated mostly to T-shirts featuring stylized portraits of serial killers and right-wing memes, and separately hosts a Proud Boys–centric podcast. There's even a company in Hawaii called Daiquiri Brothers LLC tied to the gang, but because it remains private, we may never know if they followed the easy and obvious path to profitability with that one.

They have Enrique Tarrio to thank for the business success they do have. He remains their top grifter, the kind of guy who doesn't care what he's selling or whom he's selling it to—whether the sucker on the other end of the transaction is one of his own members or one of his sworn enemies.

He owns and operates 1776.shop, a MAGA-inspired merch site that caters to the type of red-faced conservative who believes he has a patriotic duty to practice his Second Amendment rights at a school board meeting. You can find all kinds of Proud Boys merch on the site, from patches and pins to stickers, which members buy from Tarrio. It's unclear whether anyone outside the organization is buying gang merch, but there's much more to 1776.shop beyond the Proud Boys brand—you can find far-right memes from every corner of the internet here, sure to prove to everyone at the grocery store that you're an unhinged fascist.

There are shirts like the one Tarrio wore on TV at a Trump rally, declaring "Roger Stone Did Nothing Wrong," iterations of the "Pinochet Did Nothing Wrong" shirts seen at Proud Boys rallies, and threads that reveal you as an "American Supremacist" for as little as $28. You can buy a RWDS patch, short for Right Wing Death Squad, and put your authoritarian bloodlust on full display. You can sport a "Kill Your Local Pedophile" shirt, and tip your hat to QAnon, the collective of conspiracy theorists who believe that JFK Jr. is still alive and is working with Trump to bring down a pedophilic cabal of Democrats. You could opt for a Proud Boys third degree coin (though this seems redundant, given that the third degree requires a tattoo), or a $200 megaphone called the InfoWars Battlehorn that comes adorned with conspiracy theory stickers. At one point, the site peddled a T-shirt depicting an abusive meme targeting a gay journalist, which made the rounds on far-right talk shows as something to laugh at: it featured the journalist's name and face, photoshopped onto the body of Marxist revolutionary Che Guevara, displayed over the words "IS A F*G."

The site also features "charity bracelets" ranging from $25 to $5,000, which go to support the gang's cause du jour—at one point the site claimed any donations would "directly fund the NYC 9," the defendants in the GOP club attack in New York City in 2018. It's not entirely clear how much profit the Proud Boys see from the site alone, but extremism experts believe it's one of their primary sources of income. Tarrio has claimed that the site nets the gang tens of thousands each year, but that's difficult to verify.

The members put a lot back into their own economy, too. Tarrio says chapter leaders aren't required to collect dues (and previously maintained that the Proud Boys didn't collect dues at all, until their payments were revealed by data researchers), but many leaders expect them to, and evidence available suggests that most monthly dues hover around twenty dollars. Members also pool their own money for extracurriculars, such as transportation to events, room and board, and, of course, booze and cocaine. We know this because the Proud Boys are generally pretty terrible with their info security, so a lot of this information has been easily and publicly accessible online. Dozens of Proud Boys were making public Venmo payments to one another for years, and all that data was scraped up by Megan Squire, a professor of computer science at Elon University and researcher of extremist networks. She published a paper on the Proud Boys' organizational structure via data collected from Facebook and Venmo and revealed, among other things, the dues payments and a small economy shared by hundreds of extremists.

But when you look at their Venmo activity, you also get a sense of how much these guys are willing to pay out of their own pocket just for access to a like-minded friend group of men who like to fight and get loaded together. So many of the transactions mentioned booze and cocaine ("A little nose candy," one transaction receipt reads; "Doses and mimosas," reads another), while dozens upon dozens of transactions showed payments going to leaders like Ethan Nordean and Patrick William Roberts, for dues, gas, or bus rides to rallies. Ten payments went to Luke Rohlfing, a Proud Boys elder, for charges related to dinner and booze at WestFest, a national summit organized by the Proud Boys' Vegas chapter back in 2018.

Some of their revenue has come from podcasts and livestreams, which has become an extremely lucrative sector for individuals on the radical and reactionary right. It's the place where Gavin McInnes created the Proud Boys and sold them to mainstream conservatives, and it's where any extremist without the comfort of a network like Fox News can build an audience and a salary. Various Proud Boys have hosted podcasts and livestreams, but none of them have risen anywhere near the monetary success that McInnes enjoyed, in part because they were kicked off most major platforms right around the time McInnes stepped down and took his miniature media empire with him. They've since had to settle for livestreaming sites with lax content moderation like DLive, originally a Twitch-like platform for gamers that has since transformed into a bastion for racist reactionary podcasters.

But even without the audiences of YouTube or Twitch, there's still plenty of money moving around in that space, according to another study conducted by Squire into the far right's video streaming habits. White nationalist podcaster Nick Fuentes, for example, makes hundreds of dollars a day in donations on DLive and pulled in a whopping $43,822 in the last two months of 2020 alone. Her research also found that a Proud Boys–affiliated podcast called *Murder the Media*—a name that became infamous when it was scrawled across a door at the Capitol during the January 6 siege—over time cashed out more than $10,300 in total from donations to its DLive page.

Squire's research demonstrates that the Proud Boys aren't as skilled with multimedia as their bigoted peers. They're making a fraction of what other extremists are making in livestream donations and subscription numbers, suggesting that they generally aren't as savvy with new racist audiences the way white supremacists like Fuentes are. The Proud Boys are older, they don't really understand how reactionary video content works, and their politics are all over the place, Squire said, and beyond McInnes, no Proud Boy has separated himself from the lower tiers of the streaming space.

"I call it monetized propaganda, and the Proud Boys have never been very good at it," she said. "[Extremist audiences] want to hear a critique of news and a path forward as far as what to do next. There's really not a whole lot there with the Proud Boys except banter between men. Who's gonna pay for that?"

At the same time, the Proud Boys don't really need the support of the adolescent Adolf demographic. They already have mainstream appeal, afforded by McInnes' media success and their public-facing relationship to the GOP. And they know that relationship comes with a bottomless well of funding from the MAGA sector, which has demonstrated repeatedly that it will throw money at any cause anointed by Trump or his allies.

This is where they make the big bucks. They have fundraisers going at all times on crowdfunding sites like GiveSendGo, which is basically a right-wing "Christian" knockoff of GoFundMe that doesn't take a hard stance against extremist causes, so long as the cause comes with an all-American sob story.

Case in point: in the aftermath of the Proud Boys' coordinated assault outside the Metropolitan Republican Club in New York City in 2018, the gang launched a GiveSendGo campaign for John Kinsman, described by prosecutors as the "single most vicious" of the attackers that night. The campaign, titled "Christmas For Liberty," featured a photo of Kinsman with his multiracial family alongside a gushing character witness statement, apparently written by McInnes himself. McInnes wanted potential donors to know up front that Kinsman was their defender against antifa and that he had people of color in his family. A family man and a conservative, definitely not violent, definitely not racist.

"Liberty Kinsman's father is serving four years for fighting antifa," McInnes wrote. "Left wing authoritarianism has left three black kids fatherless for at least three Christmases. . . . Please help make this Christmas one to remember by donating money we can use to buy them toys and ensure John's wife doesn't have to worry about anything but loving her beautiful children."

McInnes almost always points out the Black members of Kinsman's family when garnering sympathy for the Proud Boys, even when Kinsman isn't the topic of conversation. He mentioned Kinsman's "three black children" in two separate emails to me, once after I asked him about the violence component of the fourth degree: "John, a father of three black children, separated from his family because of the propaganda people like you spread," he said, mirroring the language of the GiveSendGo campaign.

Of course, there was no mention on the campaign site that Kinsman was missing Christmas for leading a gang assault against protesters in the street. The GiveSendGo campaign had raised more than $14,000, four grand over the goal.

And that was just one fundraiser. The Proud Boys have raised hundreds of thousands of dollars from GiveSendGo campaigns alone, and plenty more when you count other crowdfunding sites. Some are smaller in scope—a "Safety and Medical Equipment" fundraiser for the Central Washington Proud Boys, for example, raised only $1,090. But the big fundraisers, which invariably come on the heels of bigger and bloodier events, pull in much, much more.

In December 2020, the Proud Boys swarmed Washington, DC, by the hundreds, ramping up demonstrations meant to raise the national temperature after the election. The Stop the Steal and Million MAGA March rallies that month were some of the most violent clashes the Proud Boys had been involved in to date.

And the fundraisers surrounding those events made them hundreds of thousands of dollars.

By the end of the worst of those rallies, the Million MAGA March on December 12, more than twenty-five people had been arrested and four people had been stabbed, a number of them Proud Boys members. If you heard the story of December 12 from the Proud Boys themselves, you might think a group of doll-faced choirboys were ambushed by antifa. Police reports, news accounts, and video evidence paint a different picture: after a long day of clashes throughout downtown DC, a video surfaced showing a lone man in a balaclava, later identified as twenty-nine-year-old Phillip Johnson, retreating from a throng of Proud Boys outside Harry's Bar, one of the gang's known hangouts. The surrounding Proud Boys shout "Fuck antifa" as they push him along. Johnson gets some separation and pulls a knife, looking back at the crowd as he continues to walk away. Someone marching with the Proud Boys grabs his hood and pulls his body back into the crowd, and the punches and kicks begin to fly. During the fracas, several people were stabbed, and Johnson was later arrested on charges of assault with a dangerous weapon. There wasn't enough evidence in the video to easily determine who instigated the melee.

But that day in DC was full of intense and aggressive mob violence exacted on the city and its residents, almost exclusively by the Proud Boys. The stabbings may have provided the gang a self-victimization narrative for the event, but no documentation of the day outside their version is friendly to the Proud Boys. Even the Rupert Murdoch–owned *New York Post*—historically forgiving to right-wing factions at Trump events—had to admit in its headline, "Proud Boys Surround Man with Knife at Violent DC Trump Rally."

The Proud Boys set up a GiveSendGo campaign after the event, titled "Medical Assistance for DC Proud Boy Victims," and raised $106,107 within days, based on this laughable tall tale about antifa plotting to attack grandmas:

> On December 12th, 2020, millions of patriots gathered in Washington DC to support President Donald J Trump. During this gathering the vile left-wing terrorists Antifa sought to attack women, children and elderly people a like [*sic*]. Patriots from all of the country came to their aid, with the Proud Boys leading the way. . . .
>
> If you are reading this and are on the fence about a donation remember the only reason these people aren't attacking you and your family is because we are standing in their way!

It's jarring enough that they were able to raise that much money off a demonstrably false narrative. But things get a whole lot more bizarre when you look at who is donating and why.

Money poured into extremist groups' wallets via GiveSendGo following the Capitol attacks, and during that same time, a colossal amount of GiveSendGo's back-end data was hacked and then released to the public by a whistleblower collective of data researchers and activists called Distributed Denial of Secrets. The leak revealed identifying information of the donors to hundreds of GiveSendGo campaigns, including those belonging to the Proud Boys and their extremist allies, the Oath Keepers. For journalists and researchers, this was an unprecedented look behind the extremist fundraising curtain. Suddenly, everyone had access to the names and email addresses of people funding far-right causes, neatly packaged in searchable spreadsheets.

And the data led to some surprising revelations. A *USA Today* investigation into the Proud Boys' GiveSendGo campaign, for example, revealed that 80 percent of the six-figure fund came from Chinese American donors. These emigrants, who had escaped communist China, supported the Proud Boys under the misguided belief that they were America's benevolent defenders against communist armies controlled by antifa and BLM—debunked conservative conspiracy theories but powerful messages nonetheless to certain sections of the Chinese diaspora.

But perhaps the biggest surprise in the Proud Boys data was just how normal everything looked on most of the donor lists. These weren't shadowy conservative megadonors, or extremist collectives supporting a like-minded cause, or bots inflating the numbers, though it's entirely possible that all of those elements have supported the Proud Boys in some way over the years. Many of these donors appeared to be everyday conservatives giving whatever spare cash they could to support a roving band of bigots who'd just made the news by storming the Capitol.

Take, for example, a $20,000 legal defense fund set up for Nick Ochs, a livestreamer for the Proud Boys who was charged with criminal conspiracy for his role in the January 6 riots. Plenty of donors clearly tied to the Proud Boys threw a few bucks toward Ochs' campaign, like Walter, who dropped $20 alongside a comment that said "Uhuru brother! Keeping fighting the good fight!"

But only a fraction of the campaign's 526 donors made reference to their membership or any connection to the crew. Anonymous tips of $20, $50, and $100 poured in alongside heartfelt messages of patriotism and prayer. Cheryl donated $20 and said, "Wish I could afford to give more. Will keep you in my prayers." Jaime gave $10 and thanked Ochs "for standing for truth. God bless your family as well." Todd left $50 and said, "Stay strong. We're with you."

There were dozens of other campaigns in the leak that were tied to the gang. Some of them were set up for members who'd been injured or jailed or to fund their events. Campaigns were also set up as defense funds for celebrity Proud Boys and elders who stormed the Capitol, including Joe Biggs, Ethan Nordean, and Ochs, and each raised upward of $10,000 or more.

These fundraisers demonstrate something crucial about the Proud Boys' rise: their monetary success—and really, much of their power—seems to rely heavily on how everyday Republicans *feel* about them, rather than their ability to do anything useful. Based on the donation messages, there's a section of the public that appears to believe the Proud Boys are fighting a war for them. For example, here are just a few of the messages left for the gang on a GiveSendGo fundraiser set up for their "travel expenses" to DC on January 6, 2021, which raised more than $5,500:

- "Thank you Patriots! Fight for our President please."
- "Love & respect. Thank you for standing up for the average American."
- "Defend the Republic. Fight for Trump!"
- "Stay safe, F antifa and blm, they don't deserve capital letters!!"
- "We need to show up in Great numbers on January 6th. Godspeed."
- "May Our Lord and Savior Jesus Christ bless you and strengthen you in this Crusade against satan followers of The Swamp."
- "Thanks for being crushers and defending the innocent! MAGA."

What's so illuminating about this particular fundraiser is that there's no plan detailing where the money might actually go, and nobody's asking for one. These donors are just supporting the *idea* that the Proud Boys are out there fighting for right-wing values. Nobody's demanding proof that their $50 went toward a plane ticket or a tank of gas. And that's a testament to how deeply this group has embedded itself into the political mainstream: there's an element of blind faith that these guys are out there doing good for people.

But none of this is to say that the total operation is a well-oiled machine. Watching them organize an event, from fundraiser to fight night, makes you wonder how they're able to zip up their pants without an egregious miscalculation. The process is a haphazard array of shakedowns, crimes, grifting, and panhandling.

A great snapshot of their operating procedure came courtesy of court documents and lawsuits stemming from all the Proud Boys' January 6 cases. There are now hundreds of pages of photos, text messages, incriminating statements, and other communications that detail the fundraising and preparedness efforts of dozens of Proud Boys and their chapters in the lead-up to the riots. They paint a picture of a group that was preparing for the big one. They called in all their favors and went through significant resources in the months leading up to January 6, the day Biden's win would be solidified by Congress and their final stand in support of Trump.

In late December, Nordean posted a link to a GiveSendGo fundraiser on his Parler account, pleading for cash to buy armor and comms equipment for the coming battle. There were several big events being planned in DC that day by other far-right figureheads, and the Proud Boys wanted to play a big role, so they planned to put as many of their guys on the ground as possible. But it wouldn't be cheap.

"Anyone looking to help us with safety/protective gear, or communications equipment, it would be much appreciated,"

Nordean wrote above a link to the fundraiser, titled "Protective Gear and Communications by Rufio Panman." "Things have gotten more dangerous for us this past year, anything helps."

The GiveSendGo leaks reveal that his campaign made $18,951 across 276 donations. In the comments, donors wished the Proud Boys "good luck" on January 6. Wrote one of them who donated $150, "Thanks for fighting the good fight! God bless you! We will be in Washington DC January 6th to fight for freedom for all."

On January 4, two days before the big day, Nordean posted again to his Parler page, this time with a video featuring him and a number of other Proud Boys covered in tactical gear, clearly enjoying their success with the fundraiser. Nordean said they were ready to go toe-to-toe with whomever crossed their path, be it antifa or police officers. He issued a warning of what was to come.

"Let them remember the day they decided to make war with us," he wrote.

———

NO PROUD BOY has better mastered their fundraising tactics than Enrique Tarrio, who on that same day was driving into DC to embark on a different kind of money-making venture. Inside his vehicle was a backpack, stuffed with two high-capacity magazines that were compatible with an AR-15 and capable of carrying thirty rounds each. They were black and customized with yellow Proud Boys logos—one with the Fred Perry laurels surrounding the letters *PB* and the other with their logo depicting a chicken weather vane pointing west, atop the Proud Boys name. Being high-capacity magazines, they were also illegal to possess within DC limits. Tarrio was planning to hand over the magazines to a paying customer who'd had some trouble receiving them in the mail.

The mission was doomed from the start. As he drove into the city, Tarrio took a call from a *USA Today* reporter named Will Carless for an interview about the Proud Boys' plans for the upcoming events on January 6. As they spoke, Carless said he heard sirens begin to wail on Tarrio's end of the call.

"They're for me," Tarrio said. "Here's something to write about," he barked before the line went dead.

The coincidence was bizarre enough that Carless wondered whether Tarrio was pulling his leg: Had he really been on the phone the moment the leader of the Proud Boys was pulled over by police? Yes, as it turned out. The sirens were real, and Tarrio's road trip ended in the custody of DC's Metropolitan Police, well before he met his buyer.

In hindsight, Tarrio later admitted in court, carrying a bag full of illegal murder merch decorated in his gang's logo was a stupid move. Making matters more idiotic, he had a warrant out for his arrest, stemming from the December 12 rally that the Proud Boys used to raise a six-figure sum. The crimes he committed at that rally, along with his arrest on the eve of January 6, would have a cascading series of effects on the Proud Boys' bottom line and implications for Tarrio's position at the helm.

On December 12, hundreds of Proud Boys and other MAGA types swarmed DC in a seething denial of the presidential election results. It was one of the biggest Proud Boys rallies yet. DC police estimated that as many as seven hundred members and supporters from across the country had been mobilized, and as usual, they were looking to fight from the start. Police were able to keep that crowd apart from counterprotesters throughout much of the day, but as night fell, the inevitable clashes began, as did assaults, arrests, and stabbings. The bars closed early as the temperature of the rally quickly rose, and Proud Boys and their supporters flooded the streets. Tarrio gathered the lot of them together and led them on a riotous march through town.

At one point, the mob stopped and took interest in Asbury United Methodist Church, a historic congregation known for its role in American civil rights: the church was once a bastion for escaped slaves on their way into free states and Canada through the Underground Railroad, and many of its congregants today are their direct descendants.

But it was the Black Lives Matter banner waving outside that caught the Proud Boys' attention. They ripped it down and paraded it through the street triumphantly, posing with it for a few pictures before throwing it to the ground. They doused it in lighter fluid, and Tarrio lit it ablaze, as the others chanted "Fuck antifa" and "USA! USA!" They marched on and pulled a similar stunt at another Black church, a group of them ripping a BLM banner in half in the doorway of Metropolitan African Methodist Episcopal Church. Four churches in total reported their property destroyed as the Proud Boys rioted.

Tarrio was arrested when DC police pulled him over a few weeks later and pleaded guilty on two misdemeanor charges, one related to the high-capacity magazines and the other over the flag burning. He later claimed at his sentencing hearing that he didn't consider the cultural implications of leading a white mob to a historic Black church and lighting things on fire out front. But church leadership, who got a chance to testify at his hearing, spelled it out for him:

"Asbury displays a Black Lives Matter banner to make a statement regarding the value of Black people: that Black lives are valued by God, and us," said Rev. Dr. Ianther M. Mills. "We display a Black Lives Matter banner to make a statement as Christians. We are not Marxist. We're not socialists. We are Christians and Methodists."

She went on: "Imagine then, if you would, a marauding band of seemingly angry white men moving about the city, apparently looking for trouble. That group happens upon Asbury, a Black church, then proceeds to rip down the church's Black Lives Matter banner, parade it down the street, and then burn it in the street while jeering and cursing. . . . In our opinion, this was an act of intimidation, and racism."

It wasn't a great look for Tarrio, the public face of the Proud Boys, whose Cuban American heritage is invoked constantly as evidence that the gang isn't racist. Tarrio was sentenced to five months in prison and later subpoenaed by Congress as he sat behind bars to answer for all of the Proud Boys' efforts during the insurrection (which he narrowly avoided, after a judge ordered him to stay outside of DC as part of his bond conditions). Meanwhile, a lawsuit filed by Metropolitan AME Church on behalf of all the targeted churches was threatening to get the Proud Boys slapped with substantial damages.

It was bad for Tarrio's bottom line, and it was looking worse for his seat at the top. Internally, his case raised suspicion among some of the rank and file about their leader. In a private Telegram chatroom among New York State Proud Boys, members wondered who in the hell would be stupid enough to cross into DC with a warrant under his belt and a pair of illegal munitions in his pack.

"Says he had high capacity magazines on him at the time of his arrest. . . . ummmm," wrote one member.

"Not sure why he would bring any kind of mag to DC," wrote another. "Dumbass confessed to bringing them into the district for a sale. Their law doesn't give a shit why you brought them."

Their suspicions were quickly drowned out by the events of January 6. That is, until weeks later, when Reuters published a destabilizing report that Tarrio had served as a key FBI informant following his arrest in 2012 over a fraud case related to the sale of stolen diabetes test kits. Feds said Tarrio's info led to thirteen high-profile prosecutions in cases involving drugs, gambling, and human smuggling. Tarrio was a "prolific" informant who, "at his own risk, in an undercover role met and negotiated to pay $11,000 to members of that ring to bring in fictitious family members of his from another country," Tarrio's lawyer argued at a hearing during his fraud case.

The Proud Boys did not like hearing this. Even McInnes, who'd purportedly been uninvolved for several years, was pissed. "He should have told me he had worked with the FBI," McInnes told me. He added that it "was stupid" of Tarrio to bring the magazines into DC.

For the other members, theories began to fly. Maybe Tarrio got arrested on purpose to avoid having a role in January 6. Maybe he's been an informant this whole time! A coalition of chapters that included Oklahoma, Alabama, and Indiana posted to Telegram that they were splintering out from under Tarrio's leadership in light of the news. They wrote: "We do not recognize the assumed authority of any national Proud Boy leadership including the Chairman, the Elders, or any subsequent governing body that is formed to replace them until such a time we may choose to consent to join those bodies of government."

He didn't have many friends in that moment. And outside the gang, there's an entire network of people working against him, dedicated to making it as difficult as possible for him and the other members to conduct their business. A loose coalition of antifascists, researchers, and other activists spend ample time online thwarting extremist groups, simply by way of surfacing the awful things they do and showing it to the companies who host them online.

They've repeatedly turned their sights on Tarrio's 1776.shop, under the impression that some portion of its profits were going toward extremist activity in their communities. It's certainly not illegal to sell racist garbage, like the "Chicago Lives Splatter" T-shirt covered in bullet holes once featured in Tarrio's store. But it's also completely within bounds to ask the companies that keep the shop running—the payment processors, the domains, the servers and security services—whether they're comfortable with supporting such a product. And that's often all it takes for activists to upend an extremist group's operations online.

"[1776.shop is] raising money for an appeal for Max Hare and John Kinsman, members of a hate group recently sentenced to four years each for assaulting protesters," tweeted Christian Exoo, an antifascist researcher who tweets under his longtime alias, Antifash Gordon. In 2019 he surfaced the shop's content directly to Square, which for a time was 1776.shop's payment processor. "This is a clear violation of @Square's Terms of Service, which prohibits anything 'threatening, harassing, hateful, abusive, or inflammatory' or that 'encourages conduct that would be considered a criminal offense or gives rise to civil liability.'"

Dozens of other researchers and antifascist accounts and onlookers boosted Exoo's and others' tweets, directed at the companies that served as the digital backbone of Tarrio's shop. And many of those companies were paying attention: over the course of about a week, Square, JPMorgan Chase, and PayPal had pulled their services from 1776.shop. Activists targeted the Proud Boys' monetary efforts online repeatedly over the years, including a sweeping campaign after the gang stormed the Capitol. Within weeks of January 6, activists had secured Proud Boys bans from a dozen or more services that supported their online deadlines, including DLive, their podcasting platform. Tarrio's bank, he said, cut off his business account. Reports indicate that he made tens of thousands less in revenue from the merch store in 2021 than in 2020, thanks largely to the deplatforming efforts of researchers and activists after January 6.

Never one to be deterred by his own failure, Tarrio told the *Wall Street Journal* that he began secretly selling leftist merchandise to pad his wallet, including T-shirts that say "Black Lives Matter" and "Impeach 45." It's not clear how much money he made off the two-timing merch scheme, but it highlighted another ace the Proud Boys seem to have up their sleeve at their worst moments: turning consequences into profit. His greatest windfall came after his arrest before January 6. The inevitable GiveSendGo campaign, launched almost immediately by the Proud Boys as he sat in jail, reached $104,000 in less than twenty-four hours.

Stories like these can make it seem like the Proud Boys are nigh invincible. Even after they're arrested, slapped with fines, and deplatformed out of their moneymaking ventures, many of them—especially leaders—still come out on top, their dignity and wallets apparently intact, despite the harm they wreak on their communities. But every now and then, the people in their personal lives decide to start fighting back, and sometimes, the scales of justice begin to tip out of their favor.

Chapter 9

FUCKING AROUND AND
FINDING OUT

In addition to being expensive, street-level extremism is a risky business. You might get arrested or doxed, or worse, punched in the face! It's much easier to do harm from the comfort and anonymity of your own home. And that's why some of the most powerful and privileged Proud Boys are keyboard warriors.

While the grunts and meatheads do the majority of the work you see in the street—the marching, the punching, the prison sentences—some of the eldest Boys get to call the shots from behind computer screens and podcast mics.

Sure, Gavin McInnes might rear his head every now and then to get a fresh taste of pepper spray at a college Republicans event. But this commander leads a battalion of jackbooted hooligans largely from a desk. He's not getting his hands dirty. He doesn't have the time—he's busy telling war stories from the old days on his podcast, while directing throngs of violent men to bring those sadistic fantasies back to life. There's often a comfortable buffer between extremist leaders and the violence they incite.

But sometimes, that barrier begins to break down, and the guys who spend most of their time issuing threats on the computer get a taste of their own product in real life. Every so often, the war gets close to home for Proud Boys leadership, when the people they terrorize decide to return the favor.

The Proud Boys like to tell you that if you fuck around, you'll find out. But sometimes it's the Proud Boys at the top who do their own fucking around and finding out.

Jason Lee Van Dyke Finds Out

Jason Lee Van Dyke, the Proud Boys' former attorney, is the human manifestation of a live hand grenade.

The cranky Texas lawyer runs hot at all times. He issues threats so regularly during casual conversation that it's difficult to tell whether he wants to sue you, kill you, or just say hello. He's so prone to exploding that even his fellow Proud Boys keep him at arm's length, for fear of getting caught in his blast radius. He even kind of looks like a grenade, ready to burst in the name of freedom: he rocks a tight Fred Perry polo stretched over a wide frame and an impressive gut, which he pairs with a bucket-sized cowboy hat, sunglasses, and skinny blue jeans.

But as it goes with any grenade, there's an extraordinary amount of power inherent in this rotund, pissed-off package.

In late 2018, around the same time as his disastrous two-day stint at the helm of the Proud Boys, Van Dyke was at the height of his power within the organization, serving as both their hyperlitigious legal counsel and the founder of Proud Boys International LLC, once their primary business connected to at least a portion of their assets. For a while, he effectively sat atop the whole operation: he had his hands on their trademark and their money, he influenced their bylaws, and he signed off on structural changes. Plus, he was an affordable and effective weapon in court, especially when it came to legal threats, which made him useful.

He absolutely loved to threaten whomever he saw as a threat to the Proud Boys. He'd send out court documents and emails full of legalese, or post to Facebook and Twitter declaring his intention to sue anyone who might disparage or criticize him or the group. His targets were all over the place and included reporters, bloggers, antifascists, random folks on social media, celebrities, or anyone else who drew his ire on a given day. The Proud Boys claim he did this hundreds of times, at no cost.

Many of the legal threats were laughably weak and fizzled out long before they made it to court, but he didn't have to win to harm his opponents. It didn't cost him or the Proud Boys much more than a bit of paperwork to harass and intimidate people with legal threats, so he deployed the strategy ad nauseam. If he could get a news org to retract some of their work, or perhaps scare someone into deleting some tweets, or even just waste a defendant's time and money, it was all gravy. And if they called his bluff or they could afford the representation to fight back, he could simply drop everything and move on to his next target. It's an intimidation tactic with its own name: a Strategic Lawsuit Against Public Participation, or SLAPP, functions to silence critics by forcing them into costly court battles and bleeding their wallets dry. Big companies like to use it against small individuals. But for someone like Van Dyke, it's a cheap, relatively low-risk, and occasionally effective weapon, especially against people who can't afford counsel. Some states—including Texas where he got his license—have anti-SLAPP statutes meant to penalize those who file them, but those didn't seem to deter the Proud Boys' lawyer at the time.

And being a member of the Proud Boys himself meant that Van Dyke conducted himself professionally the same way a Proud

Boy carries himself in the street: violence and cruelty were part of the job. Van Dyke wore them on his sleeve at all times, even before he joined the gang.

"Look good and hard at this picture you fucking n—er," Van Dyke tweeted at a Black man in 2014, alongside a picture of a noose. "It's where I am going to put your neck."

These are the words of a veteran attorney, who earned his Texas law license in 2007. And yet he was constantly threatening to murder people.

"Your kiddies are quite a nuisance," he wrote in another tweet. "My advice: run and hide. If I find you, I WILL kill both you and your family."

Those two posts were resurfaced by a defense attorney in 2017, amid a lawsuit Van Dyke himself filed against an antifascist blogger who characterized the Proud Boys as Nazis. Van Dyke argued that calling them Nazis amounted to defamation, though his case wasn't helped by his own social media posts, nor the fact that members of the Ohio chapter in question had reportedly left a bunch of swastika-laden recruitment fliers across the Ohio State University campus.

Not only did the suit fail in the end, but Van Dyke's attempts to clear the Proud Boys' name only turned more heads in his direction. Suddenly, everyone was interested in the Proud Boys' thuggish bigot of a lawyer. The Texas State Bar even took the rare step of publicly condemning one of its attorneys.

"The statements attributed to this individual are reprehensible and contrary to the values we hold as Texas lawyers," state bar president Tom Vick said. "I condemn them in the strongest terms."

Van Dyke was not humbled by the experience and didn't change a thing. He reacted the only way he knew how, by threatening everyone involved. First, he threatened a sweeping lawsuit against a bunch of people who criticized him online, including a First Amendment lawyer, a random guy on Twitter, iconic Brooklyn rapper Talib Kweli, and me, after I published a story for HuffPost about his menacing tweets. Eventually, he threatened to go postal on everyone, including the Texas State Bar for slapping him on the wrist.

"No longer welcome where I've trained for years," he wrote on Twitter at the time. "This is the final straw. Langton, White, Kweli, HuffPo—they are all getting sued first thing Monday morning. This ends now. They can disbar me if they want, I don't give a damn. If they sanction me, my property is defended with a 50 BMG [.50-caliber Browning machine gun]."

Van Dyke never did file any substantive paperwork over that legal threat, but his behavior got progressively more belligerent. His public threats were so frequent and so colorfully detailed that his social media pages verged on parody, as if he was pretending to be a grimy, over-the-top mob lawyer.

He once tweeted that a person he planned to sue "needs to lose some teeth" and then reached out to threaten the guy directly:

"This stops now—from both of us—or make your dental appointment," he wrote. "Take my offer and we walk away, or leave it and face consequences. You have 24 hours to choose starting now."

His Facebook page featured a disturbing photo in which he was standing in the woods at night with a mean mug, covered head to toe in camouflage and holding a silenced rifle. The caption read, "If you mess with my career (the one that requires me to wear a suit), I might be dressed like this the next time you see me!"

His threats tended to get a whole lot worse when he issued them in a setting he presumed to be private. He penned a scarily elaborate threat of "retribution" against Ken White, a First Amendment attorney who'd written a blog describing Van Dyke as a "dangerously unbalanced and violence-threatening" lawyer. White posted Van Dyke's email on Twitter, which read in part:

> I am going to make you a one-time offer and you get to choose.
>
> 1. I am willing to walk away. Right here. Right now. You remove the libelous blog posts about me and make whatever excuse you want. . . . You will never see or hear from me again. We both go about our lives.
>
> 2. Simply add this email to your blog post. If you do that, I want to make it very clear what is going to happen. I have a picture of you. I am going to put it on my mirror at home, near my desk, and in my truck. . . . I will make you so miserable and treat you with such extreme and completely unprecedented cruelty that you'll either kill yourself or move yourself and your family to the most remote part of the world you can. . . . There will be retribution. It may take me a year. It may take me 20 years. I may get you on my first try. But I will never stop. . . .
>
> Sooner or later, I will come for you.
>
> JASON L. VAN DYKE
ATTORNEY & COUNSELOR AT LAW

By the time Van Dyke took over as chair of the Proud Boys in 2018, he'd gone completely berserk. Other Proud Boys describe him today as if he was a liability, though they clearly liked something about him at the time because they voted him in after McInnes stepped back from the helm.

"We picked [Van Dyke] and I thought that was a horrible, horrible idea," Tarrio told me in an interview. "He didn't have the chill. The chairman position was pitched as more of a PR person, and I just felt he was too emotional."

Days later, after Van Dyke mistakenly doxed all the elders, the gang disavowed him publicly and named Tarrio as his replacement. It's unclear to this day what their disavowals actually mean in practice; several members have faced them and still continued on with the crew in some capacity, including Van Dyke. He maintained a hold on their trademark for years and had members who were loyal to him as a leader.

His removal appeared to be ceremonial, giving the Proud Boys some plausible distance from their walking hand grenade. But it also seemed to give Van Dyke a sense of freedom. He was unburdened by the responsibility and professionalism he'd clearly had to maintain as their lawyer, and now he was free to say how he really felt. He sent me this email on the day of his ouster to mark the occasion:

Subject: You

Now that I am no longer part of the Proud Boys and no longer representing them, I want to let you know that you are a despicable and evil human being. It is my hope that your duties as a HuffPo reporter bring you to the metroplex this holiday season so that I can give you the gift of a left hook.

Kiss my ass, faggot.

MR. JASON L. VAN DYKE
THE VAN DYKE LAW FIRM P.L.L.C.

This is where Van Dyke's story takes a series of dark and even more bizarre turns. He appeared to be totally overwhelmed by his anger at this point, a dangerous combo of seething rage, ego, and apathy ("not in the best state of mind," he admitted to me in a follow-up interview). And worse, he was starting to fixate on one person in particular, who would become the sole target of his vengeance. If the first half of his story was a crime drama, the second half was a homicidal fever dream.

It began with his arrest in September 2018, after he called police and claimed that a bunch of guns and camera equipment had been stolen from his truck, right outside his home in Oak Point, Texas. Responding officers grew suspicious when they talked to his roommate, whose version of events cast enough doubt on the story that they pegged Van Dyke as a liar before they even left the property. They arrested him on the spot and charged him with filing a false report. His trial was set for February, and eventually, he was released on a $1,000 bond.

But he had another personal battle to deal with when he got home: an all-consuming online beef with a guy who could only be described as his nemesis.

Thomas Retzlaff was a weird and obsessive kind of person who latched onto Van Dyke the moment they were introduced. In another life, the pair might have been friends—Retzlaff was a fellow Texan, a self-described "Trump supporter from the very beginning," according to The Daily Beast, and he had a propensity for retaliatory violence that knew no bounds. He had a laundry list of detestable convictions under his belt, including "display of harmful material to a minor," a misdemeanor assault against his wife, a violation of a protection order, tampering with government records, theft, and a felony weapons violation. He was expelled from the University of Texas at San Antonio in 2007 after he was accused of harassment and then violated a no-contact order in that case. He was, by all accounts, a bad guy.

He was fanatical and neurotic about Van Dyke and fixated on his ties to the Proud Boys. He cast Van Dyke as an existential threat to the community at large, and he dedicated a significant amount of his personal time to removing that threat.

Their blood feud began a year earlier, in March 2017, after Van Dyke accepted a job as a prosecutor with the Victoria County district attorney's office. Retzlaff got wind of the hire just before Van Dyke started and filed a complaint with the DA, urging the office to google the "crazy person" they'd just hired. If they had, he said, they might have found stories about his ongoing racism and threats, or a report alleging that he maintained an account on the hate site Stormfront (Van Dyke's handle was reportedly WNLaw, short for "White Nationalist Law," though he denied it was his), or a Southern Poverty Law Center report that detailed the domestic violence and illegal weapons charges that got him kicked out of Michigan State University in 2000.

The complaint swayed the district attorney's office, which revoked Van Dyke's job offer. Van Dyke reportedly tried to sue the DA to find the person behind the complaint, but Retzlaff wasn't keeping it a secret. His campaign was far from over. Later that year he filed another complaint, calling on the Texas State Bar to "disbar this retard ASAP." And then he filed more grievances, disbarment petitions, and court documents, all in an effort to upend Van Dyke's career.

He kept this up for *years*. He'd made a game out of fucking with Van Dyke: on multiple occasions he compiled dossiers of Van Dyke's violent exploits and mass emailed them to members of the Texas State Bar, the media, and the local legal community. He would taunt and prod Van Dyke with a flurry of emails until the man erupted and responded with a threat and then Retzlaff would forward that along, too. He seemed to delight in the whole process.

Van Dyke was exasperated. He blamed Retzlaff for his declining career and personal life, and in turn, he became violently obsessed with exacting revenge.

In early 2018, he filed a $100 million defamation suit against Retzlaff, alleging among other things that Retzlaff had a hand in getting him fired from another job in private practice by using anonymous accounts online to call Van Dyke a white supremacist and a Nazi. Retzlaff countersued using Texas' anti-SLAPP statute, and the case droned on for months. But eventually Van Dyke, citing exhaustion over the feud, dropped his case with a motion filed on December 3.

"Simply put, plaintiff lacks the time and resources to continue litigating against a lunatic," he wrote.

On December 12, Van Dyke—who was still out on bond from his false report case—sent two emails to Retzlaff that likely got him thrown back in jail. In the first, he wrote, "I promise you this motherfucker: if my law career dies, you die with it."

In the second: "Go fuck yourself and what's left of your miserable life. You have destroyed my life, and for that offense, you will pay with your own. That's not a threat. That's a PROMISE motherfucker."

His threats led the court to set a new bail hearing, which he missed (he claimed he was on a hunting trip to Alaska), and eventually he wound up back behind bars in the Denton County Jail, awaiting trial.

But just before the trial kicked off in February 2019, there came another plot twist. His roommate—Isaac Marquardt, the primary witness in his case—didn't show up to testify. Prosecutors unearthed a jailhouse phone call suggesting that Van Dyke was trying to keep his roommate quiet in the days leading up to the trial.

"Tell him don't be—if he's at my house—don't be answering the door and . . . make himself scarce," he said to his father during the recorded call.

Van Dyke was accused of witness tampering, which lost him his case. He wound up pleading no contest and was placed on probation.

Naturally, Retzlaff had been following the proceedings closely and was forwarding everything—including the threats Van Dyke had lodged against him and a series of unhinged messages from his Facebook, where he was now describing his own political views as "fascist"—to the Texas State Bar. The agency finally suspended Van Dyke for several months over the threats. It was the second of three times he was suspended from practice as a result of Retzlaff's contact with the state bar (though, even after all of that, Van Dyke was never disbarred and remains in practice as of this writing).

Their war raged on, via email and through Retzlaff's game of filing complaints. But what Retzlaff didn't know at the time—and what nobody knew until much later—is that behind the scenes, Van Dyke and the Proud Boys had been hunting him. They'd found him at the apartment he'd moved to in El Mirage, Arizona, and they were allegedly plotting to murder him.

The bombshell allegations dropped during a federal suit filed by Van Dyke against Retzlaff in 2020. Police in Oak Point, Texas, revealed that they'd been investigating Van Dyke over his ongoing threats, and they'd found something: a 2018 recording, obtained by a federal informant, in which Van Dyke detailed an elaborate plot to surveil and then assassinate Retzlaff in his own home.

In the forty-two-minute tape, Van Dyke describes how he deployed a group of Proud Boys in Arizona to find Retzlaff at his apartment complex and conduct a full security briefing on the place. He wanted minute details: what kind of car Retzlaff drove, what kind of security he had, and how many dogs were at the property.

With that information in hand, Van Dyke said he'd attempt to shoot Retzlaff dead (he preferred a "long gun" over a pistol because "most people survive a pistol shot"). Barring a clean kill, he'd instead launch a psychological campaign to scare Retzlaff into believing he was in constant danger.

"I want this guy cowering in a corner with his dogs wondering when I'm going to show up and come for him," Van Dyke said.

Much to Van Dyke's dismay, however, the Proud Boys didn't do a great surveillance job. They took pictures of the place for him, but questions about the security and Retzlaff's routine remained. So he considered other options, like waiting with a gun outside the spot where Retzlaff picked up his mail.

"The only other place we know he goes is a PO box," Van Dyke said. "There is a modest amount of parking there, but there is no place that doesn't have a significant number of cameras where I could sit up to get a clean shot with a rifle."

If that plot didn't work out, Van Dyke suggested another in which he would gear up with guns and ammo and make a big show of it on social media, leading Retzlaff to believe he was "coming straight for him." In reality, he said, he would be headed for Mazatlán in Mexico, where he would evade the police.

"The idea is to psychologically torture [him]," Van Dyke said.

It remains unclear what the informant was after when the recording was taken, or why Van Dyke emerged from the investigation unscathed. Oak Point authorities noted the plot in a police report, but they didn't press charges. It even went before a Texas grand jury in 2019, but they opted not to indict. Fortunately, in the end, the plot was never carried out. Van Dyke and the Proud Boys denied their involvement, and despite a few news stories about the plot, life went on, and months passed without much update.

And then, on September 2, 2021, Thomas Retzlaff was found dead in his apartment at the age of fifty-five. He was found in a chair in the middle of his living room, his neck opened up by multiple stab wounds. The El Mirage Police Department labeled his death a suspicious homicide.

The department declined to rule out Van Dyke or the Proud Boys as suspects but wouldn't confirm anything about the investigation, including whether Van Dyke had been questioned (Van Dyke told me he had not). And as of this writing, there's simply no publicly available evidence connecting anyone to this crime.

For his part, Van Dyke denies any involvement in Retzlaff's murder. Nevertheless, when asked about it, he said he wasn't exactly mourning over the loss.

"I celebrated with my friends over a bottle of Johnnie Walker Green Label after I learned about it during our weekly [Dungeons & Dragons] game," he told me. "That following Saturday, I had a very nice celebratory dinner at a local Brazilian steakhouse with a close friend who helped me a lot in dealing with all that Retzlaff put me through. . . . It was closure for a particularly bad chapter of my life. It was a celebration of being able to finally move on."

He also sent me a series of bank statements and credit card transactions from September 2 and 3, which he said proved he wasn't anywhere near the murder scene when Retzlaff's body was found. It's hard to tell how those records would serve him as an alibi, though, especially given that in the past he'd plotted to have Proud Boys do the work for him.

Van Dyke posted an endnote to the battle on LinkedIn, which read like a sigh of relief:

> He may have been mentally ill, but he was without a doubt the toughest opponent I have ever faced both in law and in

life generally. He was tenacious. He was cunning. He would sell his own soul and then his mother's soul to win. To defeat or even to fight him not only took skill—it took a hell of a lot of grit. Those closest to me know I almost didn't make it. . . .

So let all of us—especially his victims—resolve to live our lives in such a manner that the same cannot be said of us when our time comes.

The truly bizarre cherry on top of Van Dyke's already wild story is that in 2019, during his ongoing feud with Retzlaff, he attempted to join an infamous neo-Nazi terror group called the Base but was denied entry, members said, for being a "huge liability." Vice News got hold of a recording in which Van Dyke, using the cover name John Lee, told Base leaders on a conference call that he wanted to join to exact more violence on his enemies, and he noted in that vein that he was a skilled shot with a rifle. But he also just wanted to be more openly antisemitic than he felt he could be in the Proud Boys.

"There're plenty of people in the Proud Boys who don't believe that Jews have a place in this country, and they want to put a stop to it," he said on the call. "And whenever someone talks about doing something, they're immediately shut down or banned from the band, from the group, because, you know, the boys don't want to have that image."

Ultimately, Van Dyke was denied after members of the Base looked into his recent history, which included accidentally doxing his fellow Proud Boys, and they denied his entry.

Notably in his interview, Van Dyke criticized McInnes, who he complained wasn't actually "willing to do anything" violent from the comfort of his high castle.

Gavin McInnes Finds Out

If there's anything that pisses the Proud Boys off, it's when someone holds a mirror up to them. And Vic Berger makes a damn
fine mirror.

He's a comedian and producer, popular in part for the hilarious and awkward video mash-ups he posts online, featuring footage of political figures doing awful and heinous things,
spliced with maybe a sad trombone sound effect or an airhorn to
make a moment as cringe-inducing as possible. He characterizes
it as political commentary and satire, targeting the loudest and
most harmful people with their own words and actions. This has
naturally led him to Gavin McInnes on several occasions. For
example:

"Content warning: Gavin McInnes, Proud Boys gang leader,
says the n-word over and over and squeezes a massive dildo
out of his asshole," Berger once tweeted, atop a video featuring McInnes saying the N-word over and over and squeezing a
massive dildo out of his asshole. It's truly a sight to behold: two
and a half minutes of McInnes shouting racial epithets over and
over on *The Gavin McInnes Show*, followed by a segment from
a 2016 episode in which he stood in front of thousands of digital
audience members during a live broadcast, squirted some lube
onto his hand, pulled down his pants, and proceeded to cram a
painfully large, floppy black dildo into his body. Once you see it,
you cannot unsee it.

Berger was posting compilation videos like this as early as
2018, back when national media still hadn't picked up on the
fact that McInnes was effectively running a gang on his live show.
McInnes would go on TV and declare that his "drinking club"
was nonviolent, and Berger's videos stood in glaring contrast,

showing shot after shot of McInnes calling for violence and his gang carrying it out. It's all real footage, much of it still available on various websites dedicated to McInnes' old podcasts.

They made McInnes look like an ass, and he hated them.

"Fascists don't understand humor, and they don't like being the butt of jokes," Berger said. "They came after me."

In May of 2019, a tipster sent Berger a transcript from a private Proud Boys chat in which members were trying to find him and anyone else connected to the videos and make them pay.

"Let's get the social media profiles, phone numbers and addresses for their bosses, mothers, fathers, brothers, sisters, boyfriends, friends and get to work," one message read. "LET'S SHOW THEM THERE ARE CONSEQUENCES!!!"

And then, two weeks later, a Proud Boy goon showed up on the doorstep of Berger's home in Pennsylvania, sent to intimidate him and his family.

"When I answered the door, he seemed nervous, like he wasn't expecting me. It was the middle of the day, and my wife was home," Berger told me. "He was like, 'Hey, you Vic?' and I said yeah, that's me, and I reached out to shake his hand because I thought it was a neighbor or something. Then I noticed he was filming me. He said, 'Your videos are hurting a lot of people. You're hurting the Proud Boys, and you need to stop making these videos.'"

Berger screamed for his wife to call 911 and chased the Proud Boy back to his car, where he snapped a photo of the license plate before he got away. Later he'd learn that the brute was Kenneth Lizardo, a fifty-four-year-old self-described fourth degree Proud Boy who'd driven from Massachusetts just to threaten him.

"It was scary as hell," Berger said. "I thought this was all just bullshit from the internet; they've always harassed me online. But now they're sending thugs."

Berger didn't stop making videos. But not long after the episode, screenshots from another private chat were circulated, in which McInnes said of Berger's plight: "Play stupid games, win stupid prizes." He denied his own involvement when I asked about the house call.

"I had nothing to do with Vic's visit, and my understanding was it wasn't about me," he said. "It was about him making videos about the club."

McInnes generally enjoyed a great amount of distance between his personal life and his Proud Boys life. When he clocked out as their leader on his live show, he traveled from his studio in the city to his house in the ritzy village of Larchmont, just north of New York City. It's a beautiful and quiet upscale suburb on Long Island Sound, home to wealthy media executive types and wine-drinking liberals. There he led a peaceful life of solitude with his wife and three kids. He certainly never saw in his community the kind of chaos his gang was exacting in other places.

But after the GOP club attack in 2018, and right around the time Berger was pumping out videos about the Proud Boys, McInnes' neighbors started to take notice of the fascist gang leader in their midst, who was enjoying the comforts of their community while spewing hate and violence into others. One of them was Amy Siskind, a prominent women's rights activist and author who was a leading voice in the anti-Trump resistance movement nationally. She's also active in hyperlocal politics and activism in Westchester County. Siskind organized an antihate vigil for neighbors that, she told local news site lohud, was not directed at McInnes but would "let him know that we are inclusive and repudiate hate."

McInnes, meanwhile, was getting paranoid. He saw signs being erected in his neighbors' yards that read "Hate Has No

Home Here" and considered them a personal attack on his family, though the signs were a common sight across the country by that time. Neighbors said theirs referenced domestic terror attacks like the Tree of Life synagogue shooting in Pittsburgh, which happened that year.

McInnes lashed out, mocking his community on his podcast and calling them "retards," while still trying to keep a neighborly face on at home. His wife, Emily, defended him on message boards like Nextdoor, where she claimed that she was a Democrat and that the signs represented political intolerance and a danger to her children. Meanwhile, on the side, she harassed her neighbors with private messages and threats to sue, to the point where local police were notified. McInnes stopped short of sending his Proud Boys out to anyone's house, but he didn't need them. He made the house call himself.

Siskind said her doorbell rang one day, and when she opened her door, her blood ran cold.

"It's [McInnes] and his wife and kids in their pajamas, and his wife, she's screaming, and he's just standing there," she told me in a follow-up interview. "The moment I saw him I called the police."

She characterized the short visit as kind of a mob-like intimidation tactic, similar to the one Berger received. McInnes, for his part, claimed he was trying to reconcile with her and gave the local paper an eye-rolling story about his intention.

"Of these four people, three of them are little kids and one was holding his teddy bear," he said. "The pipe dream was that she opened the door and my wife would say, 'Look, let's talk about this. I'm a Hillary supporter. Why are you putting my beautiful children in danger?' This was not about intimidation and I was very open with everyone."

Siskind and the rest of the Larchmont neighbors still went ahead with the vigil, which had become a total fiasco after the story of McInnes' visit made the rounds. She said there were police helicopters in the air, "and local and state police, all responding to a candlelight vigil." And, she maintained, "it wasn't about him."

Today, there are more "Hate Has No Home Here" signs in Larchmont than ever before, as domestic extremist events—including Proud Boys violence—have only ramped up since 2018. McInnes remains a resident there, too, much to the chagrin of his neighbors. They, like Siskind, have turned down the McInnes family's attempts to talk things out, after McInnes repeatedly showed that he wasn't actually making amends, just trying to make himself more comfortable.

"Gavin said, 'Let's talk'—but I didn't have anything to say," one resident told me at the time. "For some people, the signs aren't up for Gavin, for others they are. But so what? You're hateful, and you reap what you sow."

McInnes seems to have gotten over the local feud, and though Larchmont residents tell me they're still concerned about the extremist leader in their community, he hasn't paid them any visits lately. He seems to have given up trying to win their approval.

It makes sense: Larchmont residents aren't his greatest threat anyway. For someone described as a fascist leader, that honor goes to antifa, the balaclava-wearing monster that keeps conservatives up at night.

Chapter 10

ANTIFA THE BOOGEYMAN

A ntifa exists.

But antifa, as it exists in the minds of right-wing pundits, is a tall tale.

If you ingested any amount of conservative media during Trump's presidency, you were bombarded with anxious rants about an anonymously evil throng of black-clad leftists who stalk the streets at night, hunting for small business owners and God-fearing Republicans. Fox News would have you believe antifa is behind every dirty plot and violent act in America's history. Tucker Carlson continues to push conspiracy theories suggesting that antifascist activists carried out the January 6 Capitol attacks, despite the arrests and confessions of hundreds of proud MAGA-hatted patriots in the months that followed.

Trump wanted his followers to believe that antifa was among their greatest threats, one that put their lives at risk and, worse, imperiled his reelection campaign. As a broad spectrum of protest movements swept the country in 2020, the president repeatedly blamed antifa for the unrest and puffed his chest on social media.

"The United States of America will be designating ANTIFA as a Terrorist Organization," he wrote in a now-deleted tweet.

The declaration was an empty gesture as far as the law was concerned, as there's no federal domestic terrorism statute on the books. But it was a powerful tool for the president, who wanted to convince his followers that a war was coming in November. Together, Trump and the conservative media machine fabricated a universe in which antifa sat atop a coalition of "outside agitators" who, among other things, were distributing shields and weaponry and black clothing to everyday protesters, hiding caches of guns and ammo in U-Hauls parked near airports, and plotting terrorist attacks on gas stations and grocery stores in residential areas.

Antifa is a lightning rod for conservative fears and anxieties and a catch-all term for acts of leftist intolerance and criminality, real or imagined. It's characterized as the lead group of a leftist army that seeks to silence the right by way of political violence, as if the Democrats have their own version of the Proud Boys. Trump has so riled his base about antifa that the mere mention of it in a tweet mobilizes his supporters after the threat, through online harassment campaigns and convoys to physical locales. And he exercises that power with abandon, often against individual people, with zero regard for the consequences.

One of those individuals was a seventy-five-year-old man named Martin Gugino, a Catholic peace activist who joined a demonstration in Buffalo, New York, over the murder of George Floyd. Video shot from an otherwise placid scene showed Gugino approach a passing patrol of police, who responded by shoving him to the ground so hard that his skull cracked on the pavement, blood oozing onto the street. He left with a skull fracture. Though the unnecessary cruelty handed down by officers was clear as day (they were briefly suspended, but a grand jury ultimately declined to indict them on assault charges), Trump went after the victim. The president tweeted Gugino's name to his millions of followers and offered up the lie that he was some kind of antifa operative attempting to interfere with police communications.

"Buffalo protester shoved by police could be an ANTIFA provocateur," Trump tweeted. "75 year old Martin Gugino was pushed away after appearing to scan police communications in order to black out the equipment."

Gugino received so many death threats that he had to be moved to a secret location to recover after his release from the hospital.

Antifa, as defined by the right, is a threat so sinister and pervasive that it justifies a violent response from the public. And it's through that lens that politicians and right-wing gang leaders feel comfortable issuing broad and generalized calls for violence against the left. Consider the words of Gavin McInnes after the Proud Boys brawled with a group of apparent antifascists outside his speaking event at New York University:

"We're the only ones fighting these guys and I want you to fight them, too. It's fun. When they go low, go lower. Mace them back, throw bricks at their head. Let's destroy them. We've been doing it a while now and I gotta say, it's really invigorating. Even when you lose, you feel great about yourself."

The Proud Boys hang on those words, but they're not the only ones listening. There are enough civilians following the fearmongering rhetoric spouted by Trump and his allies that even simple rumors about antifa can attract armed patriots by the busload, ready to face a leftist threat that may not even exist.

In 2017, a rumor made the rounds on Facebook that antifa was headed for Gettysburg, Pennsylvania, to piss on Confederate graves. A coalition of hundreds of armed Trump supporters—including the Sons of Confederate Veterans and Ku

Klux Klan—drove in from across the country and stood at attention in front of a Civil War cemetery there, scanning the horizon for an opposing force of antifa. The scene was darkly comical: the far right had mobilized an armed legion on a historical battlefield, and yet apparently none of them had done their research. If they had, they'd know that there are no marked Confederate gravestones in Gettysburg and therefore no Confederate graves to piss on. Antifa was never going to show up and certainly never did, so the MAGA legion hung out alone in a field for the day. The only violent action they saw came from one of their own, who accidentally shot himself in the leg.

The right's version of antifa is most often a boogeyman. For the Proud Boys, who angle themselves as the public's last line of defense against the boogeyman, it serves as a pretext for justified violence. For that reason alone, it is essential that the general public understand antifa and other leftist protest movements as they exist not in a right-wing fever dream but in reality.

———

ANTIFA IN AMERICA today can be broadly defined as a decentralized leftist movement, describing a full array of groups and individuals who oppose fascism in all its forms. It's an umbrella term, wide-ranging enough that it doesn't come close to describing one group or tactic, in the same way that "rock music" doesn't describe one band or genre. At an "antifa" demonstration you'll often find a range of ideologies and motivations: anarchists standing alongside communists, socialists, and liberal Democrats. You'll find black-clad antiracist protesters in the same crowd as local activists in their street clothes. In the early hours of Unite the Right, local religious leaders in clerical garb stood side by side with protesters in black bloc as they faced a crowd of Nazis. There are peaceful activists holding signs, and militant leftists much more willing to take a violent route to oppose far-right factions like the Proud Boys. There are also supermilitant, veteran groups of street-faring antifascists who describe themselves explicitly as antifa, who would not hesitate to engage in combat and might reject a liberal Democrat from their side just as quickly as they would a police officer. This movement is truly a spectrum, and there's no fully agreed-upon tactic or ideology within its loose structure beyond opposing fascism.

The militant portion of antifa is the most visible and often the only one ever featured on cable news. That's why it's the primary image evoked whenever a pundit says "antifa," whether they're speaking on CNN or Fox News. This urge to apply an easy descriptor to a whole movement is pervasive and led many news organizations to characterize a crowd of forty thousand people at the WTO protests as "anarchists." It's why today's media tend to clam up when they can't find a short and simple blanket term like *white supremacist* to fully describe a complex group like the Proud Boys.

The right uses imagery and anecdotes of militant leftism— black-clad antifascists in bloody combat with right-wingers, or Black Lives Matter demonstrators raising their fists in front of flaming police cars, for example—to establish them as the baseline for all forms of leftist activism. They use those images in an attempt to equalize the threat of the left to that on the far right and place a wide array of dissimilar elements on the left into one big bucket. There are certainly documented incidents of violence carried out by self-described antifascists in the Trump era; in one of the most oft-cited cases, a man named Michael Reinoehl shot and killed a member of Patriot Prayer in Portland during a rally in August 2020. He claimed in an interview days later that he did so in self-defense, but we'll never get more details from his side: a federal task force sent to arrest him instead gunned him down in the residential area where they found him, arguing that he pulled a gun (he did have a gun on him at the time, but witnesses told reporters that he never pulled it and that officers didn't identify themselves before opening fire).

Right-wing media latches onto isolated and incomplete anecdotes about leftist violence and plays them on repeat to drum up fear and anger about the opposing party. When the Tucker Carlsons and Andy Ngos of the world accuse someone of being sympathetic to antifa or BLM, they're not distinguishing between a journalist at a mainstream news organization and, say, a protester holding a Molotov cocktail. They're characterizing those things as one and the same, to be regarded as equal threats. They're all a part of the same antifa that Trump describes as a terrorist organization and the same BLM he called "thugs" as he sent federal enforcers in to punish them.

Amid nationwide BLM demonstrations in 2020, the Trump administration and right-wing media worked hard to paint protesters as remarkably violent and destructive. Attorney General William Barr pushed the false narrative that antifa violence had spiraled out of control at those events and that it required an unprecedented and forcible response from federal law enforcement.

"The violence instigated and carried out by antifa and other similar groups in connection with the rioting is domestic terrorism and will be treated accordingly," Barr said in May.

Fox News joined Barr in pushing the false narrative that antifa had somehow "hijacked" the Floyd protests and turned them into "riots," while other conservative outlets declared that antifa and BLM were "tearing apart our cities." By the end of the summer, conservative media was reporting from fantasyland, where metropolitan cities were fiery war zones whose liberal lawmakers had lost everything to antifa and BLM. None of it was based in reality, but misleading narratives about leftist protest movements have been pushed so consistently and for so long that they're now ingrained in the right-wing consciousness. Pundits can say *anything* about BLM or antifa and expect to be taken seriously. And I do mean anything.

"If somebody were running around with a mask that said 'KKK,' I think we'd all agree that that's abhorrent. But if you're running around with a Black Lives Matter mask, even though the group is Marxist, even though the group is anti-Semitic, even though the group hates our country, wants to overthrow it, even though it's very racist—well, there's something wrong with you," said Fox News host Mark Levin, with a straight face.

When you remove the anecdotal evidence, the mischaracterizations, and the flat-out lies pushed by the right, you get a completely different picture of the demonstrators who flooded American streets in 2020. Real data was collected from political rallies in America during that time, and there were numerous reports and studies on political violence penned by Trump's own federal agencies. Taken together, they land on three basic facts, all of which fly in the face of Trump and company's narratives about leftist violence:

1. The far right and the police are responsible for an overwhelming and disproportionate amount of violence at political rallies today.

2. Racist extremist violence remains one of the greatest domestic terrorist threats in America.

3. Far-right violence far outweighs violence ascribed to the left, even when you break out data from explicitly leftist demonstrations.

Data collected from more than 7,300 nationwide events stemming from Floyd's murder found that millions of demonstrators at the BLM protests in 2020 were, as explained by the *Washington*

Post, "extraordinarily nonviolent, and extraordinarily nonde-structive, given the unprecedented size of the movement's partici-pation and geographic scope." At 97.7 percent of those events, no injuries were reported at all, and when there were, the research found that "in many instances, police reportedly began or esca-lated the violence." Meanwhile, less than 4 percent of the protests involved property damage, and some of that wasn't even caused by demonstrators but rather vandals and looters taking advan-tage of a chaotic situation.

Essentially, the violence at leftist rallies just isn't happening anywhere close to the degree that right-wing media suggests. And the research finds that those false narratives are being used to jus-tify the "beating, gassing or kettling" of demonstrators by police, not to mention the overreaching federal police response deployed by Trump. There is simply no equivalence between violence on the left and the far right.

And let's not forget: there's no moral parity between them, either. Many of the events that conservatives have been working to downplay—Unite the Right, the January 6 Capitol attacks, and countless Proud Boys rallies—are predicated on advancing a bigoted and antidemocratic agenda by way of violence. Fox News has done a lot to sanitize those events, while pointing fin-gers back at antifascist and antiracist demonstrators.

"The both-sides narrative is easy and politically useful," said Erica Chenoweth, who coconducted the research for the Crowd Counting Consortium project. "But there's literally no moral equivalence between the claim that all humans are created equal . . . and, for example, white supremacist rhetoric and claims, which are universally considered morally abhorrent."

Even when you remove the bigoted ideology component, there's just no legitimate comparison between the far right and antifa in America. Only one of these groups is committing violence on behalf of a political party and receiving explicit support in return. And as the data show, only one of these groups is plotting and carrying out violence and destruction on a massive scale.

Federal agencies tend to agree. The American government has often failed in its preparedness and response to domestic extremist threats over the years, despite its own data and analysis repeatedly reaching the same conclusion: that far-right extremism stands alone as the nation's top terrorist threat.

FBI Director Chris Wray testified as much before Congress following the January 6 attack, which he described as an act of "domestic terrorism." He said the FBI's investigations into white supremacist violence have tripled since he took office in 2017, and that domestic terrorism and extremism are "not going away anytime soon." And while Republican lawmakers tried to goad him into shifting the blame onto antifa, Wray refused.

"We have not to date seen any evidence of any anarchist violent extremists or people subscribing to antifa in connection with the sixth," he testified.

The Justice Department and Department of Homeland Security (DHS) have commissioned numerous reports on the threat posed by far-right extremism and white supremacist violence, though a DHS whistleblower accused leaders of directing analysts to downplay that threat after Trump took office. In the months following January 6, Attorney General Merrick Garland told Congress that "racially or ethnically motivated violent extremists" were the single-greatest domestic extremist threat to the United States.

Far-right violence has been on a sharp rise over the last five years and has continued to snowball even after the Capitol attack, despite the arrests of dozens of extremists and group

leaders. Data show a colossal surge in right-wing extremist attacks and plots in recent years, the likes of which we haven't seen
in decades. At least ninety-one fatalities have been attributed to
far-right extremists between 2015 and 2021.

Thus, enter antifa, in all its various forms.

Antifascist activists have their own ways of confronting extremist violence, using a variety of tactics including research and
espionage, information warfare, and physical violence. There's
no uniform set of tactics in this space, especially when it comes to
fighting. But the glue that binds all the elements of antifa together
is the notion that, left unopposed, the violent ultranationalist and
authoritarian worldview on the fringes of the far right will fester
and grow until it can force its way into the mainstream. And
there's a body of evidence proving that notion true, even when
you focus solely on the actions of the Proud Boys. Their involvement in scores of violent political events, and the inroads they've
secured with the GOP, right-wing media, and law enforcement,
suggest to the antifascists I've spoken to that whatever structures
may exist at the government level to help stanch the rise of far-
right extremism are at best inadequate and at worst complicit
in it. They believe that in the absence of government action, the
job of thwarting the Proud Boys is up to them, and they employ
many different tactics to get the job done.

Some oppose the Proud Boys in the street. Leftist demonstrations are often a mash-up of different tactics, involving different
groups and varying levels of anonymity, depending on a protester's plans for the day and his or her level of comfort with being
identified by the far right or police. Anonymity is important to
many of them, because any leak of their personal information to
the far right can lead to harassment campaigns against them and
their families, threats, and physical violence.

An immediately useful anonymity tactic is black bloc, in which groups dress in dark monochrome at protests in the field. The sea of black clothing conceals their identities from police and extremists and also creates a confusing visual effect to their opponents, not unlike a school of fish swimming around a racist shark.

Within that crowd, there are usually a bunch of different demonstrators working different roles. Some might hold up black umbrellas at the front line to repel objects lobbed their way, while some spend their time capturing and neutralizing tear gas canisters that make it through (one low-tech way to do this, popularized by protesters in Hong Kong, is to shove the tear gas canister into a thermos filled with mud and shake vigorously). Others designate themselves as field medics, bringing water and supplies to help those who have been injured. Many activists refuse medical treatment from authorities for fear of being identified and tracked down, so field medics are sometimes forced to become field surgeons on the fly. The stories are gruesome.

On November 14, 2020, following a day of violent demonstrations among Trump supporters in DC for the Million MAGA March, familiar clashes broke out as Proud Boys attacked antifascist demonstrators outside Harry's Bar, their favorite local haunt. In an interview with me, one of the antifascists, a woman who supports medics in the field at demonstrations, recalled a harrowing scene in which a group of Proud Boys had her crew cornered and outnumbered, when one of them lunged at her:

> The Proud Boys started spraying something into the crowd. I had my respirator on, so I wasn't affected, but one girl near me got it directly in the eyes. So I'm looking at the medics, trying to get her some attention, but there wasn't much

room. Usually if you're trying to treat someone in the field, you try to take them to a safer spot, but at that point there was no safer spot. So we were in a corner.

Our shield line had been doing a fairly OK job up to that point of trying to keep the Proud Boys separated from the rest of the group, but they got overwhelmed. The shield line ended up breaking. And that's when they started charging into the crowd. I looked at the medics and I was like, 'We have to move this person, we have no choice, we have to go.'

As we started trying to move, that's when a Proud Boy— who had to have more than a hundred pounds and a foot of height on me—grabbed me and held me. He punched my arm, or at least that's what I thought, that he was punching me. And fifteen minutes later, after my adrenaline settled a bit, I realized he'd actually stabbed me.

She broke away and ran before he could land more blows. She wrapped the wound, but didn't immediately go to the hospital, until another medic, whom she described as a combat veteran, took a look. "He said, 'You don't have an option, that needs stitches, go to the hospital,' which I was severely in denial of at the time."

She showed me a picture of the gash in her arm. The knife had gone deep, well past her muscle tissue. It required stitches and weeks worth of "sobbing pain" to heal. She never did file a police report or speak openly to the press, saying she feared what officers and other Proud Boys might do with her identifying information if they found out she was antifascist.

Those concerns are paramount for all antifascist activists, but especially among women fighting back against misogynist groups like the Proud Boys. One often overlooked facet about antifascist action is that it involves the work of a *lot* of women, both online and in the street, though it's not often clear due to the anonymity requirements inherent in the job. Though there are still issues with misogyny and inequality within leftist protest movements, these women tell me it hasn't stopped them from embedding in every single facet of antifascist activism: women are opposing extremists online and in the field in a variety of roles—including infiltration—at great risk to their own safety, against forces that want to kill them.

Ashley, an antifascist activist from the New York tristate area, has infiltrated the Proud Boys. She's not a member—the gang vehemently rejects women in its ranks—but she has inserted herself into a group of women who follow the Proud Boys to bars and rallies, which she describes as a kind of roving fan club that reveres the gang for their patriotism and the protection they offer from antifa. She didn't join them to admire the gang but to record as much as she could from the Proud Boys' side of rallies and at their planning meetings to send back to her comrades.

"I wanted to keep the people that I love safe," she said.

She described herself politically as a Democrat-turned-anarchist, one who never voted until she cast a ballot against Trump during his reelection campaign in 2020. The threat posed by Trump and the far-right groups around him was so great, she said, that she got into antifascist work to directly oppose them. She went to counterdemonstrations in black bloc, where she said she faced down extremists in the street. But she always had her eye on infiltration work, which she said was dominated by men.

"I wanted to prove that women could be just as impactful and effective as men in that space," Ashley said. "I wanted to open the door for other women and encourage them to step up and push to the front if they have to, riot-girl style."

She got her chance at a bar in New York State during a night out with her activist friends. They set their sights on a crowd of

Proud Boys in uniform at the bar, and Ashley made her move to get closer to them, by "striking up a conversation and flirting a bit," she said. That's all it took. She exchanged numbers with a member, and soon enough, she was getting invites to Proud Boys events where women were allowed, which usually meant bars that were friendly to the gang or the very back of marches and rallies, where women were expected to stay throughout the day.

"They told us that physical combat is not a place for women," she said. "It was a lot of very patronizing 'we're here to protect you' kind of language."

It was frustrating to be sidelined because Ashley was there to get dirt on the Proud Boys, but she took the opportunity to get to know some of the women on the outskirts of the movement. To blend in among them, Ashley said, she had to create a character for herself, whom she described as a bubbly, over-the-top "idiot" drenched in spray tan. As she told me this, she pitched her voice upward and added a heavy dose of vocal fry, to the degree where her tone would have been a danger to a crystal wineglass.

"I'm not going to tell you her real name, but let's just call my character Candy," she said with a giggle. "She's really fucking annoying. She's absolutely obsessed with [former Trump adviser] Kim Guilfoyle, who is, like, a total style icon, and she's just really friendly and ditzy and really just wants to get out there and hold a flag and support the troops."

The character worked, she said, but not because it was convincing to the other women—they could see right through the act. But that wasn't a danger to Ashley's cover because they were *all* playing it up in the same way, to impress members of the Proud Boys. She said her character was the stereotype for the Proud Boys' perfect woman: willing to dumb herself down below their level (a difficult task, Ashley argued) and be subservient, with an understanding that misogyny was baked into the rules, like McInnes' "venerate the housewife" mantra.

What's interesting about the dynamic between the men and women in that space, she said, is that nobody ever seemed to make it past flirting, despite the fact that the women were there to "get a Proud Boy boyfriend." The groups were segregated most of the time, and women would get close to the Proud Boys who caught their eye by acting as their beer maids, walking to and from the bar with booze for the opportunity to strike up a conversation. But she never saw a situation where any of them won each other's affections. Even if that did happen, she said, most of the Proud Boys were too hammered by the end of the day to get out a sentence, much less an eloquent pickup line. This was all fine and dandy for her because she never had to worry about fending off anyone's advances. The Boys generally stuck with the Boys, and the girls with the girls.

When she was able to attend rallies, she was constantly recording video and audio. She recorded fights between the Proud Boys and antifascists, initiation ceremonies, speeches, and marching orders (all on a burner phone) and sent them back to her activist community. She showed me several of them: she had new angles on various Proud Boys moments in recent history, including a shot of the gang burning a Black Lives Matter flag outside a historic Black church in Washington, DC, on December 12, 2020.

Ultimately, she said, the surveillance was the most impactful work she was doing. The Proud Boys were a threat to not just her antifascist community but the national one, and she wanted evidence of their violence and their plots. The job came with some scary moments. She witnessed several fights she wishes she could have intervened in but couldn't—either because her cover would have been blown or because the Proud Boys wouldn't have let her anywhere near them—but getting photographic evidence was paramount.

"If someone was stabbed, I wanted to get it on camera. If some of these Proud Boys were planning serious, high-level attacks or if they were drunk and they were going to give me information that could help my friends live, I wanted to make that happen," she said.

———

THE WORK THAT happens in the street, including infiltration and militant opposition at rallies, represents a small fraction of the overall antifa movement and the groups and tactics it deploys. The primary goal of antifa is to stop Proud Boys rallies *before* they ever happen, and that takes a colossal effort from huge networks of people countering extremism online, in which researchers, activist groups, infiltrators, and everyday citizens combine their work to expose and ultimately prevent groups like the Proud Boys from organizing and promoting violence.

Antifascists and their allies have their hands in just about every facet of the Proud Boys' operating procedure. Every section of this book, and all the research therein, relies heavily on the work of researchers and activists exposing the gang's private affairs or casting light on their public actions. And that work often comes from everyday citizens lending their spare time to thwarting extremism, despite the risk involved and without an expectation of pay or prestige.

Juliet Jeske is one of those people. She's an artist and extremism researcher based in New York City who has, among other works, compiled and catalogued nearly every interview and lowlight McInnes put into the world with *The Gavin McInnes Show*. She downloaded and analyzed more than 1,500 hours of footage and detailed each in Excel spreadsheets and dossiers, which she forwarded to the press in an attempt to get the word out about the misogynist horrors she was seeing in the early days of the Proud Boys, before anyone was paying attention. Jeske isn't a mask-wearing street protester, and she doesn't have access to antifascist networks to help get her word out. She's an independent researcher, a self-described "crazy cat lady," and a journalism school graduate who said she was legitimately terrified—and pissed off—when she stumbled across McInnes' show during her research.

"Every time Gavin would look at the camera and say women are stupid, women are lazy, women are useless, it was like fire for me," Jeske told me. "It was like, OK, motherfucker, let's go."

There are many more citizen researchers like Jeske, whose work adds to a large body of research online that's drawn upon by journalists, law enforcement, and anyone else looking to better understand the far right. There are entire networks of citizen sleuths, for example, working to help the FBI identify the thousands of faces that appeared at the Capitol on January 6, 2021, by poring over terabytes of footage and other data that's publicly available but impossible to parse without a massive effort. Those citizens and groups have been cited as integral to the criminal and congressional investigations into the insurrection.

Beyond the public-facing researchers, there are layers and layers of antifascist networks working against the Proud Boys and other extremists, each one more steeped in anonymity than the last and requiring more proximity to the groups they expose.

There are tons of antifascist Twitter and Telegram accounts that compile records from the Proud Boys' communications, social media posts, and private chats and post entire dossiers of information whenever the gang has an event planned, to alert the local community. Wrote one such account, New York City Antifa, in 2019:

"This Saturday, Proud Boys and their Far Right supporters are rallying in support of two of their most violent members. To help prepare y'all coming out, we're starting a list of anticipated chud attendees."

The following posts were exactly as promised: a list of prospective attendees of a "Free the Boys" rally in support of two defendants in the Metropolitan Republican Club attack back in 2018. There were photos of Proud Boys alongside their names and, when available, a list of the crimes and threats they've been involved in. One of the posts mentioned Kenny Lizardo, the Proud Boy who showed up at comedian Vic Berger's house to intimidate his family.

"Kenny Lizardo has announced he'll be at the Saturday Proud Boy rally in NYC. Kenny likes to brag he's a '4th degree' Proud Boy, meaning he's assaulted people 'for the cause,'" the post reads, alongside a picture of Lizardo and a screenshot of his Facebook, which says, in part, "Fuck you Antifa . . . just to let you know I am a 4th degree so come get some baby."

The thread links each member to other threads written by other activists, who themselves have published their own detailed dossiers of individual Proud Boys and other groups. There are hundreds of these threads, and together they add up to a library of work covering the far right. Sometimes they're used to warn people about the violent thugs coming to town, and other times activists will tweet directly at the companies that employ them or run their websites. Many of these activists get lots of engagement, and the information they uncover ends up in news articles or charging documents. The Proud Boys liken these threads to doxing, but a solid majority of this work involves compilations of publicly available info—Proud Boys bragging on social media about their exploits, like the above Facebook post by Lizardo, is really easy to find and screenshot.

In the next layer, there are antifascists who go undercover to hassle the Proud Boys from within. They are network hackers and researchers and online infiltrators who work to collect and expose private chat logs, data from websites (like the GiveSendGo donator data uncovered by the DDoSecrets collective), and the internal documents of extremist groups.

Activists say they're able to hamper the Proud Boys more easily than some other groups because they have generally awful information security. Antifascists (and, separately, federal agents) have infiltrated just about every secret chat room run by the Proud Boys, proven by the fact that their private correspondence keeps appearing in court documents and dossiers. When activists make those chat logs public, say by posting them on Twitter or releasing them to a journalist, they can completely upend an event before it begins.

In 2019, antifascists leaked a trove of private chat logs between Proud Boys as they plotted a "Resist Marxism" rally in Providence, Rhode Island. Two months' worth of chats on Telegram showed the gang plotting to maim and kill antifascists at the event, which was set for April 6. The organizer—a gigantic brute with a thousand-yard stare named Alan Swinney—gleefully joined other Proud Boys as they discussed the weapons they'd use against the "commies" when they got there. Swinney hoped the event would inspire more "patriots" to join the Proud Boys. The rest of them were thirsty for blood.

"All I want to do is smash commies," wrote Anthony Mastrostefano, a Las Vegas–area Proud Boy who bragged about having his fourth degree. "Actually I'm lying I'm way past just hitting them. When the time comes I will stop at nothing to fully eradicate them all!"

Others posted pictures of the weapons they wanted to bring: axes, machetes, and brass knuckles were among the favorites that day.

"Group, meet Kindness," said Proud Boy Jason Cardona, showing off a black tactical axe.

They discussed bringing guns, but thought better of it after one of them noted New England's strict concealed carry laws.

"I carry but it seems like to [sic] much could go wrong with that," wrote Proud Boy Jason Lewis. "Big patriot fists and boots will do just fine."

At one point, Kyle "Based Stickman" Chapman seemed to have a moment of clarity and wondered aloud if all the premeditated violence might get them in trouble one day or end up in a book.

"I advise all of you to only speak in terms of self-defense and never speak of premeditated violence," he said. "I could be liable for what happens in Providence. So please stop making it easy for these people to prosecute us by putting threats of violence in writing that can be used against us later."

Few seemed to listen. A Proud Boy named Shaun Hufton fantasized about shooting and killing Christian Exoo, the antifascist who published Proud Boy dossiers on different members under his @AntifashGordon Twitter moniker.

"This mother fucker needs to meet a 7mm [Magnum rifle] from about 500 yards," he said. Another Proud Boy, Peter Scott, wisely replied, "Do not post any threats on here, the feds will use it against [us] in court."

Swinney was more tactful throughout the conversations and primed the others on how to make it appear as if they were acting in self-defense. He also confirmed a policy that's rarely mentioned out loud: the Proud Boys try to attack only once they're sure they have an individual outnumbered and separated from their group, to hurt them as much as possible before police or reinforcements show up. They like a three-to-one ratio.

"If any contact is made with you, that's assault. If they take your hat, spray you with silly string, spit, push. . . . It's assault. We need to have all our guys there before we retaliate though if we can. The cops aren't going to let us fight long. We need to inflict as much damage as possible in the time we have."

The plots were published just two days after the gang announced on the steps of the Lincoln Memorial in DC that they were suing the Southern Poverty Law Center for designating the Proud Boys as a hate group. Enrique Tarrio touted their age-old lie during their big announcement that "we're a drinking club that stands behind Donald Trump."

The leaks spelled trouble for almost every Proud Boy involved. The "Resist Marxism" event was canceled, Hufton reportedly lost his job at a tractor supply company over his threat, and the Proud Boys publicly disavowed Swinney to save face after they learned that he personally confirmed the authenticity of the Telegram channel to me. Like many of their renunciations, though, this one was purely ceremonial: Swinney went on to commit many more heinous crimes with the Proud Boys at their events. Two years later, at fifty-one years old, he was sentenced to ten years in prison for shooting a man in the eye with a paintball gun, aiming a loaded Ruger .357 Magnum at a group of protesters in broad daylight, and repeatedly spraying people in the face with bear mace. Prosecutors called him a "white nationalist vigilante cowboy."

Sometimes gaining access to an extremist group's private correspondence can be a relatively easy process. Their generally poor information security and lax vetting rules make for a smooth in-filtration into a chapter's chat rooms. And once you're in, there are a number of things you can do with your access: you can collect and disseminate everything you find, you can monitor event planning chats and alert others to premeditated violence, or—and this is the fun part—you can sow total chaos to make a chapter or an event implode entirely.

"One of my favorite things to do with accelerationist groups is to get on their vetting committee and just start calling everyone a fed," said Gwen Snyder, a longtime antifascist researcher who does some infiltration work online. "Or accuse other members of being antifa. Or even accuse them of being me, Gwen, and then tweet something that makes it look like yeah, maybe that person *is* me. It's a supereffective tactic."

She said most extremist groups have vetting processes by which you can make it into their private chat rooms. They'll make you "prove" yourself, sometimes by taking a photo with a gun or a sign as evidence that you are who you say. But she said it's never that difficult to mislead them, and though she's sent them pictures to get into chat rooms, she's never had to send them a picture of her face.

"They basically just want some part of your body to show you're white," she said. "Once I took a picture of my hand hold-ing a sign that said, like, 'Go Terror Organization!' and I remem-ber they made fun of me for having long fingernails. But I'd made it through vetting."

She always tries to get in using a number of different aliases so that she can spread out her efforts. If she gets enough sock-puppet accounts into a chat, she can start breeding all kinds of havoc—even by accusing herself of being a fed or antifascist infiltrator. If they kick out one of her accounts based on those accusations, her other account only benefits from more credibility. Eventually, they'll start getting paranoid.

"They'll start blocking everyone, and sometimes that can destabilize or shut down an entire event."

There's a fun and funny element to the work, she said, but the majority of it is grueling and thankless and requires you to hang out in some of the darkest places online for extended periods of time. But she does it to thwart groups like the Proud Boys who, she said, represent more of a threat to everyday people than the simple possibility of getting a knock on the door and a punch in the eye.

"The threat of the Proud Boys is less about direct violence—though that's part of it—and more about what they normalize," she said. "They're associating themselves with mainstream politicians like Trump and others like Trump, and they pose this cultural threat. They're normalizing brownshirt tactics and making them seem like acceptable politics. It's incredibly dangerous, and we need to stop it before it begins."

Regardless of your views on antifascist tactics, it is a matter of fact that the work of antifascist activists has been invaluable to journalists and law enforcement efforts over the years. Because if they're not doing it, no one is. Without that work, much of the Proud Boys' private chat logs, attack plans, and archival documents within this book would never have seen the light of day. Activists and researchers have published dossiers on hundreds of individuals and groups from the entire spectrum of far-right extremism. Those publications have led to the identification and arrests of some of the most dangerous criminals in the country and exposed white supremacists within our military and police forces. They've also exposed domestic terrorist plots and helped law enforcement build cases against the architects. And countless victims may never have seen their day in court. It took years of research by antifascist researchers to build the case against the organizers of Unite the Right, which left them in the hole for more than $25 million.

And it's because of that work that we know what the Proud Boys have been trying to obfuscate since their inception: that no extremist event, no matter how big or small, happens in isolation.

Chapter 11

THE GANG TRIES CIVIL WAR

The first person to breach the US Capitol was a Proud Boy.

Dominic Pezzola—or "Spazzo," as he was known to his crew in New York—had wrested control of a police-issued riot shield from an officer and made his way up the steps of the Capitol building to a large window that was out of sight of the main entrance. A horde of rioters were close behind him, having quickly overwhelmed a small force of officers attempting to block them at the steps. Now there was only brick, mortar, and glass between them and the members of Congress inside.

Pezzola raised the shield over his shoulder and rammed it into the window over and over until the glass pane collapsed, and then he went for another. Someone in the crowd behind him yelled "Go! Go! Go!," and they swarmed in through Pezzola's breach. Seconds later, Vice President Mike Pence was escorted out of the Senate chamber, just a few steps and a stairwell away from their position. The process of confirming Joe Biden as the new president was now on hold as Trump supporters flooded the hallways, looking for lawmakers. "Drag them out!" one of the rioters yelled. "Hang them out!"

Pezzola joined a group of people following a lone police officer as he retreated up the steps toward the Senate chamber. When they reached the second floor, the officer led them away from a nearby entrance to the chamber, a move that likely saved lives. The chamber was still full of lawmakers, and it'd be several more minutes before their evacuation began. The rioters advanced until they reached a wide hall, where they stopped for a moment to bask in their achievement. They'd just sacked the US Capitol and delayed Biden's confirmation, which was a pretty strong start to their ultimate goal of overturning the election entirely. They cheered and took selfies. Many of them were recording and streaming from their phones, including Pezzola.

He lit a cigar and turned his camera to show his face, a grin beaming out from under a tangled mess of beard and shoulder-length hair. He wasn't wearing his Proud Boys uniform—he and more than one hundred other members at the riots were told not to wear black and yellow that day to avoid detection—but in this moment of triumph he wasn't worried about laying low.

"Victory smoke in the Capitol, boys," he said. "This is fucking awesome. I knew we could take this motherfucker over if we just tried hard enough." And as if he just couldn't resist incriminating his gang, he added: "Proud of your motherfucking boy."

———

THE BIGGEST EXTREMIST events get siloed in the aftermath, pulled away from the broader conversation and studied on their own. We often remember mass shootings and violent demonstrations as solitary phenomena, each carried out in different locations by different actors, and recall them using whatever moniker stuck at the time: Unite the Right. Sandy Hook. Pulse. Tree of Life. Each attack deserves its own full-scale investigation to understand what happened, who was involved, and the ideological factors at play.

But it's important to consider individual extremist events as part of a bigger picture, stretched over a time line and analyzed alongside historical context. There's absolutely no such thing as lone-wolf extremism, and there's no single data point on the graph of far-right terror that stands on its own as an anomaly. Similarly, the story of January 6, 2021, isn't a beginning or an end point in the saga of American extremism. There are key events in the years, months, days, and minutes leading up to the sixth that predicted the assault on democracy as an inevitability, and the violent actors and sentiments involved haven't gone anywhere. The events of January 6 were premeditated, and they are ongoing.

Yet they're still being packaged as an outlier, an unusual crescendo of political violence carried out by a small number of people who, perhaps in a moment of mass hysteria, stumbled into the halls of Congress. There are all kinds of bogus narratives being spun around that day, by those with a vested interest in deflecting blame and minimizing damage to themselves. They're the usual suspects after any far-right incursion: Republican lawmakers, right-wing media, and the rioters themselves were working to distort the events of January 6 before the tear gas and smoke even had a chance to dissipate. Many of the defendants have argued in court that they were just in the wrong place at the wrong time.

The right-wing spin on January 6 hinges on three falsehoods: that there was no plot or incitement to storm the Capitol that day, that the attack was spur of the moment and therefore blameless, and that the violence and destruction were exaggerated by overzealous prosecutors and the liberal media. These are the prevailing narratives being hawked by conservative media more than a year later, despite all the evidence to the contrary. Tucker Carlson launched a three-part documentary series about the event called *Patriot Purge*, which suggested that antifa and the FBI were behind the assault, and that they were running a "false flag" operation to make Trump supporters look bad.

In reality, prosecutors allege that the Proud Boys, alongside their extremist allies, conspired in the weeks prior specifically to breach the halls of Congress and potentially other "crucial buildings" in Washington, DC. And when the day came, they certainly did so, leading thousands of people to march on the Capitol, immediately following an angry and pointed speech by their president, who told them that the election had been stolen from them and that they needed to take it back with force. The statement was crystal clear:

"Together we are determined to defend and preserve government of the people, by the people and for the people," Trump told a crowd at the "Save America" rally. "We fight, we fight like hell, and if you don't fight like hell, you're not going to have a country anymore. So we are going to walk down Pennsylvania Avenue . . . and we are going to the Capitol."

They marched, a mile and a half down Pennsylvania Avenue from the Ellipse where Trump spoke to their target, and they fought like hell. They quickly overwhelmed a small police force standing in defense of the Capitol, where Congress had gathered to certify Joe Biden as the new president. Some of them wanted to find lawmakers to kill. They chanted "Hang Mike Pence" as a warning to their vice president, who had failed to reverse the constitutionally mandated election process and reinstate Trump for an illegal second term. They smashed glass and lit fires. They took mementos, classified documents, computers, even a podium, and destroyed property in their wake.

They ripped equipment out of officers' hands and beat them with their own weapons. More than 140 cops were injured that day—one lost a fingertip in the melee, and others were clobbered with flagpoles and baseball bats or crushed by the advancing crowd. One Capitol Police officer, Brian Sicknick, died after sustaining injuries that day, and another four officers took their own lives in the aftermath.

These facts aren't in dispute. They're backed up by a repository of photo and video evidence, confessions, and court documents. And yet the counternarratives remain—right-wing pundits and politicians were still downplaying the severity of the attacks and pushing full-blown conspiracy theories a year later and beyond. They're overwhelming the narrative with misinformation in order to muddy it, a popular tactic that Trump strategist Steve Bannon accurately described as "flooding the zone with shit."

Without proper context, it's easy to get lost in the flood.

The real story of the insurrection exists in the margins, where extremist leaders spent months preparing and recruiting for a final stand against the transition of power by cranking up the heat on a long-simmering pot of American rage. The sixth was the result of a calculated and exhaustive effort to bring a small-scale civil war to the masses, and the Proud Boys were both the generals and the soldiers.

For the gang, the sixth was a culmination of everything they'd built over the previous five years, a major test of their entire apparatus: their fundraising, organization skills, coalition building, relationships with the GOP and the police and the media, and their resiliency in the face of antifascist activists and legal consequences would all be tested here.

Their road to the Capitol began at the presidential debate months earlier, when Trump told them to "stand back and stand by." The gang went absolutely ballistic when they heard their name mentioned on the big stage.

"Stand back and stand by, for when the commies start a full escalation of war and he can call on us to essentially 'let loose the dogs of war,'" one member said on Telegram after the debate.

Proud Boys leaders were ready to take orders.

"Standing by sir," Tarrio said on Parler, a right-wing social network.

"President Trump told the Proud Boys to stand by because someone needs to deal with ANTIFA . . . well sir! We're ready!!" wrote Joe Biggs, event organizer for the Proud Boys and one of Tarrio's right-hand men.

Trump and his allies scoffed at the insinuation that they'd incited a street gang, but it didn't matter what they thought. The Proud Boys were convinced they'd been mobilized by the president. They took to social media and announced their readiness for the coming civil war. They made T-shirts bearing the "Stand Back, Stand By" slogan, and they wore them to a series of rallies they helped organize over the next few months.

When Trump's election loss put an end date on their marching orders, their savagery got worse. They began targeting anyone Trump blamed for his failure, which at that point was pretty much everyone: journalists, politicians, random passersby—they didn't care. They saw the two-month span before Biden's confirmation as their final stand for Trump, and they lashed out brazenly and blindly.

On November 14, a week after most outlets had called the presidency for Joe Biden, the Proud Boys joined thousands of Trump supporters in DC for the Million MAGA March, one of several large-scale demonstrations in defiance of the election results. This one quickly devolved into a bloody, racist circus that featured a keynote speech by white nationalist Nick Fuentes, as well as appearances by a bevy of QAnon adherents and Brien James, the founder of a hard-core skinhead crew called Vinlanders Social Club, wearing a Proud Boys uniform. Tarrio later characterized the event as "the moment we really united everybody under one banner," and "the seed that sparked that flower on Jan. 6."

The gang chose the liberal media as their target that day, the same target that Trump had been harping on since his loss was called. Video shows a crowd of Proud Boys decked out in their black-and-yellow polos and military gear, marching down the street and chanting "The media sucks."

At one point, a handful of them took interest in a journalist standing on the side of the road, a cameraman named Daniel Silva-Pinto. They surrounded him in a semicircle, and one of them grabbed at his camera, shoving it downward to block his lens. Another reporter nearby caught what happened next: one of the Proud Boys—a disgraced former police officer from the Pacific Northwest named Mike Babbitt—brought up his arms without warning and sucker-punched Silva-Pinto in the face and then quickly came around with two more jabs before his victim even knew what was happening. At Babbitt's side was Dick Schwetz, the same Proud Boy running for a house seat in Pennsylvania. Schwetz lunged forward into Silva-Pinto's face.

"Back the fuck up, get the fuck out of here," he screamed, his spit flying. "How many more fuckin' punches you gonna take?"

Silva-Pinto was rattled. He said the Proud Boys chose him at random for the assault, picked out of a crowd of other journalists filming the march from a distance. Discombobulated, he looked around and locked eyes with a woman who witnessed the attack.

"This woman—she could easily be one of my mom's friends—she saw me get punched and then she saw me back off," he said. "She looked me right in the eye and she said, 'You deserved that.'"

This was the moment Silva-Pinto saw an irreversible shift among Trump supporters, in which their anger and anxiety turned to bloodlust. And not just among Proud Boys, but everyday people attending the rally. He recalled that Trump's favorite thing to do at a rally was to point out the "crooked" media standing in the risers, directing the audience to turn around and jeer at the camera crews. At the time, Silva-Pinto wasn't particularly worried about being targeted by garden-variety Trump supporters. But now the temperature had clearly reached boiling point.

"It was something I hadn't seen before," he said, "because, in general, most of these people are just regular folks, right? But in that moment, I saw things take a real turn."

He learned in a visceral way just how quickly the temperature rises whenever the Proud Boys show up. They bring an aggressive energy wherever they go that could turn grandma's bingo night into the Thunderdome within minutes. Getting regular people to go along with violence is one of the many sobering characteristics of the Trump era that the Proud Boys helped to normalize. Not only can you expect bloodshed at a rally where the gang shows up, but it's no longer surprising to see weapons and armor and fighting at *any* civic event, specifically due to this short time period.

Silva-Pinto was one of at least three journalists who were singled out and assaulted that day just for being a member of the press, and nobody batted an eye. At least twenty-two journalists were assaulted at Trump-affiliated rallies between the election and the insurrection, almost entirely at the hands of police officers and the supporters of the lame-duck president.

He was right about the shift. Every far-right extremist group under the sun was out in the street after the election. In fact, the moment news organizations predicted a Biden win, the capitol building in the new president's home state of Pennsylvania was surrounded by heavily armed members of the Three Percenters, a self-described "militia" of cosplaying army dads who sit around waiting for a justifiable moment to use their AR-15s on real people. As they sat around on this day, they spoke of civil war. "It's coming," one of them declared.

It seemed like everyone was taking up arms, gearing up for a decisive battle. The Proud Boys, QAnon conspiracy theorists, militia groups, even a MAGA-touting religious sect that worships with AR-15s called the Rod of Iron Ministries. And everyday conservatives were right there with them: almost one in five American adults at the time believed the lie that the election was stolen from Trump and that forcibly taking it back was a politically justified option. The phrase "Stop the Steal"—popularized by Roger Stone in 2016 and weaponized against Hillary Clinton—exploded again on social media, held aloft by Trump supporters as a rallying cry. It was a new coalition of sorts, in which Proud Boys, antigovernment extremists, and, perhaps most importantly, everyday Republicans gathered under the same banner against what they saw as an illegally installed liberal regime.

The Proud Boys absolutely thrive in this environment, where political anger and anxiety seep out of the digital space and begin to spill out into the street, and they were ready to take the reins of the whole operation. The wave of extremism was beginning to crest, and the Proud Boys would be riding it into shore.

Their first order of preparation, as usual, was propaganda.

One of their most skilled proselytizers was Biggs, a rabid former InfoWars employee who'd been introduced to Tarrio and the Proud Boys by Roger Stone. Biggs, thirty-seven at the time of the insurrection, was known for his ability to organize and pontificate and incite in the style of Alex Jones. Back when he worked for the conspiracy king, he helped push, among other things, the lie that shootings in America were false flag operations—a dangerous invention that led to multiple losing lawsuits for Jones and his show—and he advocated for rape and violence against trans women on social media. He got a reputation for physical violence in 2016, after he bragged on video about "pounding" a protester burning an American flag at a demonstration in Cleveland. Police initially arrested the protester for assaulting Biggs, but after the video went viral, the city had to pay the flag-burner $225,000 to settle allegations that cops falsified their reports in support of Biggs. He rose to the top ranks of the Proud Boys immediately and sat alongside Nordean and Tarrio as a gang celebrity.

Between Biden's election and January 6, Proud Boys leaders and their allies repeatedly hinted at violent uprisings in support of Trump. On November 5, two days before the networks called it for Biden, Biggs posted, "It's time for fucking War if they steal this shit." On November 7, when even Fox News had to admit defeat, Tarrio posted to Parler: "Standby order has been rescinded." The implication? It was game time.

On November 10, Biggs declared war outright. He posted a nonsensical screed as the final blog on his propaganda website, The Biggs Report, titled "The Second Civil War Is More Realistic Than You Think." It reads in part:

> If there ever was a time for there to be a second civil war, it's now. It won't be because of Trump supporters, it'll be because the [mainstream media] baited, lied and implied a Biden Victory to their lunatic base that literally believes everything that comes out of their mouth. . . . they keep spewing lies to their base, knowing that when the race is called for Trump there will be mass chaos. . . . Buy ammo, clean your guns, get storable food and water. Be prepared! Things are about to get bad before they get better. Stay safe and God bless.

Soon all the Proud Boys' posts began to read like terrorist manifestos. Nordean posted this on November 27:

We tried playing nice and by the rules, now you will deal with the monster you created. The spirit of 1776 has resurfaced and has created groups like the Proud Boys and we will not be extinguished. We will grow like the flame that fuels us and spread like love that guides us. We are unstoppable, unrelenting and now . . . unforgiving. Good luck to all you traitors of this country we so deeply love . . . you're going to need it.

The head of the Proud Boys in Philly, Zach Rehl, posted similarly disturbing stuff that same day: "Hopefully the firing squads are for the traitors that are trying to steal the election from the American people."

On the evening of December 11, the night before the Proud Boys' flag-burning episode in DC, Roger Stone stood alongside Tarrio and Nordean in front of a crowd of dozens and called on Trump supporters to continue their "fight" for the presidency.

"We will fight to the bitter end for an honest count of the 2020 election," Stone said on video. "Never give up, never quit, never surrender, and fight for America!"

Eight days later, a longtime friend of the Proud Boys named Ali Alexander announced his Stop the Steal rally for January 6 to be the main MAGA event in DC on confirmation day. Alexander is a conspiratorial far-right grifter whose suit-and-tie approach to violent extremism got him close to mainstream conservatives at the same time as he was cozying up to the Proud Boys and prominent racists like Fuentes. He made his name as a far-right voice on Twitter (before he was banned for spreading disinformation about the election). He was known for pushing violent platitudes to hundreds of thousands of followers and, in the same vein as the Proud Boys, selling merch off of the unrest he fomented.

"I am a sincere advocate for violence and war, when justified," he once tweeted. "I recognize no law above what is natural and good."

Within days of Alexander's announcement, the Proud Boys were making no secret of their excitement for January 6. On December 23, Rehl characterized it as "the day where Congress gets to argue the legitimacy of the Electoral College votes, and yes, there will be a big rally on that day." On December 29, Biggs posted to Parler, "Jan. 6th is gonna be epic."

Tarrio posted an interesting prompt to his followers on Telegram, asking, "What if we invade it?" The first reply to his post read, "January 6th is D day in America."

What we didn't know until more than a year later is that right around that time, Tarrio had allegedly gone over direct plans to occupy a few "crucial buildings" in Washington on the sixth, including the House and Senate offices surrounding the Capitol. He spoke at length with another person—someone prosecutors hadn't identified by the time of this writing—who sent him a nine-page plan called "1776 Returns" and told Tarrio that "the revolution is more important than anything."

"That's what every waking moment consists of," Tarrio said. "I'm not playing games."

It was the first big confirmation that there was a specific and coordinated plan in place to storm the Capitol prior to Trump's speech on January 6 proper. And the Proud Boys were key players in it: six of them, including Tarrio, were indicted on seditious conspiracy charges over the plot. One of the others, Charles Donohoe, a fourth degree Proud Boy and the president of a local chapter in North Carolina, pleaded guilty to his conspiracy charges in April 2022, and agreed with federal prosecutors to testify against the other members.

On January 2, Tarrio created a chat channel with sixty-five members of the Proud Boys, including his fellow leaders who would end up indicted alongside him, and they began to make final preparations. Several made references to taking the Capitol: "What would they do [if] 1 million patriots stormed and took the capital [sic] building. Shoot into the crowd? I think not," one said.

On January 3, things got even more intense. An unidentified member posted a voice note to the chat, briefing the other Proud Boys on where the vote to confirm Biden's presidency would happen: "The main operating theater should be out in front of the house of representatives. It should be out in front of the Capitol building. That's where the vote is taking place . . . ignore the rest of these stages and all that shit and plan the operations based around the front entrance to the Capitol building."

On January 4, Tarrio got arrested, and a group of Proud Boys leaders nuked their Telegram chats and started a new encrypted channel out of fear that the feds might be watching (the feds were definitely watching, as charging documents show). Donohoe issued a warning on Telegram that implied they were getting nervous about the optics of January 6 and figured their chats had been compromised:

"[I] have been instructed and listen to me real good! There is no planning of any sorts. I need to be put into whatever new thing is created. Everything is compromised and we can be looking at gang charges." He told them to "stop everything immediately" and said that "this comes from the top," though nobody was listening at that point (except maybe the feds).

Donohoe later admitted to prosecutors that by that day, two days before the insurrection, he was involved in explicit discussions with other Proud Boys about storming the Capitol. According to federal prosecutors, he "believed that storming the Capitol would achieve the group's goal of stopping the government from carrying out the transfer of presidential power," and "understood . . . that the Proud Boys would pursue their objective through the use of force and violence."

By January 5, the Proud Boys were primed and ready for battle. They created a new chat for attendees of the following day's events, called "Boots on the Ground," where they were reminded not to show up in "colors," their black-and-yellow uniforms, specifically to avoid being identified as Proud Boys. Members had been told that January 6 would be a "completely different operation" than their previous events. Many of them would wear orange beanies instead, so they could pick one another out in the crowd while maintaining the illusion that they hadn't shown up as a gang.

"No colors, be decentralized and use good judgement until further orders," one of them said.

They took another unusual step on January 6 by declaring cops as one of their opponents in the field. Their relationship to law enforcement had soured over the previous few months, after a series of rallies in which they felt they weren't receiving adequate protection. They were particularly pissed off at DC police, whom they blamed for failing to protect their boys who were stabbed amid the melee of December 12.

On Telegram, leaders reminded everyone that the police were no longer their friends: "Rufio is in charge, cops are the primary threat, don't get caught by them or BLM, don't get drunk until off the street."

Proud Boys social media and chat logs were full of anti-authority messaging by that point. Many on Telegram compared police to Nazis. On Parler, a Proud Boy named Jeremy "Noble Beard" Bertino told fellow members not to trust National Guard troops, whom he accused of colluding with counterprotesters.

"The enemy is showing their hand. The police will be arresting patriots who participate in civil disobedience," he said.

Labeling cops as a combatant for January 6 wound up being a big deal. After all, a small group of police officers were the only thing standing between thousands of Trump supporters and the Capitol building. So here were the Proud Boys, on the eve of the insurrection, untethered by their previous reverence for the cops and, in fact, ready to fight them.

One of Biggs' final messages to the group on January 5 read: "We have a plan. I'm with Rufio." The next morning, on Telegram, a Proud Boy identified in court documents only as UCC-1—an "unindicted co-conspirator"—made a bold proclamation: "I want to see thousands of normies burn that city to ash today," they said. "The state is the enemy of the people."

"It's going to happen. These normiecons have no adrenaline control," replied another. Another chimed in, "[Trump supporters] are like a pack of wild dogs."

In those final moments, the Proud Boys transformed into something bigger and more threatening than they'd ever been before. They were the leaders of a coalition of far-right groups, now so emboldened that they were willing to shed their safety net of their police relationship and, in fact, go to war against them. And with their immense talents for inciting and normalizing violence, they were bringing with them across this threshold of terror ostensibly normal people, who might not have given thought to such violence in the past.

They were at the top of their game, drunk this time not just on beer but on power.

THE PROUD BOYS sent more members to Alexander's Stop the Steal event on January 6 than any other extremist group. Their numbers made them de facto leaders of the march toward the Capitol that followed Trump's speech. Behind them was a brigade of thousands, which included everyday Republicans next to other far-right groups, like the antigovernment Oath Keepers.

Alexander, like almost everyone else connected to the assault, claimed he had "nothing to do with any violence or lawbreaking." But as he peered down on the battlefield at the Capitol steps, taking place far from his perch on a rooftop on Constitution Avenue, he seemed to take pride in the crowd gathering there.

"I don't disavow this. I do not denounce this," he said on video, pointing toward the Capitol.

Below him, an insurrection was unfolding, spearheaded by his Proud Boys pals. Some forty Proud Boys (and counting) were arrested among more than eight hundred cases in connection to the rioting and obstruction that went on that day. But the federal government clearly wanted more than a bunch of individual cases against members; they were building another case characterizing the Proud Boys as a group working in concert to carry out a planned attack. This was important not just to establish that January 6 wasn't a random event, but also that the people there were not lone wolves. The Proud Boys were a veteran street gang standing at the forefront of a movement.

To build that case, the government followed a trail of evidence that the Proud Boys had largely created themselves. It had access to Telegram chats, photos and video evidence, and confessions by different members, alongside records from 1,600 electronic devices and hundreds of thousands of tips that came in, and built a sizable conspiracy case against the Proud Boys. Conspiracy charges were filed against seventeen members, but the most prominent case focused on six leaders: Ethan Nordean, Joe Biggs, Zach Rehl, Charles

Donohoe, Dominic Pezzola, and later Tarrio—all of them except Tarrio were physically present at the riots and had an outsized role in planning and heading the Proud Boys' movements. They were charged with eight counts each, including felony obstruction charges, and accused of conspiring to delay the congressional confirmation hearings on January 6 and interfering with law enforcement, who were trying to quash the riots. And in June of 2022, the Justice Department tacked on sedition charges for all but Donohoe. Each faces decades of prison time.

The federal case is centered on the authority these men exhibited before and during the assault. They stood together as they marched to the Capitol ahead of the crowd of Proud Boys, a huge procession of Trump supporters behind them. Biggs and Rehl had walkie-talkies, and Nordean carried a bullhorn, barking orders at the rest of the group throughout the campaign.

Court documents describe it like this: as the Proud Boys reached several barricaded checkpoints leading up to the Capitol, the four leaders charged forward, ripping down metal barriers and pushing past police. Once they reached the Capitol, they spread out. Members sprayed bear mace gel at a "weak point" in a line of officers, forging a pathway for the rest of the crowd. Biggs took a video of himself, in which he said excitedly, "We've just breached the Capitol." Nordean paced in front of a line of officers, and Pezzola pushed through them, with Biggs not far behind.

At one point, prosecutors said, UCC-1 wrote in the chat, "Storming the capital [*sic*] building right now!!" and "push inside." A Proud Boy at the scene screamed, "Let's take the Capitol," which garnered the response, "Don't say it, do it" from another.

Four of the leaders forced their way into the Capitol at one point or another, clearing the way for dozens more Proud Boys and other rioters to get inside.

Afterward, each of them celebrated and took ownership of their actions online.

"I'm proud as fuck what we accomplished yesterday," Rehl posted. "But we need to start planning—and we are starting planning—for a Biden presidency."

"We stormed the Capitol unarmed," Donohoe wrote. "And we took it over unarmed."

Nordean posted an antipolice message: "If you feel bad for the police, you are part of the problem. They care more about federal property (our property) than protecting and serving the people. BACK THE BLACK AND YELLOW."

Within days, federal agents were knocking on Proud Boys' doors. They issued search warrants in several states. They arrested Biggs in Florida on the same day Biden was sworn in as president, two weeks after the insurrection. Two weeks later, they raided Nordean's home outside Seattle, with their guns drawn and flash-bangs flying. Many Proud Boys faced arrest for initial charges related to the riots, and in March, the conspiracy charges were filed against leadership.

Their lawyers attempted to get the indictment dismissed on the grounds that they were engaging in some kind of constitutionally protected demonstration that day rather than criminal conspiracy, not unlike the argument the Proud Boys used for years to obtain rally permits in Portland, Oregon. And then, in December, another Proud Boy not involved in their case, thirty-four-year-old Matthew Greene of upstate New York, pleaded guilty to conspiracy and obstruction charges and agreed to cooperate with the feds in exchange for a more lenient sentence. His lawyer said he had "very detailed discussions" with the authorities about the Proud Boys and that his plea was "an important step in taking responsibility for his actions." Then came conspiracy charges against Tarrio, and Donohoe's guilty plea.

The guilty pleas certainly didn't help the other Proud Boys fighting sedition charges. A week later, a federal judge refused to dismiss the indictment against the leaders.

"Defendants are not, as they argue, charged with anything like burning flags, wearing black armbands, or participating in mere sit-ins or protests," US district judge Timothy Kelly wrote in a forty-three-page ruling. "Moreover, even if the charged conduct had some expressive aspect, it lost whatever First Amendment protection it may have had."

Though certain federal authorities and judges have taken a new, hard-line stance against the Proud Boys following insurrection day, it remains to be seen whether the criminal justice system—or society at large, for that matter—has actually learned anything about the threat they pose. They've been heavily involved in so many of our worst incidents of domestic extremism in the last decade, and yet the penalties for that haven't yet extended beyond the incidents themselves.

Since January 6, 2021, the Proud Boys have only changed their tactics and become more of a threat. They're getting much, much worse, and their movements beyond the insurrection suggest that American extremism appears to be growing and evolving, rather than dying out.

Chapter 12

THE PROUD BOYS PLAYBOOK

You'd think the Proud Boys would have collapsed by now. A majority of their figureheads have seen the inside of a jail cell in the few short years they've been around, including their ambitious chairman, their lawyer, their elders, and some of their top bruisers. They've gone through at least three leaders. Dozens have been sent to prison for their role in the January 6 riots and other felonious brawls, and some of those who received more lenient sentences were cooperating with the feds, implying that they were rolling over on the other guys. They've been infiltrated by antifascists and federal agents. Their chairman was even revealed to have been a one-time federal informant! They've survived restructuring, a terrorist designation in at least one country, bans from social media and many of their payment platforms, and all kinds of injuries, public embarrassments, and shame.

Lesser extremist groups have rebranded or dissolved entirely in the face of lesser reverberations, like Identity Evropa after Unite the Right. But not the Proud Boys. In fact, betting on their downfall shows a fundamental misunderstanding of how they work, a lesson the federal government was finally starting to learn after January 6.

Despite agencies' ongoing acknowledgments that far-right domestic extremism is a top existential threat worth responding to, they haven't really factored the Proud Boys into that equation. A DHS official said that, up until the Capitol riots, the agency saw the gang exactly as it advertised itself: an all-male drinking club.

"There was a sense that, yes, their ideology is of concern, and, yes, they are known to have committed acts of violence that would be by definition terrorism, but we don't worry about them," said Elizabeth Neumann, who worked in threat prevention in the DHS prior to January 6, to the *New York Times*. "The Proud Boys are just the guys-that-drink-too-much-after-the-football-game-and-tend-to-get-into-bar-fights type of people—people that never looked organized enough to cause serious national security threats."

That kind of response should be maddening to anyone paying a modicum of attention. It's not like the Proud Boys are doing anything to hide their efforts: almost every crime they commit happens in public, and when it doesn't, it gets surfaced and analyzed immediately by researchers and reporters. They wear uniforms and chant their own name: "We are Proud Boys!" They're attacking demonstrators, recording their exploits, and recruiting off the videos. They're raising hundreds of thousands of dollars to pay for buses and hotels and weaponry for political riots. They're outpacing neo-Nazi factions and groups like the Ku Klux Klan in terms of attacks by a hate group. And the lackadaisical response from federal agencies has put local police departments on their heels, if they're not joining in on the Proud Boys' violence themselves.

"It has largely been left to the locals to sort things out for themselves," Mitchell Silber, former director of intelligence analysis with the NYPD, told the *Times* following the insurrection.

There's still a discussion to be had about what, if anything, we want federal agencies to do about the problem, beyond thwarting terrorist attacks. There's no domestic terrorism statute that the Proud Boys could be prosecuted with, for example, but there have been talks in the law enforcement community about whether the Proud Boys might be liable for aiding and abetting terrorists in foreign countries. In the weeks following January 6, Canada declared them a terrorist organization, and at least one of Canada's biggest chapters shut down immediately in response, on their own accord. Perhaps the Proud Boys could be pegged for aiding their own chapters in places where they're considered a terrorist organization. But do we even want such a statute? Even federal investigators worry about the implications of agencies having unbridled investigatory and punitive power. Trump showed the authoritarian extent leaders can go using what we have now by sending federal squads to disappear protesters in the night in Portland. Who might be in prison today if his accusations of "antifa terrorism" actually meant something from a legal standpoint? The power we give investigators to decide when and how to move from investigation to arrest is a touchy and unanswered problem.

"Intelligence is not intel, this is something that people don't always understand," FBI Supervisory Special Agent Jeff Fields, who works on cyber threat intelligence, told me. "They'll look at our work [on a defendant in January 6, for example] and say, well, you had an investigation into this person two years ago, why didn't you close in? Well, because there was intel, but no evidence of a crime. Do you want us to keep an investigation open indefinitely? That's just not the way it works."

The urgent truth is that we're looking at a snowballing extremism crisis in America, growing and changing so rapidly that our institutions are having a hard time keeping up. The Proud

Boys, now veterans and teachers in the extremist space, have figured out how to game the few systems in place that would thwart them—police, media, and top-tier politicians—giving them more power and influence than any of their far-right peers in America.

And though it might have looked like they were dealt a mortal blow for their involvement in the Capitol attacks, they're only getting started. Just like their allies in the GOP, they've already moved on from all that. They have simply changed tactics and dug their heels in, becoming more dangerous in the process.

Where they pulled back ever so slightly on the big national events and the "Stop the Steal" rhetoric in the year following January 6, they ramped up their efforts locally, latching onto the most contentious political flash points and fighting them out in the streets of cities across America. Research into their events by Vice News found 114 uniformed Proud Boys appearances in seventy-three cities and twenty-four states in 2021. That's thought to be a fraction of the whole picture because the data relied only on photographic evidence posted to social media and confirmed sightings of Proud Boys in uniform. Even if the actual numbers are higher, they're clearly not in hiding.

Local chapters are mobilizing at a rapid clip, latching onto any and all Republican grievances and injecting the threat of violence into everyday civic events. They've been spotted at school board meetings where things like critical race theory and curriculum about racism and slavery are being discussed. They've appeared at antiabortion rallies at women's health clinics, acting as a menacing security force on the invite of an evangelical pastor. They're onstage at capitol buildings in California and Oregon and Florida, leading Trump rallies and supporting antivax demonstrations. They're running protests against gun reform and countering leftist events and holding recruitment rallies for themselves.

And of course, the violence remains. The research found incidents of physical violence among at least a fifth of the events Proud Boys attended in 2021, whether they were the hosts or the uninvited guests. Some of the events, especially those in the Pacific Northwest, have been among their bloodiest yet—including two in which gunfire erupted and another in which a Proud Boy was shot in the leg.

They're also working to sanitize their image, at the encouragement of Tarrio, via a handful of charitable events interspersed between the melees. Because business is conducted in uniform, these events almost have a mob-like quality. They organized Christmas toy drives for terminally ill children in New York, Washington State, and California, and their Connecticut chapter attempted to donate food to several local charities (along with pictures of themselves), but they were turned away. A director at one of the social services organizations they attempted to donate to in Hartford said, "We do not accept donations or gifts from groups whose values are so far misaligned with our agency's values."

They maintain the same support they've always had within the mainstream GOP. It's exceedingly difficult to get Republican lawmakers to admit on the record that Trump lost the 2020 election, let alone decry the actions of the January 6 rioters or the Proud Boys. And right-wing politicians and pundits have continued their support of the gang well beyond January 6. Roger Stone confirmed that he still has contact with the Proud Boys, especially Tarrio, whom he characterized to me as his "friend." A follow-up investigation into Stone's movements around the riots found that Tarrio was in an encrypted group chat on Stone's phone at the time titled "F.O.S.," or friends of Stone. The Multnomah County Republican Party even signed the gang as security to patrol outside their meeting at a church in Portland, Oregon, in May of 2021. They showed up in uniform with custom Proud Boys riot shields, and neighbors said they spent the evening shining flashlights in adjacent yards and harassing passersby.

This also suggests that they haven't shied away from their own political aspirations and that they're still confident about their image on the right. Indeed, Proud Boys are still running for office in 2022: in February, Proud Boy Jeffrey Erik Perrine filed paperwork to run for California Assembly against the Democratic incumbent Ken Cooley. This is a guy who was quoted at a Proud Boys rally in 2018, shouting into a megaphone that "all the illegals trying to jump over our border, we should be smashing their heads into the concrete."

What all this means is that the Proud Boys are working as designed. McInnes and Tarrio built them with a bit of autonomy and independence in mind, initially so they could deflect blame if it ever came their way. But now the local strategy is paying off in other ways, by enabling the local chapters to pick up where the national left off once leaders began to face charges.

Some of their chapters have become more radical in the power vacuum left by Tarrio's brief incarceration. Some of their biggest Telegram channels are filling up with Nazi imagery and accelerationist memes, while others are embracing QAnon and pushing conspiracy theories. The Soufan Center, a nonprofit extremism research center, raised an alarm about this lurch further right in 2020, after Trump's "stand back, stand by" comment, and there were concerns that the smaller, more outwardly racist factions within the gang might become unmanageable for the larger group.

"Whether the Proud Boys would carry out a significant act of terrorism remains unclear," The Soufan Center wrote with sobering prescience in October 2020. "Senior leaders within the group are likely to retain a more measured approach and continue to de-flect accusations of racism. However, it remains unclear whether these leaders can tamp down the rank-and-file members who re-tain an interest in civil war and white supremacist ideology."

Leadership didn't tamp down the Nazis, at least not in a way that had any impact. They're still around, and on Telegram today you'll still find Proud Boys channels featuring cut-and-dry ethnic cleansing rhetoric and swastikas. The bigotry still exists among everyday members, too. The leader of the Proud Boys chapter in Akron, Ohio, twenty-six-year-old Andrew Walls, was arrested early in 2022 after he was caught on video brawling in the street outside a bar. He turned toward a Black woman and pointed at her, saying "N—er bitch, shut your mouth," and then sucker-punched her square in the face.

There's been some shake-up within the ranks, however. Some leaders, worried about the consequences of January 6 or the rev-elations about Tarrio's work with the government, have declared full autonomy from the wider organization. That includes the Seattle chapter, where Nordean has been replaced as the head (though claims like this, that any member has been forcibly re-moved from their position or disavowed, are almost never true and should be taken with a handful of salt). All of this suggests that there are segments of the Proud Boys that want to go harder after January 6 rather than lay low—heading away from coop-eration with the police and toward the accelerationist right-wing movements that seek to foment civil war.

There's some fragmentation happening at the top ranks, too. This happens after almost every Proud Boys incident that leads to sweeping arrests or bad optics, like the GOP club attack in 2018. But the gang isn't rudderless. In fact, McInnes appears to be back on board to some degree. Leading up to the anniversary of the January 6 riots, McInnes began making appearances in his Proud Boys attire, something he hadn't done much publicly since stepping back in 2018. And when the anniversary of the Capitol riot came, he streamed a special on his most recent attempt at a podcast, *Get Off My Lawn*, featured on the floundering MAGA site he launched in 2019 called Censored.TV.

The episode was titled "The Meandering," in reference to the way McInnes described the January 6 riots, as opposed to "The Insurrection" or any number of other more accurate descriptors of the day. In it, McInnes wore a custom Proud Boys hoodie, complete with the *PB* and laurels, the "Uhuru" slogan on his arm, and his own name embroidered across the front. He said he was "wearing Proud Boys regalia to honor our brothers behind bars." He spent much of the episode interviewing charged Proud Boys and their lawyers.

It was a two-hour disinformation job with seemingly no purpose other than to sanitize the Proud Boys' name. But it was interesting to see McInnes at the helm again, making small admissions throughout that he'd been advising the Proud Boys over the previous year and a half, including, he claims, telling them not to go to the Capitol in the first place. In my follow-up interviews with both Tarrio and McInnes, the pair tiptoed around the subject of leadership entirely: McInnes said that "leadership will be announced by the club when they deem it appropriate to do so." And Tarrio, having just been temporarily released from prison, said he was stepping down as leader but sticking with the Miami chapter. The details of the Proud Boys' new structure, he said, would be kept under wraps. He and the other leaders agreed that when the press asks about the leadership, "we're just going to make something up on the spot. That's going to be a rule."

Tarrio's short initial stint in prison following his arrest on January 4 underscored another sobering fact about the Proud Boys going forward: many of the guys who saw jail time could be out before long, and they'd enjoy the same comforts within the Proud Boys and on the right wing that they had going in. This isn't a fundamentally different gang than the one that breached the halls of Congress, nor is it different from the violent troupe of men McInnes gathered back in 2016. If anything, the Proud Boys and hundreds of other defendants swept up in the federal case from that event have become martyrs on the right, doing their time for the good of a larger cause. And when they get out, they'll likely have access to more opportunities in right-wing media and politics, not less, for their crimes.

Even though the Proud Boys represent an immediate, physical threat, the danger extends far beyond their name. If they were disbanded tomorrow, or rebranded and changed their name to "The Ancient Order of the Orange Men" as Stone suggested, or they got launched into the sun via a MAGA rocket, the playbook that they created for the next extremist movement looking for legitimacy will remain.

The Proud Boys are the most successful political extremist group in the digital age. Where the Ku Klux Klan latched onto racist white anxiety and used raw numbers to overtake political jurisdictions, the Proud Boys were able to do a lot with a little online. The numbers didn't matter as much as the propaganda machine they controlled using people like McInnes and Tarrio, the relationships they built with the authoritarian party in power and the MAGA contingent, and their willingness to go to jail for the cause even when their actions weren't popular.

In a short time, they created a rubric by which any group could feasibly go from street-level fight gang to the neofascist enforcement arm of an entire political party or at least do some work to sanitize their image. The Proud Boys playbook will continue on without them, and other, lesser extremist groups are already starting to take cues, with varying degrees of success.

Patriot Front, an explicitly white nationalist group that wears matching outfits and white neck gaiters for anonymity, has begun to test the Proud Boys playbook for themselves. They pride themselves on their flash marches, in which they march through big cities and take propaganda videos of their unopposed numbers. Lately, though, that effort hasn't gone so well: they've been run out of several towns by locals before they can even begin their goose-stepping. But in January 2022, they tried the Proud Boys method and latched onto an abortion protest in Chicago, holding American flags and a banner that read "Strong Families Make Strong Nations." Abortion is decidedly not one of their normal platforms—they're pretty much set on a Nazi-esque white ethnostate at this point—but they wanted to benefit from the attention the antiabortion folks attracted. It didn't go well either, and even the bitterly hostile antiabortion protesters had to make fun of them until they left town. "You guys are an embarrassment," one person said. "Put the shields down!"

We can only hope others won't see more success.

———

THE PROUD BOYS' future looks bright as ever, and their impact will be felt with or without them going forward.

As it stands today, we're looking at a hardened national movement of violent men, banded together over bigoted and ultranationalist causes, and now, with years of experience under their belt, leading other groups of violent men into battle. They are revered and normalized by sections of the political right, they're running for office, they have cops in their ranks and standing in their defense, and they have a supportive network of media personalities to boost them and deflect for them. They know how to make money fast, and they know how to spend it for maximum impact, despite tireless efforts to get them kicked off every platform under the sun.

Even if their reputation as the toughest political street gang in the country tapers off, there will be other movements, ones that will look to their success and build off it. There's evidence that this is already happening, and the Proud Boys' close and comfy proximity to the other burgeoning extremist movements you've heard of, like the antigovernment Oath Keepers militia, suggests that their influence hasn't waned a bit.

But while their plans for the future are of urgent concern, equal consideration has to be given to the damage they've already done. They led a wave of political violence into this country and then worked to institutionalize it. Trump may have incited violence over the years and radicalized his voters, but it was the Proud Boys who carried it out in his name and gave his base tangible acts of violence to cheer on—and, eventually, join.

Experts and activists agree that the Proud Boys' greatest impact was not in their ability to make big violent events happen— though they certainly did plenty of that—but in their successful normalization of political violence and bigoted rhetoric, pulled from the fringes of the far right and into the mainstream. They are the reason why you can expect now, at any given American protest, not just cardboard signs and sit-ins, but men covered in football pads and makeshift armor, wielding the Stars and Stripes as weapons and beating any protester who dares try to confront them.

Their playbook is now part and parcel of the American political playbook on the right. And we don't seem to have a good answer for that yet, at least not at the government level. There are no statutes to save us from domestic extremism: local governments are torn over whether Proud Boys events and membership are constitutionally protected acts, and when communities and antifascist activists try to take matters into their own hands, they get the full force of federal and local law enforcement coming down on their head.

Most distressing of all is that the savage and harmful rallies they're involved in—the Unite the Right and Metropolitan Republican Club attacks and violent event after violent event—are being distorted and obfuscated by a colossal misinformation apparatus until they're remembered as bad hangovers in the Trump era or, worse, forgotten altogether.

These destabilizing extremist events, the rhetoric surrounding them, and the violence they carry move together like waves. The last wave crashed down on January 6, 2021. That movement pulled out to sea for a few months, but today energy is gathering once again, around the Proud Boys and their playbook. Left unopposed, a new wave is guaranteed to move ashore.

ACKNOWLEDGMENTS

This book, and so much of the journalism herein, wouldn't have happened without the exhaustive, thankless, and dangerous work of countless reporters, researchers, antifascist and antiracist activists, and weird nerds on the extremism beat. You're the reason we're able to identify and react to the threats of violence and intolerance around us, and we appreciate you. Thanks to Gersh Kuntzman, Buck Wolf, and Karen Mahabir, the editors who built me up as a reporter and enabled my wild ideas. To Sebastian Murdock and Christopher Mathias, my partners in the field and in the pub. To Dan Mandel, my agent, who believed in this project from day one and listened to me whine each day after. To Sam Raim, who edited this book, helped me find my voice, and introduced me to the Oxford comma. To Nicole Pasulka, my fact checker, who fixed my blunders and helped me slow down and think about the big picture. To David Neiwert, the father of this beat, an inspiration, and a damn good guy. To Juliet Jeske, for watching all those hours of *The Gavin McInnes Show* and raising the alarm. To so many sources who accepted the risk involved in talking to me, with the intention of minimizing harm to others.

To the Slags, my crew, for keeping my morale and sanity intact. To my parents, and especially my father, Bryan, who taught me compassion and supported my dreams. And to my wife, Tess, a light in the dark since the moment we met at that one extremist rally in Charlottesville, who not only cared for me as I wrote this book but did much of the journalistic work cited throughout— I literally could not have done this without you.

NOTES

Introduction: More Violence

3   **bruises on her arm:** Amita Kelly, "What We Know: Breitbart Reporter and Alleged Assault at a Trump Event," NPR, March 11, 2016, www .npr.org/2016/03/11/470080552/what-we-know-breitbart-reporter -and-trump-altercation.

3   **McInnes, staring slack-jawed:** *The Gavin McInnes Show*, episode 120, March 3, 2016.

8   **and by their own admission:** Gavin McInnes, "I Started This Gang Called the Proud Boys," Vic Berger, YouTube video, 2:23, October 16, 2018, www.youtube.com/watch?v=G95qjjQaNho.

8   **"drinking club with a patriotism problem":** Tom Dreisbach, "Conspiracy Charges Bring Proud Boys' History of Violence into Spotlight," NPR, April 9, 2021, www.npr.org/2021/04/09/985104612/conspiracy -charges-bring-proud-boys-history-of-violence-into-spotlight.

9   **Lauren Witzke:** Esteban Parra and Brittany Horn, "Delaware US Senate Candidate Thanks Proud Boys for Providing Free Security at Rally," *Delaware News Journal* (Wilmington, DE), October 1, 2020, www.delawareonline.com/story/news/2020/10/01/witzke-thanks -proud-boys-providing-free-security-rally/5878156002/.

10   **"legitimate political discourse":** Jonathan Weisman and Reid J. Epstein, "G.O.P. Declares Jan. 6 Attack 'Legitimate Political Discourse,'" *New York Times*, February 4, 2022, www.nytimes.com/2022/02/04 /us/politics/republicans-jan-6-cheney-censure.html.

Chapter 1: The Gavin McInnes Show

13   **He'd already sat through performances:** McInnes described these and other details of this anecdote in a follow-up interview with me over email, August 3, 2021.

13   **"Fuckin' musicals, man":** *The Gavin McInnes Show*, episode 58, December 14, 2015.

14   **Hasidic Jews and Puerto Ricans:** Gentrification in NYC: Rosenberg 2018, "Williamsburg," https://eportfolios.macaulay.cuny.edu/genyc /williamsburg/.

15   **available to stream online:** The availability changes regularly, though, as McInnes gets kicked off platforms and joins new ones. Compound Media, which hosted the original *Gavin McInnes Show,* appears to have scrubbed many of McInnes' episodes during the writing of this book.

16   **"Fighting solves everything":** *The Gavin McInnes Show*, episode 130, April 4, 2016.

17   **Gavin Miles McInnes was born:** Adam Leith Gollner, "The Secret History of Gavin McInnes," *Vanity Fair*, June 29, 2021, www .vanityfair.com/news/2021/06/the-secret-history-of-gavin-mcinnes.

17   **He studied English:** Alexandra Molotkow, "Giving Offence," *The Walrus*, July 22, 2021, https://thewalrus.ca/giving-offence/.

18   **Smith wasn't far behind:** Lucas Wisenthal and Sheldon Gordon, "From Welfare to Media Empire," *McGill News*, https://mcgillnews .mcgill.ca/s/1762/news/interior.aspx?sid=1762&gid=2&pgid=933.

18   **"homeless golf pirate":** Vice staff, "Dos & Don'ts," *Vice*, December 31, 2005, www.vice.com/en/article/mv9jyn/dos-donts-v13n1.

19   **Paris Hilton and Britney Spears:** Constance Grady, "The Bubblegum Misogyny of 2000s Pop Culture," Vox, May 25, 2021, www.vox .com/culture/22350286/2000s-pop-culture-misogyny-britney-spears -janet-jackson-whitney-houston-monica-lewinsky.

19   **"The Vice Guide to Picking Up Chicks":** Gavin McInnes, "The Vice Guide to Picking Up Chicks," *Vice*, December 1, 2005, https://archive .ph/YunI2.

19   ***Vice*'s "Sex Issue":** "The Sex Issue," *Vice,* December 2005, www.vice .com/da/topic/the-sex-issue.

20   **Advertisers grew uncomfortable:** Reeves Wiedeman, "A Company Built on a Bluff," *New York*, June 10, 2018, https://nymag.com/intelligencer /2018/06/inside-vice-media-shane-smith.html.

20   **a deal with Disney:** Peter Kafka, "Disney Put More Than $400 Million into Vice Media. Now It Says That Investment Is Worthless," Vox, May 8, 2019, www.vox.com/recode/2019/5/8/18537617/disney-vice -write-off-400-million.

20   **covered the Proud Boys and McInnes critically:** Full disclosure, one of the reporters covering the gang for Vice News is my kickass wife, Tess Owen, who wasn't interviewed for this book but whose works are cited throughout.

21   **a *Vice* competitor:** Foster Kamer, "Vice vs. Street Carnage: Hipster Media's Battle Produces Draconian Non-Competes," Gawker, September 12, 2009, www.gawker.com/5358130/vice-vs-street-carnage -hipster-medias-battle-produces-draconian-non-competes.

21   **an abhorrent diatribe:** Gavin McInnes, "Transphobia Is Perfectly Natural," Thought Catalog, 2014, https://archive.ph/jACvk.

22   **racist meltdown on Twitter:** Aleksander Chan, "SiriusXM Host Claims 'Cuntrag' Assaulted Him in Racist Twitter Rant," Gawker, July 2, 2014, www.gawker.com/siriusxm-host-claims-cuntrag-assaulted-him -in-racist-1599491744.

22   **Cumia's basement:** Claudine Zap, "Radio Personality Anthony Cumia of 'Opie and Anthony' Fame Selling $3.1M NY Home," Realtor .com, October 20, 2020, www.realtor.com/news/celebrity-real-estate /anthony-cumia-selling-new-york-home/.

22   **the Proud Boys' foundation:** *The Gavin McInnes Show*, episode 1, June 14, 2015.

23   **so-called identitarian groups in Europe:** Hélène Barthélemy, "How to Write History Like an Identitarian," Southern Poverty Law Center, February 14, 2018, www.splcenter.org/hatewatch/2018/02/14/how -write-history-identitarian.

24   **On one episode just two months into the show:** *The Gavin McInnes Show*, episode 13, August 4, 2015.

25   **a source close to the company:** This source spoke to me on condition of anonymity.

25   **viewers started showing up to drink:** Alan Feuer, "Proud Boys Founder: How He Went from Brooklyn Hipster to Far-Right Provocateur," *New York Times*, October 16, 2018, www.nytimes.com/2018/10/16 /nyregion/proud-boys-gavin-mcinnes.html.

26   **the foundation for his concept of Western chauvinism:** I asked McInnes what he considered his legacy to be as it related to the Proud Boys, and he offered a passage from *Death of the West*, which he said helped him "remind men that masculinity is not toxic." The passage read in part: "In the story of slavery and the slave trade, Western Man was among the many villains, but Western Man was also the only hero. For the West did not invent slavery, but it alone abolished slavery."

26   **"pioneer of the vision that Trump ran on":** Tim Alberta, "'The Ideas Made It, but I Didn't,'" May–June 2017, Politico, www.politico.com /magazine/story/2017/04/22/pat-buchanan-trump-president-history -profile-215042/.

26   **"unrepentant bigot":** Anti-Defamation League, "Patrick Buchanan: Unrepentant Bigot," https://www.adl.org/resources/profiles/patrick -buchanan-unrepentant-bigot.

26   **blog post back in 2002:** Jonah Goldberg, "Killing Whitey," *National Review*, February 25, 2002, www.nationalreview.com/2002/02/killing -whitey-jonah-goldberg/.

27   **"Barack Obama":** *The Gavin McInnes Show*, episode 145, May 12, 2016.

27   **"n—er":** Though the Proud Boys are comfortable using this word in full, I am not, and after discussions with multiple authors and sources on the matter, I've decided to write it this way throughout the book.

27   **He referred to trans people as:** *The Gavin McInnes Show*, episode 88, February 3, 2016.

27   **"It's not wrong, big fucking deal!":** *The Gavin McInnes Show*, episode 250, November 22, 2016.

27   **the fourteen words:** Vic Berger, Twitter, November 4, 2019, https:// twitter.com/VicBergerIV/status/1191403799144849408.

28   **He called them the Proud Boys:** *The Gavin McInnes Show*, episode 153, May 26, 2016.

29   **Amy Winehouse:** Lauren Milligan, "Winehouse Wears," *Vogue*, March 11, 2010, www.vogue.co.uk/article/amy-winehouse-for-fred-perry.

29   **By the '80s, the Fred Perry polo had crossed the pond:** Hayley Spencer, "A Brief History of the Fred Perry Polo Shirt and Its Complicated Connections to Hate Groups," The Independent, September 29, 2020, www.independent.co.uk/life-style/fashion/fred-perry-proud-boys-far-right-british-brand-history-b696548.html.

29   **he threatened to sue the reporter:** Zoë Beery, "How Fred Perry Polos Came to Symbolize Hate," The Outline, June 20, 2017, https://theoutline.com/post/1760/fred-perry-polo-skinheads.

29   **a Proud Boys logo concept:** *The Gavin McInnes Show,* episode 162, June 13, 2016.

29   **the company stopped selling its black-and-yellow polo:** Fred Perry, "Proud Boys Statement," news release, 2020, https://archive.ph/ukokv.

30   **"subset of the alt-right":** *The Gavin McInnes Show,* episode 160, June 8, 2016.

30   **The term, coined by Richard Spencer:** "Alt-Right," Southern Poverty Law Center, www.splcenter.org/fighting-hate/extremist-files/ideology/alt-right.

31   **"the Jewish Question":** "The 'Jewish Question,'" US Holocaust Memorial Museum, Holocaust Encyclopedia, https://encyclopedia.ushmm.org/content/en/article/the-jewish-question.

32   **Here are a few highlights:** Juliet Jeske, "How a Crazy Cat Lady Took on the Proud Boys," Juliet Jeske blog, March 23, 2020, https://julietjeskeblog.com/2020/03/how-a-crazy-cat-lady-took-down-the-proud-boys/.

32   **"we will assassinate you":** McInnes responded to a number of the quotes in this section, claiming that they'd been cherry-picked and "lacked context." To this particular quote, he responded in part: "Silly hyperbole that is regularly encouraged on the left."

32   **"Fighting solves everything":** McInnes' response: "This is a common saying among blue-collar Americans, and you should be embarrassed you're not familiar with it."

33   **"If you're wearing a MAGA hat. . . . Him":** McInnes' response, in part: "This was from a rally where our friend . . . was approached by an antifa member who was clearly planning an ambush. . . . I was explaining how you shouldn't fall for this."

33   **racist attacks:** Andy Campbell, "Proud Boys Leader Yells Racist Slurs Before Attacking Black Woman," HuffPost, February 28, 2022, www

.huffpost.com/entry/andrew-walls-proud-boys-assault-video_n_621c 87a3e4b0afc668c2eda2.

33   **harassment campaigns against their ideological opponents:** Anna Orso, "Philadelphia Man Suspected of Ties to the Proud Boys Arrested on Harassment Charges," *Philadelphia Inquirer*, March 4, 2021, www.inquirer.com/news/philadelphia-proud-boys-harassment -krasner-district-attorney-20210304.html.

33   **death threats lodged against government officials:** Eduardo Medina, "Man Pleads Guilty to Threatening to Kill Newly Elected U.S. Senator," *New York Times*, August 16, 2021, www.nytimes.com/2021 /08/16/us/capitol-riot-raphael-warnock.html.

33   **at least one assassination plot:** Pilar Melendez and Emma Tucker, "Former 'Proud Boys' Lawyer Used Nationalist Group in Alleged Plot to Assassinate Rival: Court Docs," The Daily Beast, April 15, 2020, www.thedailybeast.com/former-proud-boys-lawyer-jason-lee -van-dyke-allegedly-plotted-assassination-of-rival-court-docs-say.

34   **formally labeled as a terrorist organization:** Ian Austen, "Canada Formally Declares Proud Boys a Terrorist Group," *New York Times*, February 3, 2021, www.nytimes.com/2021/02/03/world/canada /canada-proud-boys-terror-group.html.

34   **who ascended the ranks through acts of Catholic ministry:** Andrew Butler, "Who Are the Fourth Degree Knights?," Knights of Columbus, November 8, 2019, www.kofc.org/en/news-room/articles/who-are -the-4th-degree-knights.html.

34   **McInnes introduced them to the outside world in a blog post:** Gavin McInnes, "Introducing: The Proud Boys," Taki's Magazine, September 15, 2016, www.takimag.com/article/introducing_the_proud_boys _gavin_mcinnes/.

35   **the rantings of a neo-Nazi:** Richard Spencer, Taki's Magazine, www .takimag.com/contributor/richardspencer/69/.

35   **amid a racist rant about justified violence:** *The Gavin McInnes Show,* episode 128, April 13, 2016.

36   **the gang boasts 157 active chapters:** Tess Owen, "The Proud Boys Changed Tactics After Jan. 6. We Tracked Their Activity," Vice News, January 5, 2022, www.vice.com/en/article/z3n338/what-the-proud -boys-did-after-jan-6.

36   **"Get 'em out of here!":** Eliott McLaughlin, "It's Plausible Trump Incited Violence, Federal Judge Rules in OK'ing Lawsuit," CNN, April 3, 2017, www.cnn.com/2017/04/02/politics/donald-trump -lawsuit-incite-violence-kentucky-rally/index.html.

36   **Inciting violence became one of his recurring gags:** Amanda Terkel, "Trump Has Incited Violence All Along. The GOP Just Didn't Care until Now," HuffPost, January 11, 2021, www.huffpost.com/entry /trump-incite-violence-gop_n_5ffa6f71c5b63642b6fc7826.

37   **in a story covering Trump's inaugural celebration:** Andrew Marantz, "Trump Supporters at the Deploraball," *New Yorker*, January 29, 2017, www.newyorker.com/magazine/2017/02/06/trump-supporters -at-the-deploraball.

37   **beginning in February 2017:** Colleen Long, "11 Arrests at NYU Protest over Speech by 'Proud Boys' Leader," Associated Press, February 3, 2017, https://apnews.com/article/964cc747d67e4ae6863b07acb3c52539.

37   **"And we beat the crap out of them":** Rich Lowry, "The Poisonous Allure of Right-Wing Violence," *National Review*, October 19, 2018, www .nationalreview.com/2018/10/gavin-mcinnes-proud-boys-poisonous -violence/.

38   **storm and attack the community:** Rick Rojas, "They Created a Muslim Enclave in Upstate N.Y. Then Came the Online Conspiracies," *New York Times*, January 28, 2019, www.nytimes.com/2019/01/28 /nyregion/islamberg-ny-attack-plot.html.

Chapter 2: How to Build a Street Gang

42   **Chace is not quite like other recruits:** Chace isn't his real name; he spoke on condition of anonymity out of fear for his safety. He demonstrated his membership and the authenticity of his story with a pile of internal documentation; he provided videos of his initiation ceremonies and photo and video evidence of his association with various Proud Boys and the events they attended together, as well as a trove of chat logs only accessible by vetted members. The claims he and other infiltrators make in this book have been vetted for accuracy. Some names have been changed and small bits of information—like which New York State chapter Chace belongs to—have been omitted to protect sources' identities. But the facts presented have been verified

using journalistic standards. Conversely, unverified claims have either been thrown out or clearly identified as such.

45   **subjects newbies to a hazing ritual:** Will Carless, "They Joined the Wisconsin Proud Boys Looking for Brotherhood. They Found Racism, Bullying and Antisemitism," *USA Today*, June 21, 2021, www .usatoday.com/story/news/nation/2021/06/21/proud-boys -recruitment-targets-men-looking-community/7452805002/?gnt-cfr=1.

48   **"No wanks is a gift from the Lord":** *The Gavin McInnes Show,* episode 13, August 4, 2015.

48   **several highly disputed works:** Justin Lehmiller, "Can Abstaining from Masturbation Increase Testosterone?," *Sex & Psychology*, January 24, 2020, www.sexandpsychology.com/blog/2020/1/24/can -abstaining-from-masturbation-increase-testosterone/.

48   **"no wanks is going on forever":** *The Gavin McInnes Show*, episode 169, June 23, 2016.

49   **McInnes spelled it out during an appearance on** *The Joe Rogan Experience*: *The Joe Rogan Experience*, episode 920, February 22, 2017, https://mixes.cloud/TheJoeRoganExperience/920-gavin-mcinnes/.

49   **so toxic that it was removed from Spotify:** Todd Spangler, "Joe Rogan Podcast Comes to Spotify, but It's Missing His Episodes with Far- Right Figures," *Variety*, September 2, 2020, https://variety.com/2020 /digital/news/joe-rogan-podcast-comes-to-spotify-but-its-missing -episodes-with-far-right-guests-1234757569/.

50   **One particularly violent member named Alan Swinney:** Multnomah County District Attorney, "Alan Swinney Arrested, Charged for Recent Criminal Conduct in Downtown," news release, September 30, 2020, www.mcda.us/index.php/news/alan-swinney-arrested-charged -for-recent-criminal-conduct-in-downtown.

50   **"I got my 4th degree again today":** WANaziWatch, Twitter, July 5, 2020, https://twitter.com/WANaziWatch/status/1279651728141332480.

52   **first on Facebook, until the platform. . . dubbed them as a hate organization:** Taylor Hatmaker, "Facebook Bans the Proud Boys, Cutting the Group Off from Its Main Recruitment Platform," TechCrunch, October 30, 2018, https://techcrunch.com/2018/10/30 /facebook-proud-boys-mcinnes-kicked-off/.

53   **Proud Boys add their threatening presence to antivaccine gatherings:** Tess Owen, "The Proud Boys Changed Tactics After Jan. 6. We

Tracked Their Activity," Vice News, January 5, 2022, www.vice.com
/en/article/z3n338/what-the-proud-boys-did-after-jan-6.

55   **a vicious gang assault outside a political event back in 2018:** Christopher Mathias, "The Proud Boys, the GOP and 'the Fascist Creep,'"
HuffPost, October 17, 2018, www.huffpost.com/entry/proud-boys
-republican-party-fascist-creep_n_5bc7b37de4b055bc947d2a8c.

55   **fresh off his own arrest:** Randy Ireland, "Was Arrested in Herald
Square, NYC!," December 8, 2021, https://condemnedusa.org/?p=127.

Chapter 3: Anatomy of a Proud Boy

60   **Patriot Prayer—their smaller affiliate group:** "Joey Gibson Vows
Loyalty to 'Proud Boys' at Seattle Rally," Southern Poverty Law Center,
May 18, 2018.

61   **invited Nordean onto his show two weeks later:** InfoWars, "Rufio
Panman: Patriot Who Knocked Out Masked, Antifa Commie Thug
Joins InfoWars Live," Get It Right Media, YouTube video, 29:34,
July 7, 2018, www.youtube.com/watch?v=2orRPKbRl4M.

62   **As membership skyrocketed, so did their nationwide chapters:** David
Kirkpatrick and Alan Feuer, "Police Shrugged Off the Proud Boys,
Until They Attacked the Capitol," *New York Times*, August 23, 2021,
www.nytimes.com/2021/03/14/us/proud-boys-law-enforcement
.html.

63   **flagpoles made of wood and PVC piping and metal:** Katie Shepherd,
"Portland Police Declare a Riot After Right-Wing Marchers Begin
Beating Antifascists with Flag Poles," *Willamette Week* (Portland,
OR), June 30, 2018, www.wweek.com/news/2018/06/30/portland
-police-declare-a-riot-after-right-wing-marchers-begin-beating
-antifascists-with-flag-poles/.

63   **Some shouted racial slurs at counterdemonstrators:** PNWAWC,
Twitter, July 4, 2018, https://mobile.twitter.com/PNWAWC/status
/1014677823515123712.

63   **"smashed into the concrete":** Jason Wilson, "Who Are the Proud
Boys, 'Western Chauvinists' Involved in Political Violence?,"
Guardian (Manchester, UK), July 14, 2018, www.theguardian.com
/world/2018/jul/14/proud-boys-far-right-portland-oregon.

64   **Ross wrote in a first-person account:** Alexander Reid Ross, "In
Portland, I Witnessed the Violence of White Pride in Trump's

America," *Haaretz*, July 5, 2018, www.haaretz.com/jewish/.premium
-in-portland-i-witnessed-the-violence-of-white-pride-in-trump-s
-america-1.6225102.

64   **revoked Gibson's permits for the event:** Eder Campuzano, "Portland
Police Revoke Permit, Declare Riot as Protesters Clash Downtown,"
Oregonian (Portland, OR), June 30, 2018, www.oregonlive.com
/portland/2018/06/portland_police_revoke_permit.html.

65   **tweeted journalist Shane Burley:** Shane Burley, Twitter, June 30, 2018,
https://twitter.com/shane_burley1/status/1013253307089879040.

65   **"They fucked around. They found out":** "Proud Boy of the Week:
Rufio Panman, Battle in Portland," OfficialProudBoys.com, July 2,
2018, https://archive.ph/CqQjg.

65   **"The greatest punch in the history of Trump's presidency":** Shane
Dixon Kavanaugh, "Patriot Prayer, Antifa to Face Off in Portland
One Month After Brutal Riot," *Oregonian* (Portland, OR), August 2,
2018, www.oregonlive.com/portland/2018/08/patriot_prayer_antifa
_to_face.html.

66   **He wanted to be a US Navy SEAL:** America's Navy, "Navy SEAL,"
www.navy.com/seals.

67   **discharged after just five weeks:** Richard Read, "He Led the Proud
Boys in the Capitol Riot, Shaming His Town," *Los Angeles Times*,
May 16, 2021, www.latimes.com/world-nation/story/2021-05-16
/proud-boys-father-nordean.

67   **posting typo-laden screeds:** Judy Nordean, 2012, www.document
cloud.org/documents/20709236-judy-nordean-church-tweet
?responsive=1&title=1.

67   **Democrats and antifa were in cahoots with ISIS:** Ginger Gibson
and Steve Holland, "Trump Calls Obama, Clinton Islamic State
'Co-Founders,' Draws Rebuke," Reuters, August 11, 2016, www
.reuters.com/article/us-usa-election-trump/trump-calls-obama-clinton
-islamic-state-co-founders-draws-rebuke-idUSKCN10M146.

68   **His streetwear evolved:** Rose City Antifa, "Pacific Northwest
Proud Boys—Robert Zerfing, Travis Nugent, Caleb Stevens, Ethan
Nordean," June 7, 2018, https://rosecityantifa.org/articles/pb-1/.

68   **after he attacked a man on the sidewalk:** Tess Riski, "Proud Boy
Tusitala 'Tiny' Toese Will Be Released Early from Jail Next Week,"
Willamette Week (Portland, OR), December 16, 2020, www.wweek

.com/news/courts/2020/12/16/tusitala-tiny-toese-will-be-released-early
-from-jail-next-week-after-violating-probation-for-assault-charges.

69   **"Battle for Berkeley":** Ryan Lenz, "The Battle for Berkeley: In the
      Name of Freedom of Speech, the Radical Right Is Circling the Ivory
      Tower to Ensure a Voice for the Alt-Right," Southern Poverty Law
      Center, May 1, 2017, www.splcenter.org/hatewatch/2017/05/01
      /battle-berkeley-name-freedom-speech-radical-right-circling
      -ivory-tower-ensure-voice-alt.

69   **a hate group designation:** "Proud Boys," Southern Poverty Law Center,
      www.splcenter.org/fighting-hate/extremist-files/group/proud-boys.

69   **Ethan teamed up with a police officer:** Lewis Kamb, "Police Officer
      Partnered in Businesses with Auburn-Area Proud Boy Charged in
      Capitol Siege, Records Show," *Seattle Times*, February 11, 2021,
      www.seattletimes.com/seattle-news/police-officer-partnered-in
      -businesses-with-auburn-area-proud-boy-charged-in-capitol-siege
      -records-show/.

70   **largely cleared of wrongdoing:** Lewis Kamb, "Police Panel Clears
      Renton Officer Who Partnered in Businesses with a Proud Boys
      Leader," *Seattle Times*, May 7, 2021, www.seattletimes.com/seattle
      -news/police-panel-clears-renton-officer-who-partnered-in
      -businesses-with-a-proud-boys-leader/.

71   **Mike Nordean announced that he'd fired Ethan:** Jack Mayne, "Owner
      of Wally's Says 'Not Easy' to Disavow Son's Involvement with 'Proud
      Boys' Extremist Group," Waterland Blog, June 23, 2020, https://
      waterlandblog.com/2020/06/23/owner-of-wallys-says-not-easy-to
      -disavow-sons-involvement-with-proud-boys-extremist-group/.

72   **joined their ranks with hopes of fighting antifa:** Spencer Hsu,
      "Current, Former Police Officers Charged in New Proud Boys
      Indictment in Capitol Riot," *Washington Post*, July 16, 2021,
      www.washingtonpost.com/local/legal-issues/proud-boys-police
      -indictment-florida/2021/07/16/1fdbe642-e5a4-11eb-8aa5
      -5662858b696e_story.html.

72   **Proud Boys leader Joe Biggs screamed:** David Kirkpatrick and Alan
      Feuer, "Police Shrugged Off the Proud Boys, Until They Attacked
      the Capitol," *New York Times*, August 23, 2021, www.nytimes
      .com/2021/03/14/us/proud-boys-law-enforcement.html.

73   **hundreds more were injured, including 140 officers:** Michael Schmidt
      and Luke Broadwater, "Officers' Injuries, Including Concussions,

Show Scope of Violence at Capitol Riot," *New York Times*, February 11, 2021, www.nytimes.com/2021/02/11/us/politics/capitol-riot -police-officer-injuries.html.

74   **a disavowal of his son to the Wally's Chowder House website:** Mike Nordean, "A Message from Mike Nordean, Owner of Wally's Restaurants," 2021, http://web.archive.org/web/20210204011925 /http:/wallysrestaurants.com/statement-from-mike-nordean.

74   **posted to the right-wing donation site Our Freedom Funding:** "Financial Aid for Ethan Nordean (Rufio)," Our Freedom Funding, March 29, 2021, www.ourfreedomfunding.com/campaign/23 /financial-aid-for-ethan-nordean-rufio.

75   **Tucker Carlson, for example:** Bill McCarthy, "Tucker Carlson's 'Patriot Purge' Film on Jan. 6 Is Full of Falsehoods, Conspiracy Theories," PolitiFact, November 5, 2021, www.politifact.com/article /2021/nov/05/tucker-carlsons-patriot-purge-film-jan-6-full-fals/.

75   **Republican voters believe the lies:** James Oliphant and Chris Kahn, "Half of Republicans Believe False Accounts of Deadly U.S. Capitol Riot," Reuters, April 5, 2021, www.reuters.com/article/us-usa -politics-disinformation/half-of-republicans-believe-false-accounts -of-deadly-u-s-capitol-riot-reuters-ipsos-poll-idUSKBN2BS0RZ.

Chapter 4: Portland, the Political War Zone

77   **unprecedented surge in street-level mobilizations:** Cassie Miller and Howard Graves, "When the 'Alt-Right' Hit the Streets: Far-Right Political Rallies in the Trump Era," Southern Poverty Law Center, August 10, 2020, www.splcenter.org/20200810/when-alt-right-hit -streets-far-right-political-rallies-trump-era.

77   **an explosion of right-wing violence:** Robert O'Harrow Jr., Andrew Ba Tran, and Derek Hawkins, "The Rise of Domestic Extremism in America," *Washington Post*, April 12, 2021, www.washingtonpost .com/investigations/interactive/2021/domestic-terrorism-data/.

78   **deploying federal agents to do battle against protesters:** Steve Vladeck, "Are the Trump Administration's Actions in Portland Legal? Are They Constitutional?," *Washington Post*, July 25, 2020, www .washingtonpost.com/politics/2020/07/25/are-trump-administrations -actions-portland-legal-are-they-constitutional/.

78   **"Little Beirut":** John Locanthi, "Big Trouble in Little Beirut," *Willamette Week* (Portland, OR), May 4, 2016, www.wweek.com /culture/2016/05/04/big-trouble-in-little-beirut/.

79   **Ruckus Society hung a gigantic banner:** Gregory Scruggs, "What the 'Battle of Seattle' Means 20 Years Later," Bloomberg, November 29, 2019, www.bloomberg.com/news/articles/2019-11-29/what-seattle -s-wto-protests-mean-20-years-later.

80   **"They say, 'No, this is soup for my family'":** Luke Mogelson, "In the Streets with Antifa," *New Yorker*, October 25, 2020, www.newyorker .com/magazine/2020/11/02/trump-antifa-movement-portland.

81   **Hillary Clinton over Donald Trump by just 316 votes:** "November 8, 2016, General Election," Clark County, WA, https://results.vote .wa.gov/results/20161108/clark/.

81   **greenest and most eco-friendly cities in the nation:** "Portland— Sustainable City Leader in the United States," Green City Times, www.greencitytimes.com/portland/.

82   **whitest major city in America:** Patrick McDonnell and Melissa Etehad, "Portland, America's 'Whitest' Big City, Is an Unlikely Hub of Black Lives Matter," *Los Angeles Times*, August 2, 2020, www .latimes.com/world-nation/story/2020-08-02/portland-americas -whitest-big-city-unlikely-hub-of-black-lives-matter.

82   **quite literally as a white utopia:** Matt Novak, "Oregon Was Founded as a Racist Utopia," Gizmodo, January 21, 2015, https://gizmodo .com/oregon-was-founded-as-a-racist-utopia-1539567040.

82   **a data study on the local Black community:** Lisa K. Bates, Ann Curry- Stevens, and Coalition of Communities of Color, "The African- American Community in Multnomah County: An Unsettling Profile," School of Social Work, Portland State University, 2014.

83   **new proliferation of Confederate flags:** Emily Cureton Cook, "Central Oregonians Grapple with Racist Symbols in a Still Affordable Town," Oregon Public Broadcasting, June 9, 2021, www.opb.org /article/2021/06/09/central-oregonians-grapple-with-racist-symbols -in-a-still-affordable-town/.

83   **the founder of the Aryan Nations:** "Richard Butler," Southern Poverty Law Center, www.splcenter.org/fighting-hate/extremist-files /individual/richard-butler.

84   **neo-Nazis and even Klansmen:** Sergio Olmos, "Patriot Prayer—the New Face of 'Nativist Bigotry,'" *Columbian* (Vancouver, WA), January 30, 2020, www.columbian.com/news/2020/jan/30/patriot-prayer-the-new-face-of-nativist-bigotry/.

84   **Gibson held one of Patriot Prayer's first big rallies:** Corey Pein, "The Man Accused of MAX Double Murder Is a Portland White Supremacist Who Delivered Nazi Salutes and Racial Slurs at a 'Free Speech' Rally Last Month," *Willamette Week* (Portland, OR), May 27, 2017, www.wweek.com/news/2017/05/27/the-man-accused-of-max-double-murder-is-a-portland-white-supremacist-who-delivered-nazi-salutes-and-racial-slurs-at-a-free-speech-rally-last-month/.

85   **Fletcher survived a stab wound to the neck:** Tess Riski and Latisha Jensen, "Read the Statement of Micah Fletcher, Who Survived Portland's MAX Stabbings," *Willamette Week* (Portland, OR), July 1, 2020, www.wweek.com/news/courts/2020/07/01/read-the-statement-of-micah-fletcher-who-survived-portlands-max-stabbings/.

86   **including Proud Boys in their Fred Perrys:** Jason Wilson, "'Alt-Right' Portland Rally Sees Skirmishes with Counter-Protesters," *Guardian* (Manchester, UK), June 4, 2017, www.theguardian.com/us-news/2017/jun/04/portland-oregon-alt-right-rally-antifa.

86   **plea deal on a felony weapons charge:** Emilie Raguso, "Kyle 'Based Stickman' Chapman Takes Felony Plea Deal in Berkeley Weapons Case," *Berkeleyside*, September 24, 2019, www.berkeleyside.org/2019/09/24/kyle-based-stickman-takes-felony-plea-deal-in-berkeley-weapons-case.

86   **Fraternal Order of the Alt-Knights:** "Fraternal Order of Alt-Knights (FOAK)," Southern Poverty Law Center, www.splcenter.org/fighting-hate/extremist-files/group/fraternal-order-alt-knights-foak.

89   **"protests" against "leftist violence":** David Neiwert, "'Patriot' Rally Trolls Portland's Left for Violence, but Only Smatterings Occur," Southern Poverty Law Center, August 8, 2017, www.splcenter.org/hatewatch/2017/08/07/patriot-rally-trolls-portlands-left-violence-only-smatterings-occur.

89   **winning just 2 percent of the primary vote:** "Joey Gibson—Elections," 2018, https://ballotpedia.org/Joey_Gibson.

89   **a rerun of the Unite the Right neo-Nazi rallies:** Christopher Mathias, "Portland's Patriot Prayer Rally Could Be Most Violent Since Charlottesville, Activists Say," HuffPost, August 3, 2018, www

.huffpost.com/entry/portland-patriot-prayer-proud-boys-rally_n_5b 646217e4b0de86f4a0ba04.

90   **police were again described as the catalysts for violence:** Christopher Mathias and Andy Campbell, "Violent Proto-Fascists Came to Portland. The Police Went After the Anti-Fascists," HuffPost, August 5, 2018, www.huffpost.com/entry/portland-patriot-prayer-proud -boys-police-antifascists_n_5b668b7de4b0de86f4a22faf.

91   **possession of long rifles:** Jim Ryan, "What We Know About Patriot Prayer Gun Cache Found Before Portland Protest," *Oregonian* (Portland, OR), August 29, 2019, www.oregonlive.com/news/erry -2018/10/7d2bb561246607/what-we-know-about-patriot-pra .html.

91   **Patriot Prayer members to march:** Katie Shepherd and Mike Bivins, "Portland Streets Descend into Bedlam, Again, as Proud Boys and Antifascists Maul Each Other," *Willamette Week* (Portland, OR), October 13, 2018, www.wweek.com/news/courts/2018/10/13/portland -streets-descend-into-bedlam-again-as-proud-boys-and-antifascists -maul-each-other/.

92   **They reported seeing knives, firearms, hard knuckle gloves:** Shane Dixon Kavanaugh, "Bear Spray, Bloody Brawls at Patriot Prayer 'Law and Order' March in Portland," *Oregonian* (Portland, OR), October 13, 2018, www.oregonlive.com/portland/2018/10/patriot _prayer_flash_march_cal.html.

92   **five minutes beyond the moment he uttered his final words:** Sara B., Twitter, April 8, 2021, https://twitter.com/sara_bee/status/138018 2543211843584.

93   **in an interview with the *New York Times*:** Charlie Warzel, "50 Nights of Unrest in Portland," *New York Times*, July 17, 2020, www.nytimes.com /2020/07/17/opinion/portland-protests-federal-agents.html.

93   **caused irregularities in the menstrual cycles of dozens of people:** Catalina Gaitán, "New Study Shows Almost All People Who Responded to Survey Reported Harmful Effects of Tear Gas at Portland Protests," *Oregonian* (Portland, OR), April 27, 2021, www .oregonlive.com/health/2021/04/new-study-shows-almost-all -people-who-responded-to-survey-reported-harmful-effects-of -tear-gas-at-portland-protests.html.

93   **the Rodney King riots:** Emily Badger, "How Trump's Use of Federal Forces in Cities Differs from Past Presidents," *New York Times*,

July 23, 2020, www.nytimes.com/2020/07/23/upshot/trump-portland
.html.

94   **Berkeley denied permits:** Emilie Raguso, "Berkeley Denies 3
Rally Permits for Sunday," *Berkeleyside*, August 24, 2017, www
.berkeleyside.org/2017/08/24/berkeley-denies-3-rally-permits-sunday.

94   **it was community onlookers, not police:** Shane Burley, "Philadelphia
Bystanders Ran the Patriot Front Out of Town. It Won't Be the Last
Time," NBC News, July 7, 2021, www.nbcnews.com/think/opinion
/philadelphia-bystanders-ran-patriot-front-out-town-it-won-t-ncna
1273283.

94   **the president called him a "fool":** John Bacon and Jordan Culver,
"Oregon Gov. Kate Brown Announces Peace Plan for Portland
After Fatal Shooting of 'Patriot Prayer' Backer, Months of Protests,"
USA Today, August 30, 2020, www.usatoday.com/story/news/nation
/2020/08/30/portland-mayor-ted-wheeler-ripped-trump-1-dead-after
-protests/5673495002/.

95   **issue with federal parkland in town:** Dakin Andone and Darran
Simon, "Portland Mayor Asks Feds to Stop 'Alt-Right' Rallies," CNN,
May 30, 2017, www.cnn.com/2017/05/29/us/portland-scheduled
-demonstrations/index.html.

95   **violent plots in chat logs:** Robert Evans and Jason Wilson, "Patriot
Coalition: Leaked Messages Show Far-Right Group's Plans for
Portland Violence," Bellingcat, September 23, 2020, www.bellingcat
.com/news/2020/09/23/patriot-coalition-far-right-chat-logs
-violence/.

95   **Wheeler just seems kind of fed up with it all:** Wheeler and four
different members of his staff refused to grant repeated requests for
an interview with him for this book, over the course of more than six
months.

96   **"choose love":** Ted Wheeler, Twitter, August 20, 2021, https://twitter
.com/tedwheeler/status/1428748842573471746?lang=en.

96   **Wheeler released a statement:** Ted Wheeler, "Mayor's Statement About
Sunday's Violent Demonstrations," news release, City of Portland,
Oregon, August 23, 2021, www.portland.gov/omf/news/2021/8/23
/mayors-statement-about-sundays-violent-demonstrations.

96   **"We've wasted all their fucking resources to make this rally":** Andy
Campbell, "Proud Boys Leader Admits Their Rallies Are for Fighting

and Wasting Money," HuffPost, August 22, 2019, www.huffpost.com /entry/proud-boys-rallies-portland_n_5d5e9882e4b0dfcbd4893ee5.

Chapter 5: "Very Fine People"

100 neo-Nazi Richard Spencer: "Richard Bertrand Spencer," Southern Poverty Law Center, www.splcenter.org/fighting-hate/extremist-files /individual/richard-bertrand-spencer-0.

101 "disproportionate Jewish influence": "Jason Kessler," Southern Poverty Law Center, www.splcenter.org/fighting-hate/extremist-files /individual/jason-kessler.

101 punched in the face by an antifascist: Paul Murphy, "White Nationalist Richard Spencer Punched During Interview," CNN, January 21, 2017, www.cnn.com/2017/01/20/politics/white-nationalist-richard -spencer-punched/index.html.

102 Kessler was captured on video getting his second degree: Shawn Breen, Twitter, September 30, 2020, https://twitter.com/shawnpbreen /status/1311439463059460098.

104 ultimately decided there weren't grounds to deny him based on the messaging alone: Hunton & Williams, *Independent Review of the 2017 Protest Events in Charlottesville, Virginia,* 2017, www.huntonak .com/images/content/3/4/v4/34613/final-report-ada-compliant -ready.pdf.

106 Unicorn Riot published hundreds of thousands of its private chat logs: Chris Schiano and Freddy Martinez, "Neo-Nazi Hipsters Identity Evropa Exposed in Discord Chat Leak," Unicorn Riot, March 6, 2019, https://unicornriot.ninja/2019/neo-nazi-hipsters -identity-evropa-exposed-in-discord-chat-leak/.

106 barking orders into a megaphone: Joe Heim, "Recounting a Day of Rage, Hate, Violence and Death," *Washington Post,* August 14, 2017, www.washingtonpost.com/graphics/2017/local/charlottesville -timeline/.

106 a white polo bearing an Identity Evropa logo: Johnny Simon, "The Story Behind That Photo of a Screaming White Nationalist in Charlottesville," *Quartz,* August 15, 2017, https://qz.com/1054023 /charlottesville-torch-photo-white-nationalist-peter-cytanovic-wants -people-to-know-he-is-not-an-evil-nazi/.

108   **had pulled out a pistol:** Evan Simko-Bednarski, "Man Arrested for Firing Gun at Charlottesville Rally," CNN, August 28, 2017, www.cnn.com/2017/08/27/us/man-arrested-gun-charlottesville-rally/index.html.

108   **White supremacists beat down a Black man:** Sara Boboltz, "White Supremacist Found Guilty in Charlottesville Beating of Black Man," HuffPost, May 2, 2018, www.huffpost.com/entry/white-supremacist-found-guilty-in-charlottesville-beating-of-black-man_n_5ae9bd61e4b06748dc8e516b.

108   **Her mother, Susan Bro, sat down with me:** Andy Campbell, "Mother of Charlottesville Victim Heather Heyer: 'I'm Proud of What She Did,'" HuffPost, August 13, 2017, www.huffpost.com/entry/mother-of-charlottesville-victim-heather-heyer-im-proud-of-what-she-did_n_59907c45e4b09071f69a796c.

109   **His words were not mischaracterized:** "In Context: Donald Trump's 'Very Fine People on Both Sides' Remarks (Transcript)," PolitiFact, 2019, www.politifact.com/article/2019/apr/26/context-trumps-very-fine-people-both-sides-remarks/.

112   **He threatened to sue The Intercept:** Leighton Akio Woodhouse, "After Charlottesville, the American Far Right Is Tearing Itself Apart," The Intercept, September 21, 2017, https://theintercept.com/2017/09/21/gavin-mcinnes-alt-right-proud-boys-richard-spencer-charlottesville/.

112   **millions in damages more than four years later:** Sara Boboltz, "Jury Slaps Unite the Right Organizers with Millions in Damages over Racist Violence," HuffPost, November 23, 2021, www.huffpost.com/entry/charlottesville-unite-the-right-trial-verdict_n_6193d666e4b05e93cbb5bc7e.

Chapter 6: The Proud Boys and the GOP

116   **a "violent extremist group":** Caroline Linton, "Twitter Suspends Proud Boys, Gavin McInnes Accounts Ahead of Unite the Right Rally," CBS News, August 10, 2018, www.cbsnews.com/news/proud-boys-gavin-mcinnes-twitter-suspension-today-unite-the-right-2018-08-10/.

116   **"content to revel in their treachery against humanity":** Emilie Ruscoe, Kenneth Lovett, and Elizabeth Keogh, "Vandals Tag GOP Manhattan Office Ahead of Proud Boy Gavin McInnes' Visit; Puts Party 'On

Notice' in Warning Note," *New York Daily News*, October 12, 2018, www.nydailynews.com/news/politics/ny-pol-manhattan-republican -club-vandalized-20181012-story.html.

117 **on the lips of other authoritarian leaders around the world:** Michal Kranz, "5 Striking Examples of Politicians Around the World Starting to Sound a Lot More Like Trump," Insider, December 6, 2017, www .businessinsider.com/politicians-speaking-like-trump-2017-11.

118 **Eleven arrests were made that night:** Colleen Long, "11 Arrests at NYU Protest over Speech by 'Proud Boys' Leader," Associated Press, February 3, 2017, https://apnews.com/article/964cc747d67e4ae6863 b07acb3c52539.

118 **skinhead gangs that McInnes had reportedly associated with in the past:** Rachel Janik, "Far-Right Skinheads Join Proud Boys in Assaulting Protesters in New York City Following Gavin McInnes Event," Southern Poverty Law Center, October 14, 2018, www .splcenter.org/hatewatch/2018/10/13/far-right-skinheads-join-proud -boys-assaulting-protesters-new-york-city-following-gavin.

118 **several other attacks in New York City:** Nathan Tempey, "Right-Wing Skinheads Attack Grad Students at LES Bar over Antifascist Cellphone Sticker," Gothamist, February 13, 2017, https://gothamist .com/news/right-wing-skinheads-attack-grad-students-at-les-bar-over -antifascist-cellphone-sticker.

118 **waving his samurai sword toward protesters:** Carol Schaeffer, "Inside the Proud Boy Event That Sparked Violence Outside of Uptown GOP Club," Bedford + Bowery, October 13, 2018, https:// bedfordandbowery.com/2018/10/inside-the-proud-boy-event-that -sparked-violence-outside-of-uptown-gop-club/.

118 **Shay Horse, told HuffPost at the time:** Christopher Mathias, "Pro-Trump Gang Seen in Footage Assaulting Anti-Fascist Protesters in Manhattan," HuffPost, October 13, 2018, www.huffpost.com /entry/proud-boys-new-york-assault-gavin-mcinnes_n_5bc20d60e4b 0bd9ed55a96ee.

119 **Proud Boys had also unleashed a substantial assault in Portland:** Andy Campbell, "Proud Boys Street Gang Had a Weekend of Coast-to-Coast Violence," HuffPost, October 15, 2018, www.huffpost.com /entry/the-proud-boys-street-gang-attacked-protesters-across-the -country-over-the-weekend_n_5bc4903ae4b01a01d68cc9cb.

119   **violent acts carried out in their name:** Jon Swaine and Juweek Adolphe, "Violence in the Name of Trump," *Guardian* (Manchester, UK), August 28, 2019, www.theguardian.com/us-news/ng-interactive/2019 /aug/28/in-the-name-of-trump-supporters-attacks-database.

119   **(and whitest) neighborhoods in the city:** Where We Live NYC: Fair Housing Together, "Where New Yorkers Live," Explore Data, https:// wherewelive.cityofnewyork.us/explore-data/where-new-yorkers-live/.

120   **"They are going to be in the Tombs":** Alan Feuer and Ali Winston, "Founder of Proud Boys Says He's Arranging Surrender of Men in Brawl," *New York Times,* October 19, 2018, www.nytimes.com/2018 /10/19/nyregion/the-proud-boys-gavin-mcinnes-arrested.html.

120   **the brownshirt movements of Nazi Germany:** Colin Moynihan, "2 Proud Boys Sentenced to 4 Years in Brawl with Anti-Fascists at Republican Club," *New York Times*, October 22, 2019, www .nytimes.com/2019/10/22/nyregion/proud-boys-antifa-sentence .html.

121   **Fox News focused on the spray paint:** Fox News, Twitter, October 12, 2018, https://twitter.com/FoxNews/status/1050953019708375041.

121   **"one of our state headquarter buildings was attacked":** Dom Calicchio, "Calls for Civility After Vandalism, Violent Clashes Outside GOP Headquarters in New York," Fox News, October 14, 2018, www .foxnews.com/politics/calls-for-civility-after-vandalism-violent-clashes -outside-gop-headquarters-in-new-york.

121   **Republican state senator Marty Golden:** Jake Offenhartz, "NY Republicans Not Sure Whether Proud Boys Founder Gavin McInnes Is Good or Bad," Gothamist, October 16, 2018, https://gothamist .com/news/ny-republicans-not-sure-whether-proud-boys-founder -gavin-mcinnes-is-good-or-bad.

122   **ran interference for McInnes:** Metropolitan Republican Club, Twitter, October 14, 2018, https://twitter.com/metgopclub/status/10516221 17719060486.

122   **that the Metropolitan Republican Club "is not a hate group":** Nidhi Prakash and Tanya Chen, "Manhattan Republicans Are Defending Their Invitation to a Violent Far-Right Group," BuzzFeed News, October 14, 2018, www.buzzfeednews.com/article/nidhiprakash /ew-york-gop-defends-proud-boys.

123 **he told The Wrap:** Jon Levine, "Tucker Carlson Poses with Members of 'Hate Group' Proud Boys in Fox News Green Room," The Wrap, May 18, 2018, www.thewrap.com/tucker-carlson-poses-with-hate -group-members-in-fox-news-green-room/.

123 **looked into a camera held by members as he took the oath:** Kelly Weill, "How the Proud Boys Became Roger Stone's Personal Army," The Daily Beast, January 29, 2019, www.thedailybeast.com/how-the -proud-boys-became-roger-stones-personal-army-6.

123 **he told *Willamette Week*:** Elise Herron, "Right-Wing Provo- cateur Roger Stone Asked Proud Boys for Protection at Dorchester Conference Last Weekend," *Willamette Week* (Portland, OR), March 7, 2018, www.wweek.com/news/2018/03/07/right-wing -provocateur-roger-stone-asked-proud-boys-for-protection-at -dorchester-conference-last-weekend/.

124 **"Thank God for the Proud Boys":** Ann Coulter, "Thank God for the Proud Boys," *Marshall News Messenger*, March 2, 2021, www .marshallnewsmessenger.com/thank-god-for-the-proud-boys/article _98bfa2c0-7acd-11eb-993c-abe99a3c3e0f.html.

125 **"as an extremist group with ties to White Nationalism":** Christopher Mathias, "FBI Categorizes Proud Boys as an 'Extremist' Group, Documents Reveal," HuffPost, November 19, 2018, www.huffpost .com/entry/fbi-proud-boys-extremist-group_n_5bf317bee4b0376c9e 67be53?rqh.

125 **In a bizarre, rambling, thirty-six-minute video posted to YouTube:** David Moye, "Proud Boys Founder Gavin McInnes Quits Group," HuffPost, November 21, 2018, www.huffpost.com/entry/gavin-mcinnes -quits-proudboys_n_5bf5ec9ee4b0eb6d930b676b.

126 **"fraudulent buffoon, violence-threatening online tough guy":** Ken White, "Texas Attorney Jason L. Van Dyke: Fraudulent Buffoon, Violence-Threatening Online-Tough-Guy, Vexatious Litigant, Proud Bigot, and All Around Human Dumpster Fire," Popehat, July 9, 2017, www.popehat.com/2017/07/09/texas-attorney-jason-l-van-dyke -fraudulent-buffoon-violence-threatening-online-tough-guy -vexatious-litigant-proud-bigot-and-all-around-human-dumpster-fire/.

126 **Van Dyke scrambled to release a new set of bylaws:** Jason Lee Van Dyke, Proud Boys Redacted Bylaws, November 25, 2018,

www.scribd.com/document/394310661/Proud-Boys-Redacted
-Bylaws-Adopted-11-25-2018.

128   **threw him directly under the bus:** Proud Boys, "Proud Boys Statement
on J. L. Van Dyke," news release, November 29, 2018, https://archive
.ph/JBCjd.

128   **"The Proud Boys Are Imploding":** Andy Campbell, "The Proud Boys
Are Imploding," HuffPost, November 26, 2018, www.huffpost.com
/entry/the-proud-boys-are-imploding_n_5bfc16dde4b0eb6d9311e26d.

129   **his version as a political force:** Joshua Ceballos, "Proud Boys Leader
Enrique Tarrio Was Once a Regular Miami Kid. Now He's in Jail,"
Miami New Times, September 7, 2021, www.miaminewtimes.com
/news/proud-boys-leader-enrique-henry-tarrio-was-once-a-regular
-miami-kid-12889526.

129   **canceled Milo's $250,000 book deal:** Bonnie Malkin and Ben Jacobs,
"Milo Yiannopoulos Disinvited from CPAC After Making Comments
on Child Abuse," *Guardian* (Manchester, UK), February 20, 2017,
www.theguardian.com/us-news/2017/feb/20/milo-yiannopoulos
-denies-supporting-paedophilia-cpac-online-video.

131   **in a statement to the Federal Elections Commission:** Enrique Tarrio
for Congress, FEC Form 99, https://docquery.fec.gov/cgi-bin/forms
/C00725408/1376283/.

133   **Richard "Dick Sweats" Schwetz:** The Proud Boy didn't respond to
requests for comment for this book.

133   **Dick2022.com:** https://archive.fo/WOZ8a.

133   **"This isn't about the Proud Boys. It's about the Patriot Party":** Elle
Reeve, Samantha Guff, and Jeremy Moorhead, "Inside a 'Patriot
Party' Rally Where Trump Loyalists Search for a Path Forward,"
CNN, February 23, 2021, www.cnn.com/2021/02/23/politics/patriot
-party-trump/index.html.

134   **"fucking pussies":** Luke Mogelson, "Among the Insurrectionists,"
New Yorker, January 15, 2021, www.newyorker.com/magazine/2021
/01/25/among-the-insurrectionists.

134   **stripped of their House committee assignments:** Barbara Sprunt,
"House Removes Rep. Marjorie Taylor Greene from Her Committee
Assignments," NPR, February 4, 2021, www.npr.org/2021/02/04/963
785609/house-to-vote-on-stripping-rep-marjorie-taylor-greene
-from-2-key-committees.

134 **Edgar J. Delatorre:** Tom Schuba, "Proud Boy Present for Capitol Riot Charged with Battery in Fight at Schaumburg Anti-Biden Rally," *Chicago Sun-Times*, April 7, 2021, https://chicago.suntimes.com /metro-state/2021/4/7/22372893/proud-boy-capitol-riot-battery -schaumburg-edgar-delatorre-gonzalez-remy-del-toro.

135 **Joel Campbell:** Tim Mak, "Some Proud Boys Are Moving to Local Politics as Scrutiny of Far-Right Group Ramps Up," NPR, June 28, 2021, www.capradio.org/news/npr/story?storyid=1010328631.

135 **Josh Wells:** Sherman Smith, "Haven School Board Candidate Lured into Sharing Racist Ideology with Teenage Anti-Fascists," Kansas Reflector, July 20, 2021, https://kansasreflector.com/2021/07/20 /haven-school-board-candidate-lured-into-sharing-racist-ideology -with-teenage-anti-fascists/.

136 **"Proud Boys Standing By" T-shirts:** Neil MacFarquhar, Alan Feuer, Mike Baker, and Sheera Frenkel, "Far-Right Group That Trades in Political Violence Gets a Boost," *New York Times*, September 30, 2020, www.nytimes.com/2020/09/30/us/proud-boys-trump.html.

137 **His "dirty trickster" moniker:** Jeffrey Toobin, "The Dirty Trickster," *New Yorker*, May 23, 2008, www.newyorker.com/magazine/2008 /06/02/the-dirty-trickster.

137 **He got fired a few months later:** Olivia Paschal and Madeleine Carlisle, "A Brief History of Roger Stone," *Atlantic*, November 15, 2019, www.theatlantic.com/politics/archive/2019/11/roger-stones-long -history-in-trump-world/581293/.

137 **Citizens United Not Timid:** Stephanie Mencimer, "The Time a Trump Aide Sued a Trump Adviser over an Anti-Hillary Group Called C.U.N.T.," *Mother Jones*, September 29, 2016, www.motherjones .com/politics/2016/09/time-trump-aide-sued-trump-adviser-over -anti-hillary-group-called-cunt/.

138 **Gateway Pundit:** Daniel Dale, "Fact Check: Right-Wing Website Falsely Claims Wisconsin Assembly Voted to Withdraw Its Biden Electoral Votes," CNN, January 27, 2022, www.cnn.com/2022/01/27 /politics/fact-check-gateway-pundit-wisconsin-electors-2020-biden /index.html.

138 **openly attends their meetings and events:** Colin Wolf, "Member of Extremist Group 'Proud Boys' Considering a Run for Orange County Republican Executive Committee," *Orlando Weekly*, November 27, 2018, www.orlandoweekly.com/orlando/member-of-extremist

-group-proud-boys-considering-a-run-for-orange-county-republican
-executive-committee/Content?oid=21651001.

139 **despite characterizing himself as a journalist:** Sarah Rumpf, "How
a Roger Stone Acolyte and a 'Tiger King Tax Collector' Spawned
the Matt Gaetz Scandal," Mediaite, April 15, 2021, www.mediaite
.com/politics/its-even-weirder-than-you-thought-how-a-roger-stone
-acolyte-and-a-tiger-king-tax-collector-spawned-the-matt-gaetz
-scandal/.

139 **the pair stood together in a video address to the Proud Boys:** Zoe
Tillman, "Roger Stone's Proud Boys 'Volunteers' Have Been Defending
Him Online After the Judge Entered a Gag Order," BuzzFeed News,
February 24, 2019, www.buzzfeednews.com/article/zoetillman/roger
-stone-proud-boys-volunteers-mueller-instagram.

140 **Stone got in trouble for posting:** Andy Campbell, "Federal Judge
Says Roger Stone Faces Jail Time over Instagram Posts," HuffPost,
February 19, 2019, www.huffpost.com/entry/federal-judge-says
-roger-stone-faces-jail-time-over-instagram-posts_n_5c6c248fe4b01
cea6b89ce10.

140 **Tarrio was spotted in a live audience standing behind Trump:** Tim
Elfrink, "The Chairman of the Far-Right Proud Boys Sat Behind
Trump at His Latest Speech," *Washington Post*, February 19, 2019,
www.washingtonpost.com/nation/2019/02/19/far-right-proud-boys
-chairman-sat-behind-trump-his-latest-speech/.

141 **though he refused to cooperate with the probe:** Dartunorro Clark,
"Roger Stone Invokes Fifth Amendment in House Jan. 6 Probe,"
NBC News, December 7, 2021, www.nbcnews.com/politics/congress
/roger-stone-invokes-fifth-amendment-house-jan-6-probe-n1285569.

144 **"We have the Proud Boys across the street":** Fascist_Parler_Watch,
Twitter, July 14, 2021, https://twitter.com/RWParlerWatch/status/14
15189647127285760?s=20.

Chapter 7: The Fist Amendment

148 **by about four to one:** Christopher Mathias and Andy Campbell,
"Violent Proto-Fascists Came to Portland. The Police Went After the
Anti-Fascists," HuffPost, August 5, 2018, www.huffpost.com/entry
/portland-patriot-prayer-proud-boys-police-antifascists_n_5b668b7
de4b0de86f4a22faf.

150 **A 2006 FBI intelligence assessment:** FBI, White Supremacist Infiltration of Law Enforcement, October 17, 2006, http://s3.documentcloud .org/documents/402521/doc-26-white-supremacist-infiltration.pdf.

151 **a classified counterterrorism policy guide from April 2015:** Alice Speri, "The FBI Has Quietly Investigated White Supremacist Infiltration of Law Enforcement," The Intercept, January 31, 2017, https://theintercept.com/2017/01/31/the-fbi-has-quietly-investigated -white-supremacist-infiltration-of-law-enforcement/.

152 **Tarrio told the *Washington Post*:** Peter Hermann and Devlin Barrett, "D.C. Police Lieutenant Suspended over Alleged Ties to Right-Wing Group," *Washington Post,* February 16, 2022, www.washingtonpost .com/dc-md-va/2022/02/16/dc-police-tarrio-proud-boys-lamond/.

152 **joining in on the Proud Boys' chants of "I like beer":** Rachel Kurzius, "D.C. Police Officers Fist Bumped a Proud Boy After Clashes in Front of White House," DCist, July 5, 2019, https://dcist.com /story/19/07/05/d-c-police-officer-fist-bumps-a-proud-boy-after -clashes-in-front-of-white-house/.

153 **The flag's creator, Andrew Jacob:** Jeff Sharlet, "A Flag for Trump's America," *Harper's Magazine,* July 2018, https://harpers.org /archive/2018/07/a-flag-for-trumps-america/.

154 **it hasn't yet gone anywhere in Congress:** Avi Wolfman-Arent, "Backing the Blue or Empty Gesture? Toomey Boosts Bill to Punish Cop Killers," WHYY, May 20, 2019, https://whyy.org/articles/pa-us -senator-pat-toomey-reintroduces-thin-blue-line-act-whyy/.

154 **Trump, meanwhile, had a gigantic thin blue line flag displayed:** Reuters, "U.S. And 'Thin Blue Line' Flags Were Displayed at Trump Wisconsin Rally," October 27, 2020, www.reuters.com/article/uk -factcheck-blue-flag-trump/fact-check-u-s-and-thin-blue-line-flags -were-displayed-at-trump-wisconsin-rally-idUSKBN27C23W.

154 **officers wearing thin blue line face coverings:** Missourian staff, "No More 'Thin Blue Line' Masks for Columbia Police," *Columbia Missourian,* October 23, 2020, www.columbiamissourian.com /news/local/no-more-thin-blue-line-masks-for-columbia-police /article_2a9af262-1552-11eb-b964-a3108e9fa374.html.

155 **"The balance has tipped":** Janelle Griffith, "Police Chief Bans 'Thin Blue Line' Imagery, Says It's Been 'Co-opted' by Extremists," NBC News, January 29, 2021, www.nbcnews.com/news/us-news/police -chief-bans-thin-blue-line-imagery-says-it-s-n1256217.

155 **The piece failed to mention:** Heather MacDonald, "Police Vindicate the 'Thin Blue Line' Patch Every Day," *Wall Street Journal*, August 23, 2021, www.wsj.com/articles/police-thin-blue-line-shootings-black -homicide-crime-proactive-policing-blm-defund-11629750911.

156 **"Each skirmish appeared to involve willing participants":** Andy Campbell, "Portland Police Are Giving Up on Policing the Far-Right," HuffPost, August 25, 2020, www.huffpost.com/entry/portland-police -far-right-proud-boys_n_5f4417f6c5b6c00d03b29826.

157 **the gang took triumphant photos of themselves:** Christopher Mathias and Andy Campbell, "Proud Boys, Outnumbered by Anti-Fascists, Get Police Escort After 30-Minute Rally," HuffPost, August 18, 2019, www.huffpost.com/entry/proud-boys-portland-rally_n_5d59390ee4 b0eb875f2539c4.

157 **Text messages between Portland police:** Katie Shepherd, "Portland Police Chief Says Protesters Went Off to 'Whine and Complain' Last Week Because Officers 'Kicked Your Butt,'" *Willamette Week* (Portland, OR), August 15, 2018, www.wweek.com/news/courts /2018/08/15/portland-police-chief-says-protesters-went-off-to-whine -and-complain-last-week-because-officers-kicked-your-butt/.

159 **a sheriff in Washington State who wore a Proud Boys sweater:** Katie Shepherd, "Clark County Sheriff Deputy Fired After Wearing a Proud Boys Sweatshirt," *Willamette Week* (Portland, OR), July 20, 2018, www.wweek.com/news/courts/2018/07/20/clark-county-sheriff -deputy-fired-after-wearing-a-proud-boys-sweatshirt/.

159 **cop named Rick Fitzgerald who rallied with the gang:** Hannah Knowles, "California Police Fire Officer Who Was a Proud Boy, Saying They Have No Tolerance for 'Hate Groups,'" *Washington Post*, April 11, 2021, www.washingtonpost.com/nation/2021/04/11 /fresno-rick-fitzgerald-proud-boys/.

160 **Kristen Clarke, president of the group:** Stanley Augustin, "Lawyers' Committee for Civil Rights Under Law Calls for Removal of Officer Linked to 'Proud Boys' from East Hampton, Connecticut Police Department," Lawyers' Committee for Civil Rights, October 16, 2019, www.lawyerscommittee.org/lawyers-committee-for-civil-rights -under-law-calls-for-removal-of-officer-linked-to-proud-boys-from -east-hampton-connecticut-police-department/.

161 **"Only what I searched on the internet":** Michael Kunzelman, "Chief: Officer's Proud Boys Membership Didn't Break Policy," Associated

Press, October 15, 2019, https://apnews.com/article/business-race
-and-ethnicity-racial-injustice-12ece8cedbf045259dcddebf61914
1e7.

161 **Chicago Antifascist Action released a dossier on Bakker:** CAFA,
"Chicago Proud Boys Telegram Chat Logs Identify Chicago Police
Officer Rob Bakker as Proud Boy," Chicago Anti-Fascist Action, May
25, 2020, https://antifascistchicago.noblogs.org/post/2020/05/25
/chicago-proud-boys-telegram-leaks-chicago-police-officer-rob
-bakker/.

163 **"a provocative club . . . to the alt-right":** Jemima McEvoy, "Who
Are the Proud Boys, the Group Behind the Controversial Portland
Rally?," *Forbes*, September 26, 2020, www.forbes.com/sites
/jemimamcevoy/2020/09/26/who-are-the-proud-boys-the-group
-planning-a-controversial-portland-rally/?sh=6cfa672c654a.

164 **They fired pepper spray and three tear gas canisters:** Hawes Spencer
and Matt Stevens, "23 Arrested and Tear Gas Deployed after a K.K.K.
Rally in Virginia," *New York Times*, July 8, 2017, www.nytimes.com
/2017/07/08/us/kkk-rally-charlottesville-robert-e-lee-statue.html.

166 **A ten-minute-long ABC News feature:** Paula Faris, "Proud Boys
Founder Denies Inciting Violence, Responds to Whether He Feels
Responsible for Group's Behavior," ABC News, December 12, 2018,
https://abcnews.go.com/US/proud-boys-founder-denies-inciting
-violence-responds-feels/story?id=59758209.

167 **"A Voice of Hate in America's Heartland":** Richard Fausset, "A Voice of
Hate in America's Heartland," *New York Times*, November 25, 2017,
www.nytimes.com/2017/11/25/us/ohio-hovater-white-nationalist.html.

169 **"January 6 is not the greatest threat to America":** Hannah Grossman,
"Jan. 6 Is Not the Greatest Threat to America—It's the Democrat Party,"
Fox News, January 9, 2022, www.foxnews.com/media/mark-levin
-comments-january-6-not-greatest-theat-america-its-democrat-party.

169 **"no arrests were made":** Louis Casiano, "Antifa Marches Through
NYC as Fears of Political Violence Heighten," Fox News, January 11,
2021, www.foxnews.com/us/antifa-nyc-violence-fears.

169 **Fox News and the Trumpian right:** Justin Baragona, "Fox News Stars:
America Had It Coming. Also Antifa Did It," The Daily Beast, January
7, 2021, www.thedailybeast.com/fox-news-stars-tucker-carlson-laura
-ingraham-sean-hannity-say-america-had-it-coming-and-also-antifa
-did-it; Haaretz and the Associated Press, "Proud Boys' Violence Spills

onto New York City Streets—Fox News Blames Antifa," *Haaretz*, October 15, 2018, www.haaretz.com/jewish/fox-news-blames-proud-boys -violence-in-new-york-city-on-antifa-1.6554300; BBC, "Antifa: Trump Says Group Will Be Designated 'Terrorist Organisation,'" BBC News, May 31, 2020, www.bbc.com/news/world-us-canada-52868295; Jaclyn Peiser, "'Their Tactics Are Fascistic': Barr Slams Black Lives Matter, Accuses the Left of 'Tearing Down the System,'" *Washington Post*, August 10, 2020, www.washingtonpost.com/nation/2020/08/10/barr -fox-antifa-blm/; Sabrina Siddiqui, "Donald Trump Strikes Muddled Note on 'Divisive' Black Lives Matter," *Guardian*, July 13, 2016, www .theguardian.com/us-news/2016/jul/13/donald-trump-strikes-muddled -note-on-divisive-black-lives-matter; Brandy Zadrozny and Ben Collins, "As Wildfires Rage, False Antifa Rumors Spur Pleas from Police," NBC News, September 11, 2020, www.nbcnews.com/tech/security /wildfires-rage-false-antifa-rumors-spur-pleas-police-n1239881; Brian Flood and Tim Molloy, "Glenn Beck, Richard Spencer Among Those Blaming Black Lives Matter for Chicago Kidnapping," The Wrap, January 4, 2017, www.thewrap.com/black-lives-matter-chicago -kidnapping-glenn-beck-richard-spencer/; Marc A. Thiessen, "Yes, Antifa Is the Moral Equivalent of Neo-Nazis," *Washington Post*, August 30, 2017, www.washingtonpost.com/opinions/yes-antifa -is-the-moral-equivalent-of-neo-nazis/2017/08/30/9a13b2f6-8d00 -11e7-91d5-ab4e4bb76a3a_story.html; Jeremy Diamond, "Trump: Black Lives Matter Has Helped Instigate Police Killings," CNN, July 19, 2016, www.cnn.com/2016/07/18/politics/donald-trump-black -lives-matter/index.html; Media Matters staff, "Laura Ingraham: 'These Wanton Acts of Violence Are Part of a Coordinated Effort to Eventually Overthrow the United States Government,'" Media Matters for America, June 1, 2020, www.mediamatters.org/laura-ingraham /laura-ingraham-these-wanton-acts-violence-are-part-coordinated -effort-eventually.

170 **Protesters have been shot repeatedly at political events:** Ashley Hiruko, "Gunman at Seattle Protest Charged with First-Degree Assault," NPR, June 10, 2020, www.kuow.org/stories/gunman-at -seattle-protest-charged-with-first-degree-assault.

170 **nineteen incidents of vehicles plowing into crowds:** Neena Satija, Emily Davies, and Dalton Bennett, "Amid Massive Demonstrations, Vehicles Striking Protesters Raise Disturbing Echoes of 2017 Charlottesville Attack," *Washington Post*, June 15, 2020, www.washingtonpost .com/investigations/2020/06/15/cars-ramming-protests/.

171 **shared approvingly on Twitter by Mercedes Schlapp:** Marc Caputo, "Chainsaw-Wielding Racist Gets Boost from Top Trump Aide as Race Protests Sweep the Nation," Politico, June 6, 2020, www.politico .com/news/2020/06/06/racist-boosted-by-trump-aide-mercedes -schlapp-race-protests-sweep-nation-304633.

171 **and Stone replied:** Dalton Bennett and Jon Swaine, "The Roger Stone Tapes," *Washington Post*, March 4, 2022, www.washingtonpost.com /investigations/interactive/2022/roger-stone-documentary-capitol-riot -trump-election/?itid=hp_special-topic-1.

171 **pipe bombs started showing up at the addresses:** US Department of Justice, "Cesar Sayoc Pleads Guilty to 65 Felonies for Mailing 16 Improvised Explosive Devices in Connection with October 2018 Domestic Terrorist Attack," news release, March 21, 2019, www .justice.gov/opa/pr/cesar-sayoc-pleads-guilty-65-felonies-mailing-16 -improvised-explosive-devices-connection.

172 **hit with a milkshake, punched, and kicked:** Andy Campbell, "Far-Right Extremists Wanted Blood in Portland's Streets. Once Again, They Got It," HuffPost, July 1, 2019, www.huffpost.com/entry/andy -ngo-quillette-antifa-proud-boys_n_5d1a1275e4b07f6ca5811e0c.

172 **he wrote an op-ed for the *New York Post*:** Andy Ngo, "Inside the Suspicious Rise of Gay Hate Crimes in Portland," *New York Post*, March 30, 2019, https://nypost.com/2019/03/30/inside-the -suspicious-rise-of-gay-hate-crimes-in-portland/.

172 **far-right troll named Eoin Lenihan:** Luke O'Brien, "Twitter Still Has a White Nationalist Problem," HuffPost, May 30, 2019, www .huffpost.com/entry/twitter-white-nationalist-problem_n_5cec4d28e 4b00e036573311d.

173 **maintains questionable relationships:** E. J. Dickson, "How a Right-Wing Troll Managed to Manipulate the Mainstream Media," *Rolling Stone*, September 3, 2019, www.rollingstone.com/culture/culture -features/andy-ngo-right-wing-troll-antifa-877914/.

Chapter 8: Funding Political Violence

177 **There's even a company in Hawaii:** Tess Owen and Greg Walters, "The Black Church That Could Bankrupt the Proud Boys," Vice News, April 8, 2021, www.vice.com/en/article/4avgvd/the-black -church-that-could-bankrupt-the-proud-boys.

179 **She published a paper on the Proud Boys':** Megan Squire, "Understanding Gray Networks Using Social Media Trace Data," in *Social Informatics: 11th International Conference; Socinfo 2019, Doha, Qatar,* ed. Ingmar Weber, Kareem M. Darwish, Claudia Wagner, Emilio Zagheni, Laura Nelson, Samin Aref, and Fabian Flöck (New York: Springer, 2019), 202–217, www.researchgate .net/publication/337268223_Understanding_Gray_Networks_Using _Social_Media_Trace_Data.

179 **WestFest, a national summit:** Ben Schreckinger, "Trump's Culture Warriors Go Home," Politico, November 2018, www.politico.com /magazine/story/2018/10/29/trump-cernovich-milo-yiannopoulos -richard-spencer-alt-right-2018-221916/.

180 **another study conducted by Squire:** Megan Squire, "Monetizing Propaganda: How Far-Right Extremists Earn Money by Video Streaming," arXivLabs, Cornell University, May 2021, https://arxiv .org/abs/2105.05929.

181 **launched a GiveSendGo campaign for John Kinsman:** "Christmas for Liberty," GiveSendGo, https://givesendgo.com/christmasForLiberty.

183 **"Proud Boys Surround Man with Knife at Violent DC Trump Rally":** Elizabeth Elizalde, "Proud Boys Surround Man with Knife at Violent DC Trump Rally," *New York Post,* December 13, 2020, https:// nypost.com/2020/12/13/one-person-stabbed-during-massive-proud -boys-brawl-in-dc/.

184 **A *USA Today* investigation into the Proud Boys' GiveSendGo campaign:** Will Carless, "Proud Boys Saw Wave of Contributions from Chinese Diaspora Before Capitol Attack," *USA Today,* May 4, 2021, www.usatoday.com/story/news/nation/2021/05/04 /proud-boys-chinese-americans-community-support-donations /7343111002/.

187 **Nordean posted a link to a GiveSendGo fundraiser:** US District Court for the District of Columbia, *United States of America v. Ethan Nordean,* Criminal Complaint, January 6, 2021, www.justice.gov /opa/page/file/1364196/download.

189 **Tarrio took a call from a *USA Today* reporter:** Will Carless, "Proud Boys Leader Arrested on Charges Related to Burning of Black Lives Matter Banner, Police Say," *USA Today,* January 4, 2021, www .usatoday.com/story/news/nation/2021/01/04/proud-boys-leader -arrested-ahead-dc-protests-support-trump/4135703001/.

189 **It was one of the biggest Proud Boys rallies:** Peter Hermann, Marissa Lang, and Clarence Williams, "Pro-Trump Rally Descends into Chaos as Proud Boys Roam D.C. Looking to Fight," *Washington Post*, December 13, 2020, www.washingtonpost.com/local/public -safety/proud-boys-protest-stabbing-arrest/2020/12/13/98c0f740 -3d3f-11eb-8db8-395dedaaa036_story.html.

190 **Tarrio lit it ablaze:** Ford Fischer, Twitter, December 13, 2020, https:// twitter.com/FordFischer/status/1338004715456573440.

191 **Tarrio was sentenced to five months in prison:** Paul Duggan, "Proud Boys Leader Henry 'Enrique' Tarrio Sentenced to Five Months in Jail," *Washington Post*, August 23, 2021, www.washingtonpost .com/local/legal-issues/tarrio-proud-boy-jail-sentence/2021/08/23 /df06b84a-041b-11ec-a266-7c7fe02fa374_story.html.

191 **published a destabilizing report that Tarrio:** Aram Roston, "Proud Boys Leader Was 'Prolific' Informer for Law Enforcement," Reuters, January 27, 2021, www.reuters.com/article/us-usa-proudboys-leader -exclusive/exclusive-proud-boys-leader-was-prolific-informer-for -law-enforcement-idUSKBN29W1PE.

193 **Christian Exoo:** Antifash Gordon, Twitter, October 28, 2019, https:// twitter.com/AntiFashGordon/status/1188870637449891843.

194 **revenue from the merch store in 2021 than in 2020:** Rebecca Ballhaus, Khadeeja Safdar, and Shalini Ramachandran, "Proud Boys and Oath Keepers, Forceful on Jan. 6, Privately Are in Turmoil," *Wall Street Journal*, June 16, 2021, www.wsj.com/articles/proud-boys-and-oath -keepers-forceful-on-jan-6-privately-are-in-turmoil-11623859785.

Chapter 9: Fucking Around and Finding Out

196 **connected to at least a portion of their assets:** Tess Owen and Greg Walters, "The Black Church That Could Bankrupt the Proud Boys," Vice News, April 8, 2021, www.vice.com/en/article/4avgvd/the -black-church-that-could-bankrupt-the-proud-boys.

198 **Van Dyke tweeted at a Black man in 2014:** Andy Campbell, "Lawyer Suing Anti-Fascist for Calling Him Nazi Sent Death Threats, Racial Slurs on Twitter," HuffPost, November 14, 2017, www.huffpost.com /entry/lawyer-anti-fascist-lawsuit_n_5a0aefbee4b0b17ffce028fe.

198 **fliers across the Ohio State University campus:** Gerry Bello, "Neo-Nazi Group Targets Residents in South Campus Area," *The Mockingbird*,

http://www.mockingbirdpaper.com/content/neo-nazi-group-targets
-residents-south-campus-area.

199 **then reached out to threaten the guy directly:** Ken White, "Texas
Attorney Jason L. Van Dyke: Fraudulent Buffoon, Violence-Threatening
Online-Tough-Guy, Vexatious Litigant, Proud Bigot, and All Around
Human Dumpster Fire," Popehat, July 9, 2017, www.popehat
.com/2017/07/09/texas-attorney-jason-l-van-dyke-fraudulent-buffoon
-violence-threatening-online-tough-guy-vexatious-litigant-proud-bigot
-and-all-around-human-dumpster-fire/.

200 **White posted Van Dyke's email on Twitter:** Popehat, Twitter, July 22,
2017, https://twitter.com/Popehat/status/888832772516626432.

202 **his arrest in September 2018:** Andy Campbell, "Proud Boys Lawyer
Arrested for Lying to Cops, Can Still Practice Law," HuffPost,
September 19, 2018, www.huffpost.com/entry/proud-boys-lawyer
-jason-van-dyke-arrested_n_5ba26515e4b0823ea19a61d5.

202 **"Trump supporter from the very beginning":** Kelly Weill, "'Proud
Boy' Lawyer Wants $100M from Man Who Cost Him His Job," The
Daily Beast, September 18, 2018, www.thedailybeast.com/proud-boy
-lawyer-wants-dollar100m-from-man-who-cost-him-his-job.

204 **$100 million defamation suit:** US District Court, Eastern District
of Texas, Sherman Division, *Jason Lee Van Dyke v. Thomas
Retzlaff*, Memorandum Opinion and Order, April 7, 2020, www
.courthousenews.com/wp-content/uploads/2020/04/attorneyaccused
ofbeinganazi.pdf.

205 **In the forty-two-minute tape:** Brett Barrouquere, "On Recording,
Former Proud Boys Leader Jason Van Dyke Lays out Plans for
Stalking, Terror Campaign," Southern Poverty Law Center, June 2,
2020, www.splcenter.org/hatewatch/2020/06/02/recording-former
-proud-boys-leader-jason-van-dyke-lays-out-plans-stalking-terror
-campaign.

208 **join an infamous neo-Nazi terror group:** Ben Makuch and Mack
Lamoureux, "A Proud Boys Lawyer Wanted to Be a Nazi Terrorist,"
Vice, December 8, 2020, www.vice.com/en/article/wx8xp4/a-proud
-boys-lawyer-wanted-to-be-a-nazi-terrorist.

210 **Kenneth Lizardo:** I reached out for comment at the time, and Lizardo
blocked me on social media.

211 **Siskind organized an antihate vigil for neighbors:** Gabriel Rom, "Amy Siskind Warns That Far-Right Leader Gavin McInnes Lives Here," lohud, October 29, 2018, www.lohud.com/story/news/local /westchester/2018/10/29/amy-siskind-warns-far-right-leader-gavin -mcinnes-lives-here-proud-boys/1810446002/.

212 **harassed her neighbors:** Andy Campbell, "Gavin McInnes' Wife Threatens Neighbors over 'Hate Has No Home Here' Signs," HuffPost, January 8, 2019, www.huffpost.com/entry/gavin-mcinnes -emily-mcinnes-neighbors-over-anti-hate-signs_n_5c34c117e4b05d4 e96bcc88d.

Chapter 10: Antifa the Boogeyman

215 **Tucker Carlson continues to push conspiracy:** Bill McCarthy, "Tucker Carlson's 'Patriot Purge' Film on Jan. 6 Is Full of Falsehoods, Conspiracy Theories," PolitiFact, November 5, 2021, www.politifact .com/article/2021/nov/05/tucker-carlsons-patriot-purge-film-jan-6 -full-fals/.

216 **fabricated a universe:** Alexi Cardona, "Miami Police Dispel Rumors About Antifa Election Riots," *Miami New Times*, November 3, 2020, www.miaminewtimes.com/news/miami-police-say-rumors-of-antifa -election-attacks-are-false-11724381.

217 **Gugino received so many death threats:** Ben Feuerherd, "Protester Martin Gugino Recovering at 'Undisclosed Location' Amid Death Threats," *New York Post*, June 18, 2020, https://nypost.com /2020/06/18/martin-gugino-to-recover-at-undisclosed-location-amid -death-threats/.

217 **Consider the words of Gavin McInnes:** Ted Cox, "Gavin McInnes, Conservative Pundit, Banned by DePaul," DNAinfo, May 19, 2017, www.dnainfo.com/chicago/20170519/lincoln-park/gavin-mcinnes -conservative-pundit-banned-by-depaul/.

218 **accidentally shot himself in the leg:** Christopher Mathias and Andy Campbell, "Guns and KKK Members at Gettysburg Confederate Rally, but No Foes to Fight," HuffPost, July 2, 2017, www.huffpost .com/entry/gettysburg-confederate-rally-kkk-antifa_n_59592 bd8e4b05c37bb7f0ca4.

219   **characterize a crowd of forty thousand people:** L. A. Kauffman, "Who Were Those Masked Anarchists in Seattle?," *Salon*, December 10, 1999, www.salon.com/1999/12/10/anarchists/.

220   **sent federal enforcers in to punish them:** Safia Samee Ali, "'Not by Accident': False 'Thug' Narratives Have Long Been Used to Discredit Civil Rights Movements," NBC News, September 27, 2020, www .nbcnews.com/news/us-news/not-accident-false-thug-narratives-have -long-been-used-discredit-n1240509.

220   **"The violence instigated and carried out by antifa":** Tyler Olson, "Barr: Violence from Antifa, Other Groups 'Is Domestic Terrorism and Will Be Treated Accordingly,'" Fox News, May 31, 2020, www.foxnews .com/politics/barr-george-floyd-violence-from-antifa-other-group-is -domestic-terrorism-and-will-be-treated-accordingly.

221   **said Fox News host Mark Levin:** Media Matters staff, "Fox News' Mark Levin Says Black Lives Matter Is Equivalent to the KKK," Media Matters for America, January 11, 2022, www.mediamatters.org /mark-levin/fox-news-mark-levin-says-black-lives-matter-equivalent -kkk.

221   **Data collected from more than 7,300 nationwide events:** Erica Chenoweth and Jeremy Pressman, "This Summer's Black Lives Matter Protesters Were Overwhelmingly Peaceful, Our Research Finds," *Washington Post*, October 16, 2020, www.washingtonpost.com /politics/2020/10/16/this-summers-black-lives-matter-protesters-were -overwhelming-peaceful-our-research-finds/.

223   **"not going away anytime soon":** Brian Naylor and Ryan Lucas, "Wray Stresses Role of Right-Wing Extremism in Hearing About Jan. 6 Riot," NPR, March 2, 2021, www.npr.org/2021/03/02/972539274 /fbi-director-wray-testifies-before-congress-for-1st-time-since-capitol -attack.

223   **to downplay that threat after Trump took office:** Zolan Kanno-Youngs and Nicholas Fandos, "D.H.S. Downplayed Threats from Russia and White Supremacists, Whistle-Blower Says," *New York Times*, July 1, 2021, www.nytimes.com/2020/09/09/us/politics/homeland-security -russia-trump.html.

224   **Data show a colossal surge:** Robert O'Harrow Jr., Andrew Ba Tran, and Derek Hawkins, "The Rise of Domestic Extremism in America," *Washington Post*, April 12, 2021, www.washingtonpost.com /investigations/interactive/2021/domestic-terrorism-data/.

224 **can lead to harassment campaigns:** Micah Lee, "How Right-Wing Extremists Stalk, Dox, and Harass Their Enemies," The Intercept, September 6, 2017, https://theintercept.com/2017/09/06/how-right -wing-extremists-stalk-dox-and-harass-their-enemies/.

225 **one low-tech way to do this:** Colin Groundwater, "'Pack an Umbrella': Hong Kong Protesters Share Their Best Strategies and Tactics," *GQ*, June 4, 2020, www.gq.com/story/hong-kong-protest-advice.

231 **working to help the FBI identify the thousands of faces:** Sara Morrison, "To Catch an Insurrectionist," Vox, January 6, 2022, www.vox .com/recode/22867000/january-6-fbi-search-facebook-google -insurrection.

232 **Wrote one such account, New York City Antifa:** New York City Antifa, Twitter, November 15, 2019, https://twitter.com/nycantifa/status /1195539726926827520.

233 **"All I want to do is smash commies":** Andy Campbell, "Leaked Proud Boys Chats Show Members Plotting Violence at Rallies," HuffPost, May 22, 2019, www.huffpost.com/entry/proud-boys-chat-logs-pre meditate-rally-violence-in-leaked-chats_n_5ce1e231e4b00e03 5b928683.

235 **at fifty-one years old, he was sentenced:** Michael Levenson, "Self-Proclaimed Proud Boys Member Gets 10 Years for Violence at Portland Protests," *New York Times*, December 10, 2021, www.nytimes .com/2021/12/10/us/proud-boys-alan-swinney-sentenced.html.

Chapter 11: The Gang Tries Civil War

243 **More than 140 cops were injured that day:** Michael Schmidt and Luke Broadwater, "Officers' Injuries, Including Concussions, Show Scope of Violence at Capitol Riot," *New York Times*, February 11, 2021, www.nytimes.com/2021/02/11/us/politics/capitol-riot-police -officer-injuries.html.

243 **"flooding the zone with shit":** Sean Illing, "'Flood the Zone with Shit': How Misinformation Overwhelmed Our Democracy," Vox, February 6, 2020, www.vox.com/policy-and-politics/2020/1/16/20991816 /impeachment-trial-trump-bannon-misinformation.

244 **"'let loose the dogs of war'":** David Gilbert, "'Trump Basically Said to Go Fuck Them Up': Here's How the Proud Boys Reacted to Trump's Comments," Vice News, September 30, 2020, www.vice.com/en

/article/n7wxxk/trump-basically-said-to-go-fuck-them-up-heres-how
-the-proud-boys-reacted-to-trumps-comments.

244 **readiness for the coming civil war:** "IntelBrief: The Proud Boys Viral
Moment—Will It Devolve into a Virulent Threat?," The Soufan
Center, October 6, 2020, https://thesoufancenter.org/intelbrief-the
-proud-boys-viral-moment-will-it-devolve-into-a-virulent-threat/.

245 **hard-core skinhead crew:** ADL, "Behind the American Guard:
Hardcore White Supremacists," March 30, 2017, www.adl.org/blog
/behind-the-american-guard-hardcore-white-supremacists.

245 **"the seed that sparked that flower on Jan. 6":** Joshua Kaplan and
Joaquin Sapien, "New Details Suggest Senior Trump Aides Knew
Jan. 6 Rally Could Get Chaotic," ProPublica, June 25, 2021, www
.propublica.org/article/new-details-suggest-senior-trump-aides
-knew-jan-6-rally-could-get-chaotic.

245 **a disgraced former police officer:** RoseCityAntifa, Twitter, December
14, 2020, https://twitter.com/rosecityantifa/status/1338360817230
598145.

246 **At least twenty-two journalists were assaulted:** "Assaults," U.S.
Press Freedom Tracker, https://pressfreedomtracker.us/physical
-attack/?endpage=21.

247 **they spoke of civil war:** Luke Mogelson, "Among the Insurrectionists," *New Yorker*, January 15, 2021, www.newyorker.com
/magazine/2021/01/25/among-the-insurrectionists.

247 **even a MAGA-touting religious sect:** Tess Owen, "MAGA Gun
Church That Worships with AR-15s Has Bought a Giant Mountain
Property in Tennessee," Vice News, October 12, 2021, www.vice
.com/en/article/4avkdw/rod-of-iron-ministries-purchases-property
-in-tennessee.

247 **one in five American adults . . . believed the lie:** NPR, "After the Riot:
The Extremism That Fueled the Capitol Insurrection," January 5, 2022,
www.npr.org/2022/01/05/1070675200/after-the-riot-the-extremism
-that-fueled-the-capitol-insurrection.

247 **Biggs, a rabid former InfoWars employee:** David Kirkpatrick and
Alan Feuer, "Police Shrugged Off the Proud Boys, until They Attacked
the Capitol," *New York Times*, August 23, 2021, www.nytimes
.com/2021/03/14/us/proud-boys-law-enforcement.html.

247   **shootings in America were false flag operations:** Media Matters
      staff, "A Day After Hosting Trump, Alex Jones Calls San Bernardino
      Shooting a 'False Flag,'" Media Matters for America, December 3,
      2015,   https://mediamatters.org/alex-jones/day-after-hosting-trump
      -alex-jones-calls-san-bernardino-shooting-false-flag.

248   **advocated for rape and violence:** Media Matters staff, "New Host
      for 'Unofficial Version of Trump TV' Encouraged Date Rape and
      Punching Transgender People," Media Matters for America, January
      4,   2017,   www.mediamatters.org/right-side-broadcasting/new-host
      -unofficial-version-trump-tv-encouraged-date-rape-and-punching.

248   **Proud Boys leaders and their allies repeatedly hinted:** US District
      Court for the District of Columbia, *United States of America v. Ethan
      Nordean, Joseph Biggs, Zachary Rehl, Charles Donohoe, Enrique
      Tarrio, Dominic Pezzola*, Second Superseding Indictment, February
      14, 2022, www.justice.gov/usao-dc/press-release/file/1480801/down
      load.

248   **Biggs declared war outright:** Joe Biggs, "The Second Civil War Is
      More Realistic Than You Think," The Biggs Report, November 10,
      2020,   https://web.archive.org/web/20210224011815/https:/www
      .thebiggsreport.com/2020/11/the-second-civil-war-is-more-realistic
      -than-you-think/.

249   **"Never give up . . . fight for America!":** Ryan Goodman and Justin
      Hendrix, "New Video of Roger Stone with Proud Boys Leaders Who
      May Have Planned for Capitol Attack," Just Security, February 6, 2021,
      www.justsecurity.org/74579/exclusive-new-video-of-roger-stone
      -with-proud-boys-leaders-who-may-have-planned-for-capitol
      -attack/.

254   **far from his perch on a rooftop:** Luke O'Brien, "How Republican
      Politics (and Twitter) Created Ali Alexander, the Man Behind 'Stop
      the Steal,'" HuffPost, March 8, 2021, www.huffpost.com/entry
      /republicans-twitter-ali-alexander-stop-the-steal_n_6026fb26c5b6f8
      8289fbab57.

256   **agreed to cooperate with the feds:** US Department of Justice, US
      Attorney's Office, District of Columbia, "New York Man Pleads
      Guilty to Conspiracy and Obstruction Charges Related to Jan. 6
      Capitol Breach," news release, December 22, 2021, www.justice.gov
      /usao-dc/pr/new-york-man-pleads-guilty-conspiracy-and-obstruction
      -charges-related-jan-6-capitol.

257 **Timothy Kelly wrote in a forty-three-page ruling:** "Judge Refuses to Dismiss Charges Against Proud Boys Leaders over Jan. 6 Riot," Associated Press, December 29, 2021, www.nbcnews.com/news/us -news/proud-boys-leaders-jan-6-charges-upheld-rcna10296.

Chapter 12: The Proud Boys Playbook

260 **"we don't worry about them":** David Kirkpatrick and Alan Feuer, "Police Shrugged Off the Proud Boys, until They Attacked the Capitol," *New York Times*, August 23, 2021, www.nytimes.com/2021/03/14/us /proud-boys-law-enforcement.html.

260 **"We are Proud Boys!":** Tony Norman, "The Great American Coup Attempt of 2020," *Pittsburgh Post-Gazette*, December 14, 2020, www .post-gazette.com/opinion/tony-norman/2020/12/15/Trump-rally -Proud-Boys-secession-sedition-election-coup/stories/202012150014.

262 **Research into their events by Vice News:** Tess Owen, "The Proud Boys Changed Tactics After Jan. 6. We Tracked Their Activity," Vice News, January 5, 2022, www.vice.com/en/article/z3n338/what-the -proud-boys-did-after-jan-6.

263 **attempted to donate food:** Eric Bedner, "Proud Boys Making Push in Connecticut," *Journal Inquirer* (Manchester, CT), January 29, 2021, www.journalinquirer.com/connecticut_and_region/proud-boys -making-push-in-connecticut/article_168ee330-6243-11eb-b94a -730e91987896.html.

263 **difficult to get Republican lawmakers to admit:** Jennifer Bendery, "A Year Later, GOP Lawmakers Still Won't Say If Joe Biden Is Actually President," HuffPost, January 5, 2022, www.huffpost.com/entry /january-6-republicans-overturn-election-capitol-riot_n_61d35f59e4 b0bcd219561a94.

263 **investigation into Stone's movements:** Dalton Bennett and Jon Swaine, "The Roger Stone Tapes," *Washington Post*, March 4, 2022, www .washingtonpost.com/investigations/interactive/2022/roger-stone -documentary-capitol-riot-trump-election/?itid=hp_special-topic-1.

263 **Republican Party even signed the gang as security:** Sophie Peel, "Multnomah County Republican Party Signed Agreement with Proud Boy–Affiliated Security Team at Portland Meeting," *Willamette Week* (Portland, OR), May 10, 2021, www.wweek.com /news/city/2021/05/10/multnomah-county-republican-party-signed

-agreement-with-proud-boy-affiliated-security-team-at-portland
-meeting/.

264 **The Soufan Center wrote with sobering prescience:** "IntelBrief: The
Proud Boys Viral Moment—Will It Devolve into a Virulent Threat?,"The
Soufan Center, October 6, 2020, https://thesoufancenter.org/intelbrief
-the-proud-boys-viral-moment-will-it-devolve-into-a-virulent-threat/.

265 **sucker-punched her square in the face:** Andy Campbell, "Proud Boys
Leader Yells Racist Slurs Before Attacking Black Woman," HuffPost,
February 28, 2022, www.huffpost.com/entry/andrew-walls-proud
-boys-assault-video_n_621c87a3e4b0afc668c2eda2.

266 **featured on the floundering MAGA site:** Zachary Petrizzo, "Proud
Boy Founder Gavin McInnes' Far-Right Media Site Apparently
Collapsing," Salon, May 13, 2021, www.salon.com/2021/05/13
/proud-boy-founder-gavin-mcinnes-far-right-media-site-apparently
-collapsing/.

268 **they tried the Proud Boys method:** Carter Sherman, "White Supremacist Group Patriot Front Showed Up at an Anti-Abortion March,"
Vice News, January 10, 2022, www.vice.com/en/article/7kbkjd
/patriot-front-anti-abortion-march.